THE NEW Start With $1000

THE NEW Start With $1000

Do-It-Yourself Investment Strategies

J. J. Brown, PH.D.
Jerry Ackerman, PH.D.

Macmillan of Canada
A DIVISION OF CANADA PUBLISHING CORPORATION
Toronto, Ontario, Canada

Table in the middle of p. 280 from Jerome B. Cohen and Arthur W. Hanson. *Personal Finance: Principles and Case Problems*. Fourth edition. ©Richard D. Irwin, Inc. 1954, 1958, 1964, and 1972. Reprinted by permission.

CANADIAN CATALOGUING IN PUBLICATION DATA

Brown, J. J. (John James), date.
The new start with $1000

Bibliography: p.
Includes index.
ISBN 0-7715-9619-7

1. Investments – Canada. I. Ackerman, Jerry, date. II. Title.

HG5152.B76 1987 332.6′0971 C86-094955-9

Design: The Dragon's Eye Press

Cover design: Brant Cowie/Artplus

Macmillan of Canada
A Division of Canada Publishing Corporation

Printed in Canada

First edition published 1982
Reprinted November 1982
First paperback edition 1983
Reprinted June 1983, October 1983, March 1984, October 1984, June 1985
Second edition published in paperback April 1987
Reprinted August 1987, November 1987, January 1989

Contents

PART IV: INVESTMENT ANALYSIS AND PLANNING

APPENDIXES

THE NEW
Start With $1000

The Authors

WHO ARE THESE FINANCIAL EXPERTS?

With all thy getting, get understanding. PROVERBS 4:7

DR. J. J. BROWN

I came near to being crippled for life financially by growing up in the Depression in Windsor, Ontario. Windsor was the centre of the automobile industry, and therefore one of the areas of Canada hardest hit by the Depression. I decided very young that I would have nothing to do with the chicanery, swindles, and jungle warfare of the business world. I was going to be a learned man, a scholar, sitting calm above the storm in my ivory tower. From time to time I was going to issue dicta to a waiting world, letting people in on what I had been thinking, and making my final solutions available to the waiting public.

What a plan! Before I even got my union card as a college teacher I discovered that the academic world was a much fiercer jungle than business.

My father, from Old Ontario farming stock, was an orphan driving a baker's wagon by the time he was twelve, so he had little chance for education. But he was an honest man and a hard worker with a good wife, so by the 1920s he was a wealthy man, owning a large store on Ouellette Avenue in Windsor, a beautiful home in the posh suburb of Walkerville, two cars, a summer home – the works. But, having been very poor, he was very careful and conservative with money. He owned only banker's investments: blue-chip stocks, government bonds, and mortgages on revenue properties. So in the Depression he was wiped out. He had to give quit-claim deeds to all his properties (i.e., give them away), sell his equities at bottom-of-the-market prices, and move to a small rented home. His efforts during the hungry thirties to find ways of supporting a wife and four children made an indelible impression on me. I still don't think it is easy to make a living, even though it has been years since there has been any need for me to worry about such matters.

My dark memories of the Depression include answering a help-wanted ad in a Detroit paper. Bright and early one morning I crossed the river, walked to the Penobscot Building, and took the elevator to the twenty-second floor. The elevator was crowded, and it turned out that everyone wanted to get out at the same floor – twenty-two. When the doors opened, not a single person could get out. Even at eight o'clock in the morning the corridor was completely jammed with job hunters, all feverishly answering that little classified ad. In those days people really wanted work.

Picked clean by lawyers and swindlers as he tried increasingly desperate ventures, my father nevertheless made a new start, and by the time he died in 1950 he had educated his children and accumulated a fair estate. He was always cheerful, customers liked him, and he had a certain shrewd intuition about how to make a business go.

But living with his adventures and disasters came close to keeping me out of finance. I took refuge in the Walkerville Public Library, the gift of the Hiram Walker family, and studied poetry, drama, philosophy, religion – anything but business and finance. This continued through college and graduate school and to the beginning of a teaching career at Cornell University. Then a good thing happened, although it looked like a major disaster at the time. During the year, I was forced out of Cornell because, being a Quaker, I was a pacifist (there was a war on), and I fled back to Canada on the midnight train. I then had to enter the real world, make a living for my wife and child, and learn a little about how business really worked. I got a job as a technical writer, wrote a true but unpublishable book on the life-insurance business, and began to meet people who were skilled in science and technology. This last influence forced me to think about the problems of beginning businesses: capital formation, make-or-buy decisions, test marketing, and so on. But by this time I was an old man of thirty, no longer flexible and quick to learn. So I am a very late starter in business and finance. I was thirty-two before I overcame my terror of debt sufficiently to buy a house in Montreal and take out a mortgage for $8,000.

But once I had a regular paycheque coming in from a large corporation and had overcome my pathological fear of debt, I began to make serious moves. I bought an apartment house, using the lowest possible cash down-payment (borrowed from the bank) and heavy mortgages. Three months after the year end, I was able to repay the bank loan with the money I had thereby saved on income tax.

In 1950 I lost my savings in an ill-conceived venture in Mexico City. My fault. I thought it up and made all the major mistakes. But by that time I owned a house in a fancy suburb of Montreal, so bankers thought it safe to lend me money. In the late 1950s I lost my shirt again on a mirror factory in Vermont. Again, my fault. Not enough preliminary research on either production or marketing, poor choice of personnel, etc., etc. But I was learning. Besides, by this time I had a major interest in two more apartment houses which provided tax shelter for all my income and substantial cash flow that looked good to bankers.

As soon as my sporadic earnings from investments, together with my wife's steady salary from her profession, were enough to support a home with a maid, I gave up nine-to-five work for the corporation and began eight-to-midnight work for myself. I became adept at keeping twenty-seven coloured balls in the air at once. This exposed me to the charge of being a jack of all trades and master of none, but it also allowed me to survive while Canadians were making their slow way to understanding new concepts like automation, term insurance with separate savings plans, entrepreneurial history, tax-sheltered real estate, and intrinsic-value analysis. Had I focused exclusively on any one of these, I would have starved to death for sure. In the 1960s I was writing books and magazine articles on all these subjects and was investing in them as opportunities arose.

At a certain point I had another stroke of good luck. I slipped my fifth lumbar disc, was unable to walk, and ended up flat on my back in a hospital for a couple of weeks. This meant no books, no telephone, no writing materials. So, for the first time in years I was able to do some uninterrupted thinking. I thought about many things which left no traceable residue, but I did make some investment decisions. At this time KLM Royal Dutch Airlines was effectively bankrupt, but it had not yet defaulted on its bonds. Staring at the hospital-room ceiling for clues, I could not believe that the practical Dutch government would allow its official carrier, with its long and honourable history in aviation, to go under. Nor would the pride of the Dutch people allow it. So I made up my mind.

As soon as the doctor let me up, I stopped off in New York on my way to Bermuda for a rest in the sun. The New York brokers to a man thought anyone would be crazy to buy KLM, either the convertible bonds (exchangeable for stock) or the stock. I bought the bonds, because I could borrow 90 per cent of the money needed from the bank, whereas this would be, at best, 50 per cent if I had been buying stock. I offset the interest on the loan by the interest on the bonds. This proved to be a delightful investment in quite a short time. The company was rescued, and the stock moved from $30 to $90 a share. I got out near the top, which made my back feel better.

This money allowed me to make some foolish moves, and some good ones, but the really important result was to give me confidence. I began to think, for the first time, that I knew what I was doing. I could afford to ignore the so-called experts.

About 1964 I began to get into the big time. I learned of a very large building (420 suites) in Ottawa that was in such trouble it could be bought by taking over its mortgages. I asked one of my investment clients in Ottawa to visit it for me, and he wrote back: "Dilapidated, dirty building, slum district, awful people for tenants, crooks in management. Forget it." So I bought it, but I had to, or thought I had to, bring in some partners to supply enough working capital to pull it through. This caused untold grief later on.

The same year I made the investment that indirectly made me a multimillionaire. For nearly twenty years I had been following the up-and-down fortunes of a small electronics company founded by two friends of mine in Toronto. In 1964, after many problems and disappointments, I was able to arrange the initial public financing of this company, and I received options and some shares for my pains. I also bought shares on the market, until I owned 100,000 shares. After four years of adventures, some hair-raising, others merely scary, the company finally got out a great frontier technology product, and the stock took off. At the high of $34 a share I should, of course, of *course*, have sold all. But in the meantime the apartment house in Ottawa that I had bought with bank loans secured by the electronics stock was looking reasonably solid, and I had bought a second, so I thought I could afford the risk. Moreover, I was married up to the little company, loved its people, its products, its prospects. In my infatuation I was no longer capable of rational thought. So, in the early 1970s I followed the stock down to $16, to $4, and finally, as the company went under in 1974, to zero. This is not an example I cite when trying to convince people of my financial expertise. But I still had the apartment houses in Ottawa.

The Ottawa buildings did prove to be worth a couple of million more than we had paid for them, and by this time I owned nearly fifty per cent of the largest one. When we sold out in 1971, to avoid taxes on capital gain, there was a bitter period of betrayal, recrimination, and hatred, followed by killingly expensive lawsuits between the partners. But I finally got most of my money, and am still a millionaire.

The final event in this particular chronicle is that in 1970 I decided I had to leave the country. It happened like this: When the electronics stock kept rising and the apartment houses were turned around, my tax lawyers gave my company a freeze operation. This was to fix the value of the assets for tax purposes at their then market price. But soon thereafter the market turned down with a vengeance, and the lawyers tried to negotiate with the fisc (the tax-collecting branch of government) about the prices at which the assets had been taken into the frozen company. This proved impossible. The fisc said the electronics stock had been valued at market at $16 a share, and the fact that it was now selling for $4 had nothing to do with it. This meant that I couldn't afford to die. The succession duties on this holding alone would be more than the value of all the remaining assets. So, after all my work, I would leave a bankrupt estate, and even our family properties would have to be sold to pay the taxes. So I decided to be like E. P. Taylor and the Crothers family and many others, and accept the government's award of the overseas medal. From 1971 to 1983 I was a resident of Monaco, where I took advantage of foreign residence to get out from under most of my money. Now I am back in Canada, enjoying retirement, grandchildren, and dogs.

DR. JERRY ACKERMAN

When Dr. Ackerman first went to Purdue University to continue his post-graduate work in economics, he was the proud owner of a sixteen-year-old car and $1,000 in cash he had saved from working the previous year. He had a research assistantship that paid $150 a month and a wife who was working until the first baby came. At this time he began to write "the best book ever written on finance", namely the little black book that contained his own investment record year by year.

The story begins in January 1957, when he bought 25 shares of Howe Sound, a diversified mining company. How sound, indeed. They cost $18 each, or $450. Why did he buy? The company had paid a quarterly dividend for twenty-five years, the $1 dividend seemed high, the stock had sold as high as $29, and the copper business was important. The results: in February the dividend was cut to 10¢; in August it disappeared entirely. The stock dropped to 5¾, while the price of copper continued its downward movement. He sold out with a net loss of 63 per cent.

Next, he took the idea of buying Consolidated Electronics to his broker. The broker talked him out of it, saying that Sperry Rand was much better, what with its Univac and its military contracts. So he bought $500 worth at $23 a share. The results: at first the stock went to $26, but soon earnings fell, and the stock fell too, to $17. After waiting two years, he sold at a profit of $1.49 on $500.

Battered, but still game, he next bought Chrysler at $80 a share. Why? Well, the company earned $5 in the first quarter, so the stock should have gone back to $105. Cars were selling well, and the mutual funds were buying the stock. The result: second-quarter earnings *were* $5, but the market didn't notice, and the shares dropped to $44. He sold a year later at a 32 per cent loss.

Was it time to throw in the towel? In early 1958, after three chapters of his black book had been written – with less than glorious results – Dr. Ackerman was living in a church centre with his wife and child, in a room supplied in exchange for cleaning services. His wife had had a very conservative Southern upbringing: no card-playing, no investing, no risk-taking. It was beginning to look as if she had a point. But, on the other hand, he was taking a course on investing, and doing lots of library work trying to prove his professor wrong.

On April Fool's Day, 1958, he bought 100 shares of Northwest Airlines at 13½, or $13.50 a share plus commission, for $1,368.50, using $1,000 cash and the rest on margin. (Don't worry for the moment about "margin" and other technical terms used. They will be explained in due course.) Basis for buying: both book value and cash flow were the highest of any airline per $1 invested. They had sold off their old aircraft in 1957 and had taken on DC6s and DC7s, then the latest and last gasp. They had a new route to Florida, where everyone wanted to go, and new management, namely Donald Nyrop, the former chairman of the Civil Aeronautics Board, and therefore a certified expert on how to get new routes. Management was buying shares, and Nyrop had come in with lots of stock options. With all this good news, Dr. Ackerman plunged for 100 shares instead of his usual 25. Results: in November the company issued a convertible preferred, with common shareholders being given first chance to buy 1 share for each 3 held. After nine months he sold the common shares at a profit of 189 per cent, and the convertible (bought on 75 per cent margin) at a profit of 204 per cent. This was more like it.

Now, twenty years later, without inherited money, with an academic salary that started at $7,000 in 1960 and some income from investment counselling, he has a substantial net worth.

Dr. Ackerman's view is that the important thing is not how much he has now, but that clients who have listened to his advice in the past have done extremely well on their investments – even in perilous times. In his twenty-year experience of counselling, there was tremendous success through 1968, a holding operation during the debacle of 1969 and the decline to 1975, and relative prosperity in the period since.

Preface

A man without money is a bow without an arrow.
THOMAS FULLER (1608–61)

Some people seem to be able to make money go further than others. Two men working for about the same salary and with the same number of dependants often live on entirely different scales. One will be well dressed and will have a beautiful home, a new car, and lots of spending money; the other, living in a rented flat, will always seem shabby and pressed for funds. Now, if you were hiring one of these men for a job in which the ability to manage money was important, you would be tempted to take the first man and reject the second. This decision would be made simply on the basis of appearance.

The trouble is, you might be dead wrong. When you are dealing with men, you can't be sure that the first man's higher standard of living is the result of his ability to manage money. He may have other sources of income besides his job. Maybe his father left him a trust fund. Maybe his wife's father owned large chunks of Toronto real estate. Maybe his aunt in Calgary sends a cheque for $2,000 every Christmas as a token. On the other hand, maybe the second candidate, who always looks so scruffy, got that way because he is spending all his money putting his two younger brothers through college. Since men don't publish annual financial statements in which they set out the source and application of their funds, there is really no way of judging a man's financial ability by appearances.

Companies, however, are different. They are required by law to publish an annual report. In this report they have to say where their money came from and where it went. This fortunate circumstance makes it possible for us to weigh one company against another and decide which one is making the best use of its funds.

When you invest, you are in effect hiring a company to work for you. If you choose your company wisely, your money will be returned with a dividend. Finance is an important part of business, so one of the first things you want to know about your company is how good it is at handling money.

Before you can judge another's performance, you must know the elements of the subject yourself. This book attempts to teach the ABC's of investing: the elementary facts you need as you attempt to handle money intelligently.

Personal security is to a large extent a state of mind, and this state of mind can be achieved by several methods. One of the most comfortable kinds of personal security comes as the result of possessing marketable skills. If you can do something well – better than most other people – you can usually compete in the labour market. This is true, however, only if your skill is one that satisfies a basic human need, because during times of business depression only essential services can be sold. If you are a trainer who has specialized in training dicky-birds to yodel, you will find it difficult to get a job no matter how good you are at your chosen profession.

This brings up the question of versatility. Being able to do one thing well is a good kind of insurance, but if you can do two things reasonably well you are that much safer. The man who is a skilled operator in two different fields, both of which render essential service, is in a very secure position indeed.

Another very important kind of personal security is the result of what might be called self-possession. This is something that has nothing to do with whether or not you have a job or whether or not you have any money. Many bums and artists have it. Many millionaires do not. This kind of security arises out of having a philosophy of life that enables you to discipline your desires.

When we speak of freedom we mean the ability to do as we please. Most people don't recognize that there are two possible ways of succeeding in this. The first is to obtain more money so we can do anything we like. The second is to limit the number of things we really want to do. If, for example, I have a consuming yen for a Rolls-Royce, there are only two things I can do about it. I can slave day and night to accumulate the money to buy one, or I can discipline my desires to the point at which I decide that I don't really want a Rolls-Royce after all.

Discipline, besides helping you to see your real needs, makes it possible for you to save. To do without things you want today in order to have something you want in the future takes courage. Self-discipline is also a basic prerequisite for becoming a successful investor. It takes courage to buy when everyone else is selling, and to sell when the crowd is buying.

Still another kind of personal security is familiar to everyone. It is the security that arises from having money in the bank, and real-estate deeds and bonds and stocks in safety-deposit boxes. There is no denying that money, or something that can quickly be converted into money, is an important source of personal security. Money isn't everything, but it can be used to soften many of life's foul blows.

This book is about financial security, rather than about personal security arising from the possession of marketable skills or from a particular philosophy of life. Financial security, unlike the other two kinds, is relatively easy to learn. Training in any field takes years, and developing self-possession is the enterprise of a lifetime, but anyone can work toward financial security by the regular application of a few relatively simple rules.

Throughout this book we have tried to use round numbers and illustrations that clarify the point at issue. For this reason, you will find many figures that are not exactly right and many illustrations that are some years old. These illustrations are used, not to tell you what to buy today, but to make clear a principle. The rounding of figures is sensible because, in such things as tax rates, government policy changes from year to year. Thus, even if you have the correct figure in the year this book is published, it might be wrong before another year has passed. Various types of academic, government, and corporation nit-pickers can have a picnic going through the book, pointing out that instead of 3.4 per cent, it should be 3.7, and instead of being a ratio of 3 to 1, it's really a ratio of 3.156 to 1. This is an entertainment we provide for readers of this type at no extra charge.

We would be sorry to have any reader believe that just because we write books on financial matters we believe that money is important either as a means or as an end. Many people live useful and happy lives without paying any attention to money. But ours is a money society. Hence, if you want to live graciously in it, you should have a certain minimum amount of information about money and how it grows.

Whether we like it or not, money poses psychological problems for all of us. We can all be placed on a scale somewhere between the extremes of pathological miserliness on the one hand and pathological open-handedness on the other. Whether we normally tend to be close-fisted or open-handed is in a large measure beyond our control. It depends on our heredity and upbringing. But no matter at what point on the scale we fit, some elementary facts about money and its uses can be extremely valuable.

It may even be argued that the person who takes the trouble to learn something about money and investments can thereby free himself from excessive worry about them. This book is designed to give you all the elementary facts you need about the various ways of investing money. On each topic, of course, there is much more to be said. For example, a whole book could be written on the art or science of speculating with bonds on margin.

Extra space is devoted to two topics: investing in common stocks, and portfolio management. This was done because common stocks are perhaps the most widespread means of investment for ordinary people; and once you own common stocks, all the problems of portfolio management fall on your head at once.

Our excuse for writing a book about money management is that both opinion surveys and our own experience indicate that money is a very serious problem. A 1981 Gallup poll, posing the question "What would you say is the greatest problem facing you and your family at the present time?", came up with the result that 46 per cent of the respondents cited "money" and the "high cost of living". The next-highest factor mentioned was housing, with 7 per cent, and this again is largely a financial problem.

Material difficulties are not those causing us deepest anguish, but they are the ones that cause the greatest volume of trouble for the greatest number of men. Their hurt is not deep but wide. Most people worry about money because they think they don't have enough, but at the same time they waste a large part of the money they have because of their ignorance of the elementary facts of mathematics and finance. Whenever the individual citizen has to make a deal involving money, he has to compete with professionals, and of course he always loses. Today, investment analysis, like the practice of medicine, is largely an art. Nevertheless, as in medicine, science can help.

After giving you some general hints on how to introduce some rationality into the financial side of your life, we want to get specific and

1. Indicate the *resources* of financial analysis, the sources of information: periodicals, individuals, institutions, and books.
2. Describe effective *methods* of financial analysis and market analysis in use today.
3. Help you learn a *system* of financial analysis which has proved useful, and which seems to hold out most promise for improvement in the future.
4. Show the *limitations* of financial analysis and discuss the areas in which a purely analytical approach falls down.
5. Teach methods of *applying* the art of security analysis to the specific problems of portfolio management.

Don't give up when you hit a bump. You'll never learn to fly if you do that.

And don't insist on *complete* understanding of a sentence before you go on to the next one. The authors themselves can't claim that. Push on through thick and thin and you will often find that we explain the puzzling term or concept a page or so further on.

We can't say everything at once, so you have to go along with us on pure faith from time to time. But eventually, as you gain confidence, the loose threads will be picked up.

Finally, it should be emphasized that market prices are the result of human feelings, and these are unpredictable. We have often thought that anyone in the investment business should paste the following passage in his hat. It is from Ralph Ellison's novel *Invisible Man*:

Once I saw a prizefighter boxing a yokel. The fighter was swift and amazingly scientific. His body was one violent flow of rapid rhythmic action. He hit the yokel a hundred times while the yokel held up his arms in stunned surprise. But suddenly the yokel, rolling about in the gale of boxing gloves, struck one blow and knocked science, speed and footwork as cold as a well-digger's posterior. The smart money hit the canvas. The long shot got the nod.

PART I: INTRODUCTION

CHAPTER ONE

Introduction

The ability to weigh two duties, and balance them against each other, is the measure of human worth and dignity.
ROBERT CHAMBERS (1802–71)

As we see it, a book on investing should result in what Carl Rogers, the noted psychologist, calls "significant learning". It should change your behaviour. To the reader who says, "But investing is risky," we say, "Yes, but the risks of not investing are also high, and they take their toll in blasted hopes, vanquished dreams, and unused human potential."

To the reader who says, "But I've never *done* any investing," we say, "All right, we'll get you started by showing you what pitfalls to avoid, where to go for information, and how to analyse it."

To the reader who says, "But whom shall I trust?", we say simply, "Trust yourself."

This book is about personal investing–investing yourself (your mind, some muscle, somebody's money) in order to grow both as an individual human spirit and as an asset to your community.

Investing consists of two major parts: saving, and adding brainpower to the money saved to put it to constructive creative use.

HOW TO SAVE

Whenever we begin to talk about investments, we are greeted by the plaintive cry: "Where am I going to get the dough?" You can't perform efficiently under the capitalist system unless you have capital. So your first goal is to get hold of some.

There are many ways to do this, but the only way that is both ethical and legal is to save it systematically out of income. Money mounts up quickly if you save a little each day. How do you save?

Sell your car and buy the cheap monthly bus ticket.

Give up smoking or taxis or other habits that cost money and wreck your health, and put the proceeds into a separate bank account.

Save out of each paycheque, and out of each windfall, at least 10 per cent (before or after taxes). If you can manage 20 per cent, so much the better.

Do you think you have as much moral character as the average West German or Japanese? They save, on the average, 20 per cent of their salaries each year. If you can bring yourself to put all of a windfall, or even half of it, into your savings plan, this is even better than 20 per cent.

One quick way to get instant money for your savings plan is to take your name off the list of suckers who own permanent life insurance. First you must replace it with the amount of term insurance you currently need, paying not more than $2 or $3 a thousand. Then turn in your old policies and use the money for some serious investment.

In a word, live conservatively. Avoid conspicuous consumption and the neighbourhood battle of invidious comparisons. Avoid cash-value life insurance, government bonds, and other types of institutionalized waste. Develop spending skills and saving skills in addition to the usual money-making skills. Remember that garage-sale purchases are tax free. Do you really need a suit nowadays? If you don't, why buy one? Most important of all, join without delay the voluntary forced-savings plan outlined in Chapter 4.

DEVELOPING MONEY SKILLS

There is no short route to saving, but there are a few rules that will help you, once you have made up your mind to save. One way in which these rules can help is by setting controls on your expenses, to give you a better idea of where the money goes.

The first rule is to ask questions. Some good questions are: "What am I getting for this money?" "What will the product do for me?" "What will it be worth next year, the year after, ten years from now?"

Another important question to ask might be: "Is the first cost the last cost?" Many purchases not only take an amount of your capital out of circulation, but commit you to large upkeep costs each year. Automobiles, boats, even cameras, fall into this class. You should get into the habit of figuring the total cost of any contemplated purchase.

A second rule for fiscal competence is to figure in the earning power of your own invested capital. If you spend a thousand dollars on a boat or other piece of real property, the first item in its annual cost to you is the interest that the thousand dollars could have earned each year if you had invested it. As a minimum, this will be $100 a year forever. Under some conditions, it might be $200 a year forever.

A third rule is to get everything into percentage. The object of this is to take the emotion out of buying. Don't say, "This debt is costing me $45 a month," but say rather, "I'm paying 23 per cent a year on the amount owed." Don't say, "My food costs for the family are $250 a month." Say, "Thirty per cent of my net income after taxes goes for food." Don't say, "This car will cost me $8,000." Say, "This car will cost 80 per cent of my net income after taxes." By doing this you can learn how many months you will have to work to pay for the car. If they pay $1.95 for an article in one store and $2.95 for the same article at another, most people say the difference is only a dollar, and what's a dollar? The right way to say it is that one store charges 50 per cent more than the other for the same article. This should give you ideas about where to buy.

Numbers and dollars are charged with emotion and can easily fool you. Percentage figures are accurate and colourless and tell you exactly where you stand. A good example of this is a bit of radio dialogue during a debate on hospitalization plans between Morris Fishbein, then head of the American Medical Association, and Henry Kaiser, a prominent businessman who from small beginnings had worked his way up to being a millionaire many times over:

MORRIS FISHBEIN: "Over 4,000,000 people in the United States have prepaid hospital care today." (Sounds like a lot.)

HENRY KAISER: "About 3 per cent of the people of the United States have prepaid hospital care." (Sounds like only a few, which it is.)

The fourth basic rule for fiscal competence is to have a budget. There are books on household budgets, telling you how to work them out in greater or less detail, which you can get from your public library. But the essential point about budgets is to write down on one piece of paper a list of all the money coming in (income), and on another piece of paper a list of all the money going out. This second list should be divided into two parts. The first part contains all unavoidable expenses such as housing, food costs, insurance premiums, health and recreation, and so on. This total shows you the amount of money you put aside to maintain the various commitments you have made. The second part of the list should be avoidable expenses such as vacation costs, entertainment items such as television sets and movies and payments on your stereo, and all other items that can be dropped if the going gets really rough. If the total of all anticipated expenses of both types is greater than the total of your yearly income, you start paring away at this second list until the amounts come within reason.

The fifth rule is to consolidate all debts. It is a commonplace today to say that we are all in debt. But some of us are in debt in smarter ways than others. Anyone who buys anything on time is in debt. But instalment buying is usually one of the most expensive ways to borrow money. Department-store credit in the form of charge cards costs 21 per cent. This charge may be called something other than interest, such as a "service charge", an "accommodation fee", or whatever – some of the names given to these packing charges are quite ingenious – but whatever the name, you lose.

The way to avoid buying on time and thus avoid high interest rates is to consolidate all your small debts into one large one. What happens when you do this is that you get the lower interest rates, because the cost of administering one large debt is lower than the cost of administering several small debts. Also, you get a clear idea of how much you owe. When you are trying to consolidate your debts, you must shop around for credit the way you shop for a used car. You have to know cars and must be willing to spend some time shopping around before you pick up a bargain. The same thing is true of credit. Don't take the first loan offered. You must know the field and be aware of the various possibilities open to you.

BORROWING

The first thing you must know when borrowing money is how to look behind interest rates. People who lend you money are providing a service, and expect to be paid for it. You must pay for this service, but you want to pay as little as possible. Since customers don't like to pay high interest rates, some companies have worked out ingenious methods of making the interest look smaller than it really is. Say, for example, that you want to borrow $1,000 for one year at 16 per cent. One commonly used method of figuring out the repayment of the loan is to add the $160 interest to the $1,000 to get $1,160. This amount is to be paid back in twelve equal instalments, which works out to $96.67 a month. The company then subtracts the first return payment of $96.67 from the $1,000 and hands you a loan of $903.33. By this method, although you are paying interest on $1,000, you never receive a $1,000 loan but a loan of a little over $900. Over the one-year period the true interest rate on the unpaid balance, figured on a monthly payment schedule, adds up to over 35 per cent, rather than the 16 per cent you thought you were paying.

What you think you pay is called the "nominal" interest rate; what you really pay is called the "effective" interest rate. In the example given, the effective rate is double the nominal because of two factors. The first is that the borrower of $1,000 gets only $903.33; the second is that the interest is calculated as if the borrower had the use of all the money for a full year. Actually he is paying part of it back each month, and by the end of the year will have it all repaid. Part of the interest he pays each month is on money he has already repaid.

In some countries this method of computing interest is legal, so you must be on your guard against it.

Despite the introduction of "truth in lending" laws, which force the lender to disclose the real interest rate, many people are still being robbed blind by institutional lenders and issuers of credit cards. In fact, one good simple rule for savers is "keep away from plastic".

The first rule about going into debt is "fear not". Throughout this book we are going to be advising you to get into debt – but for *investment*, not for consumption. The rest of the world borrows money to buy a new car, which loses one-third of its value the moment it is driven off the display-room floor. *You* borrow so that the money can immediately begin earning income and capital gains for you. Moreover, when you borrow for investment, some of the interest may be tax deductible, and hence is paid in part by the government in taxes saved.

It is perfectly natural for you to be afraid of debt if you are not accustomed to it. We are all afraid of the unknown. But debt is like sex, in that, if your first experience has been a good one, the next time around you are not so timid. The ability to brave the psychological pressures of debt is the *sine qua non* of success in business. When Henry J. Kaiser, the successful businessman quoted earlier, applied for his first loan, from a Vancouver banker, he requested $25,000. Asked what he would put up as collateral, he said simply, "I know how to build roads." The heroic banker lent the money, Kaiser made $19,000 on a road-building contract, and he was on his way. When he died in 1967, the companies he had founded showed a net profit of $100 million a year.

Your object in borrowing from the bank is to establish a credit rating. The rule is, if the banker doesn't raise an eyebrow, you haven't asked for enough. Borrow whether you need it or not, just for the practice, and to lay the groundwork for the credit rating you will need (sometimes badly) for the rest of your life.

Your bank or credit union is not the only place where you can borrow money. We are going to recommend that, as soon as you know what stocks to buy, you open a margin account with a broker. This means you put up at least half the money to buy the stock, and the broker lends you the rest. If later on you are caught up a tree, and have to raise money for an emergency, the broker with your margin account can give you a cheque immediately, if you are not already fully margined.

The unfamiliar words "margin" and "margined" bring up a problem of exposition not easily solved. If we stop continually to tell you what such words mean, it will interrupt the flow; besides, you may know what they mean already, and hence be insulted. If we use a footnote to explain at every first use of a new term, the publisher is going to be unhappy with high production costs. The third alternative is to use a "glossary of terms", and, where terms cannot be explained with a phrase, this is the one we have chosen. It is on page 283 and should be consulted as required.

One thing your banker will want before he gives you a loan for investing rather than for acquiring consumer goods is a net-worth statement. We show you how to make one out later in the book. Actually, you should have two net-worth statements, one which takes an optimistic view of the current value of your assets (for the banker) and a second which values them with harsh realism (for yourself).

Collateral is the name given to the property you give to the bank or other lender as security for your loan. This collateral can be real-estate deeds, stock certificates, or bonds. Even in stores, if you insist on buying on time, always use the "loan" rather than the "conditional-sale contract" form. Under a conditional-sale contract the laws against usury do not apply, so any rate of interest that the seller can get away with can legally be charged. Also, if you don't pay for the television set or other appliance you have bought under a conditional-sale contract, the seller can not only take the set back, but sue you for the amount owing plus interest and collection charges. Under a loan contract the law protects you against excessive interest charges, and you are responsible only for the amount of the loan.

WAYS TO GET MORE MONEY

There are only three ways in which you can increase your stock of worldly goods. The first is by selling your services for a fee or salary. The second is by lending your accumulated capital in such a way that it earns annual interest. The third is to put your money out at risk, and get paid for having taken more than normal risks with your capital.

Most people use all three methods at one time or another during their lives. Depending on your age and situation, you may find that risking capital is your chief source of income. Or it may be selling services.

These services consist of mind or muscle or a combination of the two. The world seems to have an adequate supply of muscle, but mind is definitely in short supply. Hence, you should try to sell management services, which will be better paid.

The proper balance between these three elements for increasing your capital tends to change automatically as you get older. The young person will normally begin by selling only services; then he will sell services and at the same time risk some capital in order to increase his net worth. The older person will take less and less risky with capital. The retired person will cease selling his services, and live almost entirely on the income from money lent.

CASH OR CHARGE?

The key question that must be answered by every investor before he sets sail on the ocean of finance is, "How are my investments going to be bought?" This is simply a matter of how much risk you think you can stand. If you are a risk-taking individual, and can afford substantial losses, you will buy investments in quite a different way from the person who is very conservative and, moreover, cannot afford to lose.

The most conservative way to buy any investment is for cash. If you buy for cash and your judgment of the investment proves to be wrong, you simply stash the share certificate away in your safety-deposit box and forget about it. You have lost your capital, but you have not made an undertaking to pay anything beyond it.

Buying on margin (investing with borrowed money) can be more or less risky depending on how you do it. It is certainly much more risky in every case than investing with cash. The risk in margin buying depends to a great extent on what you buy. If you borrow money from the bank at 15 per cent in order to buy bonds that pay 16 per cent, you can be home free with 1 per cent profit. If, on the other hand, you borrow money at 15 per cent to put into a less certain venture, your risk is much higher.

Again, margin buying can be done with or without a cash reserve. If you speculate in bonds on margin, paying less than 30 per cent of the cost out of your own pocket, and the bonds go down, you will have to find an amount of cash perhaps equivalent to your original investment, in order to protect your capital. If you start out with a cash reserve equal to the amount invested, it won't matter so much if the bonds go down.

Margin levels can be high or low. If you pay 80 per cent of the cost of your stock, you are obviously taking less risk than if you use the maximum margin allowed and pay only 50 per cent.

PUTTING SAVINGS TO WORK

Saving is the easy part. It takes only character. When you have some money put aside you have to invest it, and to do this well requires both skill and hard work. Successful investing is one of the most highly specialized of all undertakings. The security analyst knows that there is no magic formula for success in this field, especially in times like the present when things are changing rapidly. The skilful investor must search for facts, and not be discouraged because they become obsolete rapidly and must be replaced. He must be sufficiently organized to make use of scientific methods of analysis, yet must not allow emphasis on method to smother his imagination.

The growing profession of security analysis is working toward making investment more of a science and less of an art. Benjamin Graham of Columbia harped for thirty years on the theme that we should be analysing the intrinsic value in a security rather than analysing trends in market prices. To do this effectively, more dependable measurements of securities are needed. We also need to develop simpler and more accurate analytical methods. These will be discussed later.

You can put your money into two basic kinds of investments: debt or equity. The traditional debt investments such as bonds, savings-bank accounts, mortgages, and trust certificates all have a fixed dollar value. Equity investments – real estate, commodities, jewellery, art objects, and common stocks – have constantly changing dollar values.

Trustees of institutional funds, bankers, and insurance company managers, whose obligations are in fixed dollars no matter what the dollar may buy, are still able to cling chiefly to fixed-dollar ways of investing. But the individual investor has to do something about the invisible erosion caused by inflation. Here the thrifty person faces a difficult problem. In the twenty years between 1958 and 1978 the purchasing power of the dollar dropped to about forty-five cents. Part of this was caused by the inflation that normally comes after every major war, but part of it was the result of government fiscal policy. The person who saved with fixed-dollar investments experienced a serious loss of purchasing power.

EQUITY INVESTMENTS AS A CLASS

If you can afford to risk your capital and are young enough to wait out any unfavourable long-term changes in the market, you will probably favour equity investments. The particular type of equity you will buy depends on many factors. If you fear civil uproar as well as inflation, you might well buy art objects and jewellery. If you foresee world-wide food shortages, you might buy commodities. If you see eventual shortage of land for urban use, you will probably buy real estate. If you see a rosy future ahead for your country, you will probably buy common stocks.

Art and Valuables

In buying art objects as an inflation hedge, you have to remember that they must be stored, and that they earn no money. Besides, you have to pay insurance on them. Silver, gold, Oriental rugs, furs, paintings, and diamonds are the usual valuables bought for the long haul. Jewellery is perhaps the most convenient because it is small, light, easily stored, and doesn't go out of style.

In times of violent inflation, jewellery has often provided a complete livelihood. A First World War Russian refugee in Berlin rode out the collapse of the mark quite comfortably by pawning a diamond necklace, and redeeming it as prices rose by pawning a sapphire brooch. This process was repeated as many times as was necessary to keep the good lady in groceries.

Real-Estate Ownership

Many skilful investors have bought real estate since 1945 and have found it to work very well as an inflation hedge. But millions of dollars have been lost in real estate during depressions. Since most people own real estate at one time or another, we have devoted Chapter 7 to a brief outline debate on this type of investment.

Real estate has been the traditional investment of large institutions, churches, insurance companies, and universities. Today, however, we may be seeing the beginning of a trend away from this class of investment, because it is often cheaper to rent than to buy.

Commodities

Basic raw materials of industry, such as wheat, coffee, cotton, and metals, have been used by many as a means of investment. There are special commodity exchanges corresponding to the stock exchange, where bulk lots of these raw materials can be bought and sold. Such investments are usually for the shorter term. They are also of a more speculative nature, and are based on shorter-term price fluctuations. Commodities will be discussed in more detail later.

Common Stocks

A favourite type of equity investment is common stock. In recent years legislators have recognized that certain common stocks have a capacity for growth that can offset the declining buying power of the dollar. Shares are notoriously sensitive to investor opinion; hence their prices fluctuate. Yet they have one very important advantage: liquidity.

This means that they can be bought in large or small quantities and sold for cash within a few hours. You may be more or less locked into a real-estate holding for years; in a bad slump, jewellery and commodities often can't be sold at all. With stocks, you can cut your losses, or take your profits at will.

HOW TO BEGIN INVESTING

Life Insurance

The only correct use of life insurance is as protection against the risk of dying prematurely. The gap between assets and what is required to pay all debts and support your financial dependants should be covered in the simplest and most economical way. This is done by term insurance and by no other.

For a discussion of life insurance, see Chapter 5.

Investment Portfolio

Every investor is looking for certainty, income, and appreciation in value caused by genuine growth. Appreciation in value is preferable to income, because it is taxed at a lower rate.

The basic problem is how to find such investments, or how to test securities to make sure they fit these requirements. In this book we are going to spend a lot of time describing and applying such tests.

Problems Afflicting the Investor

Preconceived ideas and lack of system are two rocks on which beginning investors often founder.

Preconceived ideas are a serious obstacle for the investor. For some years we have been collecting the old saws mouthed by the financial community, and putting beside them examples from real life proving the opposite. Actually, such pearls of wisdom as "No one ever went broke taking a profit" or "The market is its own best forecaster" or "No tree grows to the sky" are meaningless until applied to specific cases and often are used by the broker for his own ulterior motives. If he can persuade you to sell, that generates a commission for him, and probably another when you reinvest. Sometimes it is wise to take a profit, sometimes not. Logical reasoning, like virtue, will probably win out in the end, but before an undervalued stock can rise, the fact that it is undervalued must be recognized by others. This often takes time.

Conclusions reached through an impeccable process of logic are a form of preconceived idea, and equally disastrous in the stock market. In the market valuation of stocks, economic theories often fail, either because they have been thoroughly discounted in advance, or because of the existence of some overriding factor you failed to see. For example, take the relation between income and price moves. While as a general rule prices of stocks tend to rise ahead of the trend in earnings, they quite often do not. Some companies earn more and more, and their stock goes down and down.

The decade before 1982 was terrible for the stock market. The best security analysts began to look more and more like idiots. Between the late sixties and the early eighties, one tool of stock analysis, the ratio of the average stock's price to its earning power, which stood at 10 to 15 historically, dropped to less than 10. Obviously, a low price-earnings ratio makes a stock attractive. One of the reasons we are backing away from the market *now* (1986-7) is the fact that price-earnings ratios are not at liveable levels.

A second major obstacle facing the investor is lack of system. The average person invests in the market the way he plays the horses –

by a combination of intuition and hot tips. This is the basic reason why the average investor in common shares loses all or part of his capital. There seems to be something about the stock market that hypnotizes the investor and makes him throw his common sense out the window. Persons who will take the trouble to compare prices and make sure they get good value when buying a $60 pair of shoes fail to take even elementary precautions when investing $6,000. Even businessmen, who can be extremely hard-headed about their own businesses, making realistic appraisals of risks versus possible gain, tend to forget their business sense when they come to invest their money. At bargain sales, where prices are low, people buy anything but stocks. Company shares are popular only when they are high; and the higher the better.

Intelligent investing can be done only by those who have the basic financial data on a company at their fingertips, and who know how to use these data to get meaningful indicators.

You want to be right in your investments for the right reasons. If your success is accidental, you are fooling yourself. You are less wise than before, even though you made money.

For example, when the price of oil went through the roof, it was easy to see that the airlines would lose money and their stock prices would fall, because fuel accounts for 30 per cent of airline operating costs. Conversely, when crude-oil prices dropped precipitously in late 1985, it was reasonable to think that the airlines would recover and their stock prices would rise. They didn't, but that doesn't alter the fact that investment in airline stocks at that time was an intelligent move. When fuel prices dropped by 40 per cent, airline profits should have doubled. They still haven't really moved, in spite of one of the strongest stock markets in history. You can be right for the wrong reasons, and wrong for the right reasons.

The problem is:

1. to know what information you want and how to get it;
2. to know what to do with the information once found;
3. to build up your confidence so you can act upon what you know.

The best piece of positive advice we can give is this: Start right now to write your own book of finance. Get a little black book (permanently bound, not looseleaf, so there can be no cheating), and each time you buy or sell write down what you are doing, and why. Also write down what you expect, and how soon. These immortal words, read one or ten years later, will teach you much, such as, "Was my success accidental or deliberate?" This little black book is such an intimate source of learning that it will quickly become the world's best book on finance for *you*.

Finding investment values takes work. If it didn't, everybody would find them and there would be no such thing as an undervalued stock. To pick out a bargain in any industry you have to make an intense study of the financial and commercial affairs of the companies in it.

Elements of a Workable System

A workable system of security analysis must fulfil two basic requirements. First, it must be based on an adequate but not overwhelming body of carefully digested statistics. Second, it must be possible to subject these statistics to a comprehensive series of meaningful tests. These tests will have as their end result a clear picture of a company's investment merits, management policy and prospects, the degree of risk attached to it, and where it stands as an investment in relation to other companies in its industry.

We need a technique that is conceptually sound and basically simple, yet provides enough information so that judgments about the company are based on facts. The statistical raw materials used must be readily available from company reports, and in a form which allows you to compare them with criteria already established.

Most important, the system of analysis used must leave the investor with a specific directive telling what to do with any particular stock.

The slogan "Investigate, then invest" is all very well, but unless the investor has specific directions about what to investigate, procedure to follow in doing so, and specific information on how to interpret the results of these investigations, he can never become an intelligent investor.

We propose to show the reader how to analyse financial statements and how to use this information to make investment decisions. Proper use of such information makes it possible for you to invest for intrinsic value. Using it, you can analyse most businesses with the same intimate knowledge, and by the same methods, that you use in analysing your own.

Intrinsic-value analysis permits you to choose your investments independent of the level of the market. The question we propose to answer in this book is not "Is the market high or low?" but "Does this particular stock at today's price meet my particular criteria?"

CHAPTER TWO

Elementary Mathematics of Finance

Some truth there was
But dashed and brewed with lies
To please the fools
And puzzle all the wise. JOHN DRYDEN (1631–1700)

INTRODUCTION

Before you begin, it is important that you have a few basic mathematical tools at your service. Don't let the phrase "mathematics of finance" scare you. At the levels we plan to discuss, the mathematics is mostly simple arithmetic. This means addition and subtraction and, more rarely, multiplication and division. This is all grade-school arithmetic, and should present no difficulty. But when we get to ratios we have to use calculations of "interest" and "discount". You may have forgotten about these matters in the years since you took elementary algebra in high school. Skim this chapter if you remember your high-school math. It is elementary, and designed only to help those for whom math holds hidden terrors.

First, let's review quickly per cent, interest, and discount.

In judging investments we are usually faced with two types of problems:

1. Understanding the situation at one point in time, namely today.
2. Understanding the developing situation over many points in time.

For describing the static situation, that is, at one point in time, we usually use ratios, which show the size relationship between two numbers. These may be expressed by saying "x is 4 times y", or by using per cent (y is 25 per cent of x).

Before you can understand the dynamic situation, the trends and changes of any economic factor over a period of time, you need to know a little about the various ways of depicting changing quantities. This is what the calculus is about, but there are many simpler ways to show the results. Perhaps the most useful way of all is by means of graphs; hence we should spend a little time on the various methods of graphical representation. In addition, you should know something about correlation – how to compare graphs to see the story they tell.

Finally, you need to know a bit about detective work on statistics – how to ferret out sources of distortion and error before pinning your faith on the figures.

The object of this chapter is to make you generally familiar with the basic mathematical tools and procedures used in investment analysis. The examples chosen are for the purpose of illustrating the use of the tools only. We don't expect you to emerge with a complete knowledge of how to use bond-yield tables, or of how to value the conversion privilege of a convertible bond. What we want to cover in this chapter is a survey of the usual methods by which we apply mathematics to come at the valuation of a security.

REVIEW OF PERCENTAGE, INTEREST, DISCOUNT

Percentage

This is a basic tool of any sort of financial analysis. Perhaps the most important rule for the individual in developing fiscal competence is: "Get everything in per cent." But one thing to watch when figuring in per cent is the shifting base. A good example of this is the method most druggists use to figure percentage profit on sales. For various economic reasons, the retail druggist must make a high profit on individual sales, yet at the same time, and for equally good public-relations reasons, he must guard against being considered a man who makes an excessive profit out of other people's physical suffering. In this dilemma, he turns to the shifting base. Most people figure profit as a percentage of cost price. That is, if we buy an item for $1.00 and sell it for $1.20, we figure we have made a profit of 20 per cent. The druggist, however, figures his profit on the selling price. If he sells an item for $1.20 and makes 20 cents profit on it, his percentage profit is not 20 per cent but 16⅔ per cent. If he buys a pill for 1 cent and sells it for a dollar, the profit is either 99 per cent or nearly 10,000 per cent, depending on which base he uses. The beauty of choosing the selling price as the base is that, no matter how high the actual profit, it can never be more than 100 per cent, since the item always costs something.

Percentage also has some other interesting properties – and dangers. For example, in percentage a rising market always sounds more bullish than a falling market sounds bearish. Saying this another way, it takes a drop of only 16.7 per cent to wipe out all the gains made by a previous rise of 20 per cent. This again is because of a shift in the base. For example:

1. Market quotation rises from $5 to $6 a share, or $1 in $5.

   Therefore: $\frac{1}{5} = \frac{1 \times 20}{5 \times 20} = \frac{20}{100}$ or 20% (multiply top and bottom by the number that will make the bottom 100)

2. Market quotation falls from $6 to $5, i.e. $1 in $6.

   Therefore: $\frac{1}{6} = \frac{1 \times 16.7}{6 \times 16.7} = \frac{16.7}{100}$ or 16.7%

Here are the two basic cases for figuring per cent:

1. Market quotation rises from 13 to 16.
   Change is 16 – 13 = 3

   Therefore: % change is $\frac{3}{13} \times 100 = \frac{300}{13} = 23\%$ up.

   Or – another way to say it – the new price is 123 per cent of the old.
2. Market quotation falls from 16 to 13.
   Change is 3

   Therefore: % change is $\frac{3}{16} \times 100 = \frac{300}{16} = 18\frac{3}{4}$ per cent down.

Interest

Money is like a tree. Properly placed, it grows and grows, producing a large crop of new money called "interest". The speed at which money grows if interest is allowed to accumulate is called the "interest rate". In some countries people have religious or other scruples against having money earn interest automatically without the owner of the money doing any work. They don't think it is fair. In most Western countries, however, we have drawn a line between what we call a "fair" rate of interest and an "unfair" rate. Taking too high a rate of interest from a person who borrows money is called "usury", and many countries have passed laws against it.

People who undertand that money earns interest often die rich. There are two kinds of interest, simple and compound. In simple interest the money earned by the principal is not added to the principal at the end of each year. Thus, if you lend someone $100 at simple interest of 6 per cent, at the end of the first year he owes you $106 and at the end of the second year he owes $112.

With compound interest the interest payment itself begins to earn interest at the end of the first year. If you put $100 into an investment that pays 6 per cent compounded annually, then:

FIGURE 1: **How Money Grows**

After	1 year the amount will have grown to	$	106.00
"	2 years " " " " " "		112.36
"	3 " " " " " " "		119.10
"	10 " " " " " " "		179.08
"	20 " " " " " " "		320.71
"	30 " " " " " " "		574.35
"	50 " " " " " " "		1,842.02
"	80 " " " " " " "		10,579.60
"	100 " " " " " " "		33,930.21

At 6 per cent, money doubles at compound interest every twelve years.

Figure 2 on page 38 is a graph showing how money mounts up at various rates of compound interest (B & C), compared with simple interest (A). One point to note is that, in the beginning, simple interest and compound interest are not greatly different. The two lines A and B, representing simple and compound interest at 6 per cent, start out close together in the early years, but then diverge more and more as the years pass.

Another thing to notice about the compound-interest curves is that they are exponential. That is, in the beginning they rise rather slowly, but their rate of rise increases all the time until in later years the amount of money is increasing very quickly.

Individuals tend to neglect interest because the amount of money at stake seems rather small. At the end of the second year, for example, the difference between simple and compound interest on

FIGURE 2: **Simple Interest vs. Compound Interest**

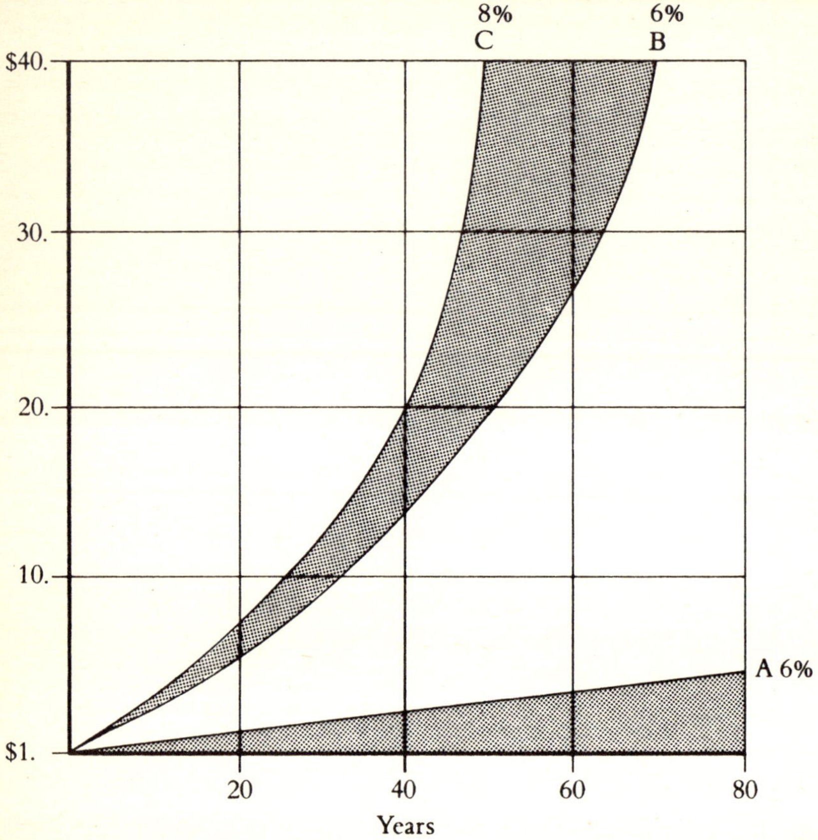

$100 is only 36 cents. But financial institutions such as banks and insurance companies never neglect interest, and neither should you.

To calculate what $13 will be worth 27 years from now, at a compound interest rate of 5 per cent, you look up the proper interest table (compound amount of one), which can be obtained at any library, bank, or broker, and find the intersection of the column marked 5 per cent and that marked 27 years. The number at this intersection is 3.73. This is the amount that one dollar has become in that time. Since you started with $13, you simply multiply 3.73

FIGURE 3: **How Money Can Accumulate**

Time	Rate 5%	7%	9%	11%	13%	15%	17%
A. One sum of $1,000, annual compounding							
5 Years	$1,276	$1,402	$1,538	$1,685	$1,842	$2,011	$2,192
10 Years	$1,628	$1,967	$2,367	$2,839	$3,394	$4,045	$4,806
15 Years	$2,078	$2,759	$3,642	$4,784	$6,254	$8,137	$10,538
20 Years	$2,653	$3,869	$5,604	$8,062	$11,523	$16,366	$23,105
25 Years	$3,386	$5,427	$8,623	$13,585	$21,230	$32,918	$50,657
30 Years	$4,321	$7,612	$13,267	$22,892	$39,115	$66,211	$111,064
35 Years	$5,516	$10,676	$20,413	$38,574	$72,068	$133,175	$243,503
B. An annual investment of $1,000 with annual compounding							
5 Years	$5,525	$5,750	$5,984	$6,227	$6,480	$6,742	$7,014
10 Years	$12,577	$13,816	$15,192	$16,722	$18,419	$20,303	$22,393
15 Years	$21,578	$25,129	$29,360	$34,405	$40,417	$47,580	$56,110
20 Years	$33,065	$40,995	$51,160	$64,202	$80,946	$102,443	$130,032
25 Years	$47,727	$63,249	$84,700	$114,413	$155,619	$212,793	$292,104
30 Years	$66,438	$94,460	$136,307	$199,020	$293,199	$434,745	$647,439
35 Years	$90,320	$138,236	$215,710	$341,589	$546,680	$881,170	$1,426,491

by 13, to get $48.49. With the new electronic calculators that can be programmed, you don't even need the tables. Just punch in the figures and touch the "compute" and "future value" buttons.

Compound Amount of 1 Per Annum:
If, instead of depositing your $13 in the fund just once, you make the same deposit each year, the money will mount up faster. The table used to calculate this case is called "compound amount of 1 per annum". Taking the same conditions as in the first example, the figure at the intersection of 5 per cent and 27 years is 54.669. Multiplying this by $13 as before, we get $710.70.

Figure 3 shows how money grows at various rates of compound interest.

Discount: How Money Shrinks
If interest is about how money grows, discount is about how money shrinks.

If you promise to pay a man $100 five years from now, your debt to him is not $100 but only $82, because $82, deposited now in an investment earning 4 per cent, will amount to $100 at the end of five years. Similarly, when an insurance company promises to pay you $1,000 at the end of twenty years, it is not promising you $1,000, or anything like it. Its commitment is $456. To find out how much a single payment at some later date is worth now, you use the table in Figure 4, "Present Value of 1".

FIGURE 4: **Present Value of 1**

Number of years	Rate:	4%	8%	12%	16%
1		.9615	.9259	.8929	.8621
2		.9245	.8573	.7972	.7432
3		.8889	.7938	.7118	.6407
and so on for 50 years					

Say you want to know the present value of $10,000 to be paid three years from now, and money is worth 8 per cent. Look in the 8 per cent column across from 3 years and get the figure .7938. This means the present value is $7,938. This table is used when you are finding the present value of the face amount of a bond.

To find out how much a *series* of yearly payments beginning at some later date is worth now, use the table in Figure 5, "Present Value of 1 Per Annum".

FIGURE 5: **Present Value of 1 Per Annum**

Number of years	Rate:	4%	8%	12%	16%
1		.9615	.9259	.8929	.8621
2		1.8860	1.7832	1.6901	1.6052
3		2.7750	2.5770	2.4018	2.2459
and so on for 50 years					

Say you are promised a payment of $1,000 a year for three years, and money is worth 12 per cent, and you want to know how much the deal is worth right now. Look under 12 per cent and across from 3 years and get the figure 2.4018. This means the present value is $2,401.80.

This table is used when valuing an annuity, or when finding the present value of the coupons of a bond.

MATHEMATICS OF THE STATIC SITUATION

Ratios for Judging the Quality of a Security

As you develop investment skills, you will devote more and more time to studying balance sheets and income statements for clues about the intrinsic value of a company's securities. The results of this study will for the most part be expressed in ratios. Sound capitalization (a proper balance between debt and common stock), for example, is one of the factors making for high quality or low risk. One way of measuring the soundness of a company's capitalization is through the ratio of bonds and preferred to total capitalization. In Gulf Canada, for example, the ratio is 336 / 2048 or 17 per cent, which is conservative for companies in the oil industry. Of course, this fact can't be used alone. You must relate it to all the other facts you have about the company before you draw any conclusions.

Another commonly used ratio is the current ratio (total current assets divided by total current liabilities). Crane Company, with figures of $458 and $210 million respectively, has therefore a current ratio of 2.2. Depending on the industry, ratios of 1.5 to 4 are considered reasonable. Normally, the higher the ratio, the safer the investment.

Current assets of course include inventory, and under some circumstances inventory cannot be sold. Hence, a more severe test of a company's current position is to subtract inventory from current assets. This gives the figure called "net quick assets", and the "quick ratio".

Some other ratios derived from the balance sheet are:

Cash / current liabilities (to show liquidity)
Gross property / depreciation reserve (to show the extent to which the fixed assets are depreciated)
Net income / sales (to show profitability)

Ratios that chiefly aid in judging growth potential, but may also be useful in judging quality, are derived from the income statement. The earnings ratios (net income / equity, and cash income / equity) are basic indicators. Here again you have to look at this ratio while keeping other factors in mind. Maybe the ratios are high because the company understates the equity figure.

If the company gives sales figures, a useful ratio is that of net income / sales. If the figure is high, it is usually a good sign.

Schlumberger, the oil industry service company, had a ratio of net income to sales of 475 / 2570, or 18½ per cent. This is unusually high, even for a service business.

All these ratios will be discussed in the sections on investment analysis.

Ratios Showing Return on Invested Capital

Bonds

Current Yield

This is simple interest, but it changes with the changing market price of the bond. An 8 per cent coupon attached to a \$1,000 bond is worth \$80 when cashed. This amount is paid no matter what the current market quotation of the bond may be. Even if the bond itself is selling for only \$600 on the market, the coupon is still worth \$80.

Thus, the bond is yielding not 8 per cent (its coupon rate) but considerably higher. The current yield at a purchase price of \$600 would be

$$\frac{80}{600} \times 100 = 13.3\%$$

Yield to Maturity

In order to compare bond values we have to determine how much the bond is worth over its whole life until redemption. This value is made up of two parts:

1. The present value (p.v.) of the redemption price.
2. The p.v. of the total interest payments.

You can figure this out using interest and discount tables as above. In actual practice, when you want to know what a bond at a given price will yield to maturity, you use bond-yield tables (again, to be found in libraries, brokers' offices, and banks), such as the Sprague, Johnson, or Equitable Trust Rapid Bond Tables. If you know

1. the market quote,
2. the market rate,
3. the length of time yet to run before maturity,

you can simply look up a bond table and get the yield directly.

In fact, if you know any three of the four factors you can find the missing one.

However, like all mathematical tables, bond tables have the disadvantage of seldom having the exact figure you need. It is obviously impossible to set down yields for every possible market price and for every possible length of time to maturity. Time, for example, is usually given in half-years, so if your bond has three and one-eighth years to run, you have to interpolate from the tables. This is not a difficult matter, but it is time-consuming. People in the bond business will make the fine calculations for you if needed.

Stock Yields

Stock yields are much simpler than bond yields, since the return of the principal sum is not promised for any particular time. The rule is: divide the current dividend rate by the price at which the stock is selling on the market.

For example, Fruehauf Canada pays $.45 dividend per year and sells for about $22.50, hence the yield is:

$$\frac{.45}{22.50} \times 100 = .50\%$$

This rate obviously changes every day, with the change of the market quotation. It is also wise to think of it as a current, not a fixed, yield, because the dividend itself may change with the changing fortunes of the company.

WAYS OF DEPICTING MATHEMATICAL QUANTITIES

Tables

After you have collected a set of facts, the standard way of exhibiting them is in columns one under the other. These tables are a useful form, and a practised eye can read them quickly. But to the casual student, meaning doesn't exactly leap out of tables. They have to be studied carefully, and even then they sometimes fail to give up all the information they contain.

Pictorial Methods

For the general public, the simplest way to show the trend of figures is by means of pictures. These can take the form of bar charts, or pie charts, or little men, or bags of gold. As we shall see later, there are dangers in each of these methods, but they are a standard means of presenting statistical information.

Graphs

The graphic method of presentation is extremely useful because it permits large amounts of information on trends to be shown in a small space. The usual type of graph is linear, that is, equal spaces represent equal amounts of money or time.

How To Read a Graph

A picture is the best way of getting a quick bird's-eye view of a large subject. The type of picture best suited to demonstrating facts that have to do with numbers is a graph. Take for example a simple natural phenomenon that everyone has noticed: the fact that it gets hot in the middle of the day and is cold at morning and night. The man at the weather bureau puts this information in the form of long tables or lists of numbers which look something like this:

Time	Temperature in degrees
2 a.m.	12
4	8
6	12
8	20
10	22
12 noon	24
2 p.m.	23
4	21
6	18
8	16
10	13
12 midnight	10

But it is simpler to make a picture or graph. So we mark off a sheet of paper in equal squares and say that the horizontal lines represent time, the vertical lines temperature. If we begin in the lower left-hand corner, time will pass as we move horizontally to the right, and the temperature will increase as we move upward.

This square sheet with its labelled lines is called the "grid". Now take a pencil and transfer the information on the table to the grid.

FIGURE 6: **Graph of a Normal Summer Day**

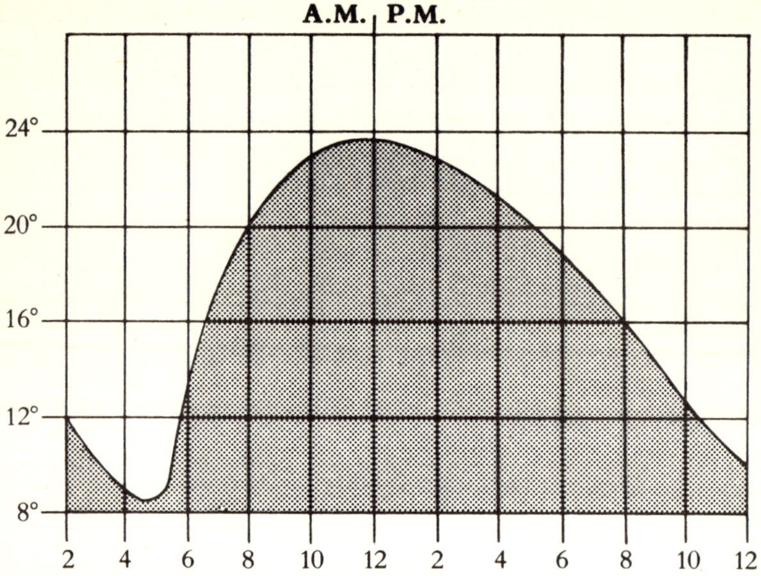

FIGURE 7: **Graph of an Unusual Summer Day**

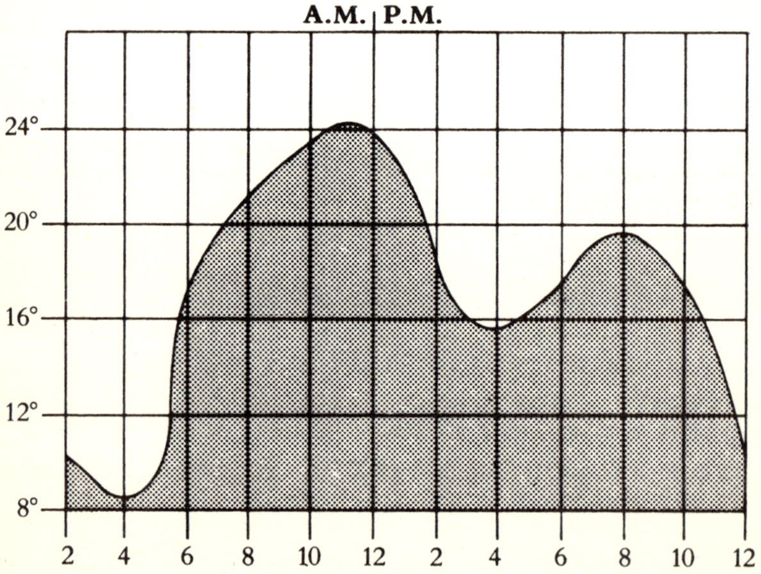

First we see that at 2 a.m. the temperature was 12 degrees, so we make a dot at the point where the line representing 2 a.m. crosses that representing 12 degrees. We do the same for all the pairs of numbers in the table and join the dots with a curved line. This gives a graph something like the one in Figure 6.

By glancing at a picture like this you can see immediately what kind of day it has been. If the graph in Figure 6 is considered a normal summer day, then when a graph like the one in Figure 7 appears, you know at once that the day has been unusual.

A graph, then, is simply a picture of a set of figures. It lets you know the trend of the figures without getting bogged down in the details. In Figures 6 and 7 we have plotted temperature against time. But any one set of things that change can be plotted against any other set. In talking about financial security we usually plot "dollars" against "time". But there are many other possibilities. Graphs of changing market prices of shares, or of the various economic indicators, are just as easy to make as graphs of the weather.

Non-linear Graphs

If quantities are changing greatly, as for example a growth mine that goes from 15¢ to $10 a share, linear graphs have the disadvantage that the lines run off the top of the page and are not seen again. To get around this we can use log or semi-log paper, where equal spaces do not represent equal amounts. In Figure 8, for example, is a hypothetical stock that moved from 15¢ to $10 a share, and yet remained on the paper.

Another important advantage of semi-log paper (that is, paper with a log scale on one axis and a linear scale on the other) is that lines of equal slope represent equal percentage rises, or a single vertical distance (say one inch) represents the same percentage change no matter where it is measured on the chart. Thus both low- and high-priced stocks look the same on the graph if they are acting the same.

The publication *Value Line* makes intelligent use of this type of graph.

FIGURE 8: **A Graph on Semi-log Paper**

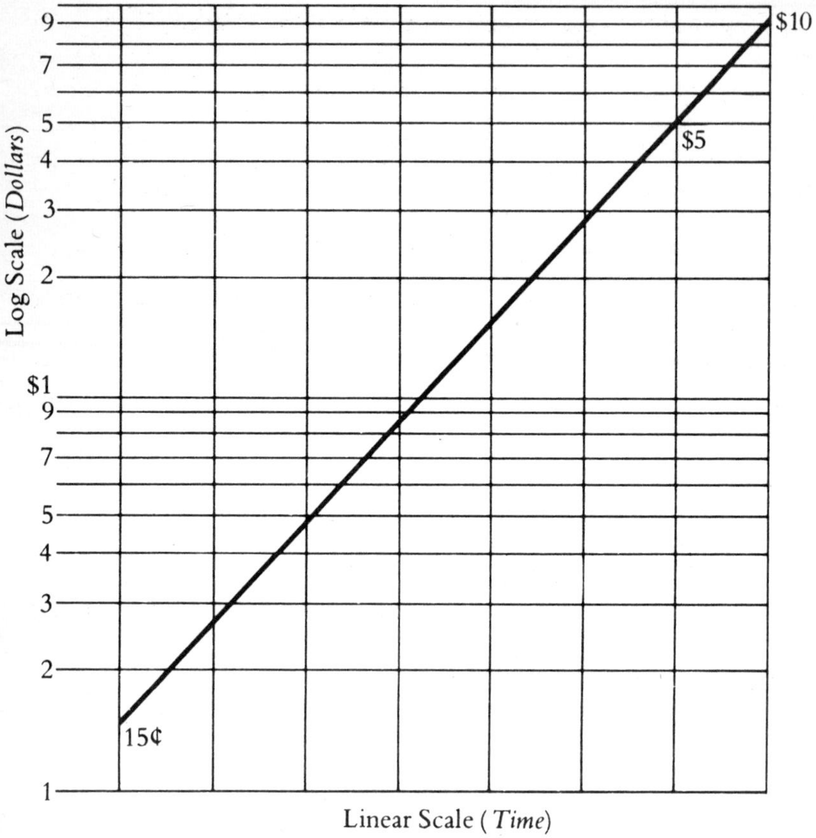

MATHEMATICS OF THE DYNAMIC SITUATION

Trends

One of the quickest ways to see how a particular industry is progressing in relation to the average of all industries is to superimpose a graph of one on the other. If the two graphs are made on the same scale, you can see immediately whether the industry in question is doing better or worse than its contemporaries.

In the same way, a particular company's operation can be compared with the average results in its industry. This shows immediately where your company stands in relation to the rest of the industry.

Graphs of the basic economic indicators, such as carloadings (the number of tons of goods that are moving) and consumer credit, will show trends in a most dramatic way. If they all turn down together, it's a pretty clear warning of a major reversal in the trend of stock prices. Remember, one of the functions of investment analysis is to spot major trends. Proper use of graphs will help you to do this.

Types of Correlation in Graphs

Correlation means that there is a causal relationship between the factors represented by two graphs. This relationship between the variables may be indirect (for example, they may both be affected by the same cause), but nevertheless it must be demonstrated or there is no correlation. Neglect of this point is the source of many popular abuses of statistics.

A classic case of correlation is that of the business index with the employment index. As levels of business rise, more people are employed, and vice versa. This is what is called a direct correlation, where the two variables move together in the same sense, either up or down.

Inverse correlation is where the variables move in the opposite way. An example of inverse correlation is the business index (A) with the commercial-failures index (B), which gives a graph like the one in Figure 9, in which, as one variable rises, the other falls.

FIGURE 9: **Inverse Correlation**

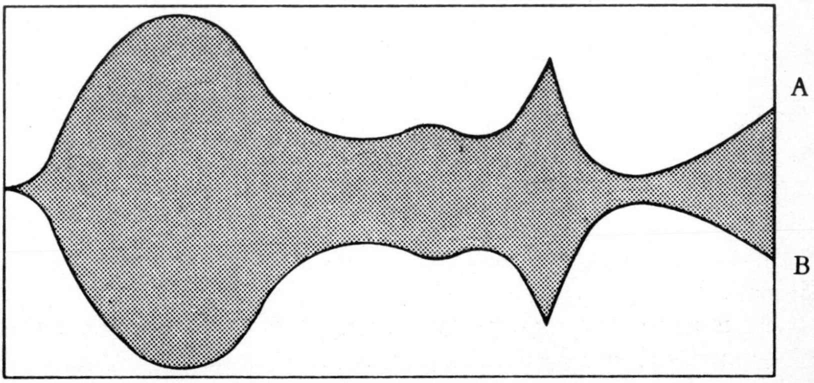

False correlation is an important hazard. The stock averages sometimes seem to rise with the hemline of women's skirts, but this may be an accident. You can't generalize from any correlation until you are sure that it is not an accident.

Detective Work on Statistics

Here's how to peer behind an impressive façade of figures to see what is really going on.

Sampling

This is a big field, and not one to be completely covered here. Suffice it to say that before taking the results of surveys to heart, you must look very closely at such things as:

- what is the size of the sample?
- selection of sample (when? how broad? from what group?)
- who did the interviewing?
- are there slanted questions in the questionnaire?

What Is Omitted?

1. It is true that one honest test found A to be B. But what about all the other tests?
2. Deviation from norm. It is true that most automobiles come equipped with engines, but what about the used car *you* bought?

Averaging

One area of great confusion is averaging. We read of the "average" this and that every day. But there are three main kinds of averages, all usually different. Here is a list showing how much each of ten families spends on housing:

Family	1	$62,000
	2	15,000
	3	15,000
	4	15,000
	5	8,000
	6	8,000

7	6,000
8	6,000
9	4,000
10	1,000
	$140,000

The various averages are:

1. The arithmetic mean is $\frac{140{,}000}{10} = \$14{,}000$

   This is a straight arithmetical average, and is usually meaningless. The financial situation of the man paying $62,000 is not helped by the knowledge that "average" families pay out $14,000 a year.
2. The median is $8,000. Five families pay this amount or more, and five pay this amount or less.
3. The mode is $15,000. This means that the housing cost that occurs most frequently is $15,000.

Featuring Meaningless Variations

Cigarette advertising thrives on this. One multimillion-dollar campaign some years ago was based solely on determinations of nicotine content so small as to be within the range of experimental error.

Graphical Misrepresentation

1. Truncated – only parts of the curves are shown.
2. Changed proportion between the vertical and the horizontal lines of the graph (to make a factor look large or small).
   What you have to remember is that there are many methods of graphing. Any method can be used, and any method is honest if you say what you are doing. But watch out for graphs that don't say clearly what method is used.
3. Extrapolation and interpolation.

When you have a graph like the one in Figure 10, made up from genuine figures (o's), you feel an almost irresistible temptation to extrapolate. This means you say to yourself, "Since the lines are

FIGURE 10: **Interpolation and Extrapolation**

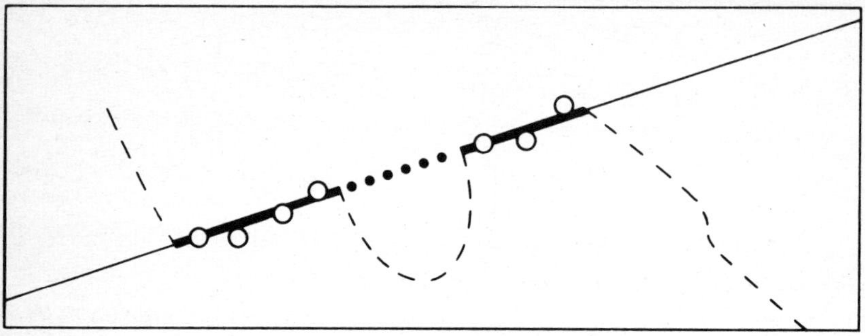

trending in this direction, they will continue in this direction" (solid lines). Or, you want to interpolate and make the graph look as if you had all the figures (dotted line). Graphs look neater this way. But both these suppositions are highly dangerous. You do not know anything for sure about the graph outside the areas where you have figures. For all you know, the graph in those areas may look like the dashed lines.

After the Reagan–Carter presidential election of 1980 it is perhaps superfluous to warn against taking pollsters too seriously, but the advertising business still makes good use of fraudulent figures and misleading graphs. One good antidote is to read Darryl Huff's book, *How To Lie with Statistics*.

CHAPTER THREE

Dealing with the Broker

The number of useful and productive laborers is everywhere in proportion to the quantity of capital stock which is employed in setting them to work, and to the particular way in which it is so employed.
ADAM SMITH (1723–90)

Another thing you should know before you begin investing is how to deal with a broker. You must be aware of what his position is in the market and what he can and cannot do for you.

THE STOCK MARKET

A market is a place where buyers and sellers meet. The Saturday morning farmers' market in most towns is where the farmers from the surrounding district come to sell their produce to buyers wanting various kinds of food. The stock market is a place set aside for the buying and selling of shares in companies. In each country there are stock exchanges in the leading cities. Stockbroking companies that are members of the stock exchange are the only ones allowed to buy and sell shares. The individual buyer or seller places his order with a stockbroker, who receives a commission for carrying out the order.

Whenever a stock is bought or sold on the exchange, its name, the number of shares, and the price are recorded on a tape. The information on this ticker-tape is sent to brokers' offices all over the country, where it is flashed on a screen.

Since the value of a stock depends on the opinion of various investors about the company's prospects, the price of the stock moves up and down every day. Investors are people, and not all people think alike. One investor will think the company's prospects are good and want to buy the stock. At the same moment another investor will think the company is on the downgrade and will want to sell.

The stock exchange provides a convenient system for getting buyer and seller together so that both parties can do what they want. Actual sales of stocks take place between brokers who act as agents of the owners. The seller telephones his broker, telling him that he wants to sell his stock at a certain price. The broker has bought the privilege of dealing on the floor of the stock exchange, and has a man stationed there to whom he communicates the selling order. This "floor trader" walks over to the booth where this particular kind of stock – steel, railway, chemical – is traded, and shouts that he has a certain number of shares of this company for sale at a certain price. Other brokers, acting for people who want to buy the stock, have their floor traders standing at the same booth. The two traders reach an agreement with each other, and then telephone their respective offices indicating that the sale and purchase have been made.

This price will be recorded on the screens in brokers' offices across the country. No one has any control over stock prices of major corporations today. Fifty years ago large fortunes were made by men who organized "pools" in certain stocks. They would buy up shares on the market, spread a rumour that the company was about to make a fortune, and then when the public began clamouring for the shares and the price was forced up would sell their holdings at a handsome profit. Today there are government bureaus, such as the Securities Exchange Commission and the Ontario Securities Commission, that regulate the operation of the stock market and prevent the formation of pools. Price manipulation is still possible, however, with penny stocks. This is another good reason to avoid them.

Prices on the stock market fluctuate – they go both up and down. This is one of the most important points to remember about the stock market. Another important fact about the market is that it has conflicting currents. At a time when most of the stocks are going down, individual shares may be going up, and vice versa.

But the most important point to remember about the stock market is that prices on the exchange represent the average of what thousands of people are thinking about a given stock at a given time. Since the price is made by the actions of crowds, it is emotional rather than rational, and for this reason no one knows what the price of a given stock will do. Price movements either up or down tend to become more severe because of the influence of crowd psychology. When people standing around brokers' offices see a stock's price declining, they often stampede to sell. This drives the stock's price down still more. The converse happens when people stampede to buy.

It is easy to buy or sell shares of large corporations because they are all listed on the exchange, and both buyers and sellers are usually easy to find. Small companies, however, are not usually listed on the stock exchange. This means that the owner of such shares must himself take on the job of finding a buyer who is willing to invest in the shares. This is sometimes a difficult and time-consuming process.

The price of shares listed on the stock exchange is determined mainly by owners and would-be owners, for whatever reason, notion, or emotion.

The important thing is what individual investors think about the prospects of an individual company. If the majority of investors think a company's prospects are poor, its share price will tend to fall, even though the market averages – representing the average share price of twenty to four hundred representative companies – are rising. The price of a stock on the market is the result of every scrap of information that every interested person can obtain about it, discounted as far into the future as people are able to see. This is why stock prices often behave in a queer way, going up on receipt of bad news and down with good news. In the former case, the market price had already been adjusted to take care of all possible bad news, and thus could only move up after the blow had fallen.

Listed and Unlisted Securities

Most stocks you hear about are traded on the listed market: that is, they are listed on the big board at the New York, Toronto, and other stock exchanges, and every transaction in the stock appears on the ticker-tape.

As mentioned, other things being equal, there is usually less trouble and delay in either buying or selling a listed stock than there is in buying or selling unlisted stocks. Thus, if you are trading, and the success of your transactions depends on the speed with which they can be carried out, you would normally stick to listed stocks.

Stocks that are not listed on such exchanges as the New York or the Canadian exchanges are called "over-the-counter", or unlisted. The unlisted market is vastly larger than the listed. In other words, most of the companies that have issued shares to the public are not registered on any of the stock exchanges. The National Quotation Bureau, which issues daily quotes on unlisted securities, gives prices on about 5,000 stocks each day. In the course of the year something like 25,000 different unlisted securities are traded. By comparison, there are fewer than 5,000 listed securities on all U.S. exchanges.

The fact that a company's securities are not listed is in no sense a reflection on the integrity or prospects of the company. There are a hundred reasons why a company feels it doesn't require its securities to be listed.

If a company is doing business chiefly in one local area, not much is gained by having it listed on the national exchanges. Some companies are well enough known that there is always a market for their stock among well-informed investors, both private and institutional.

One advantage of over-the-counter securities is that you can be sure they are not being promoted. The first thing a stock promoter does is get his company listed on a major exchange. This opens up opportunities for pushing it by means of publicity, and all the other tricks of the trade.

The chief danger in over-the-counter securities is buying from a small local broker who has no skills or facilities in this field. The large brokerage houses in the United States and Canada keep a market in several hundred over-the-counter securities. This means that they will buy shares in these companies at the going market price for their own account, and then keep them to sell to others at a mark-up. This is just like the retail grocer buying commodities, stocking them on his shelves, and then selling them at a profit. This is a valuable service.

INVESTING WITH BORROWED MONEY

Margin requirements differ with the type of security and government regulations in force at the time you buy. Most brokerage houses will finance government bonds or Treasury bills on 5 per cent or 10 per cent margin. Stocks and preferred shares are always bought on higher margins than bonds because they are more risky. In Canada, the normal brokerage margin level at the present time is 50 per cent.

Many people are afraid of margin buying because they have heard stories of people being wiped out during the 1929 market crash. These stories are true, but the fact that some people have been killed in automobile accidents does not necessarily prove that the automobile is harmful. Buying on margin is a useful device, perhaps even a necessity, for people who know what they are doing and can afford the increased risk.

Buying on margin seems excessively risky to most people because they are unfamiliar with it. But essentially it is no different in principle from buying a house and then taking a first mortgage on it. If you do not keep up the principal and interest payments on your mortgage you will lose your investment in the house. True, there is no danger that the mortgage lender will come to you and ask you to put up more collateral if the price of houses drops. Nevertheless, people without adequate capital must take this kind of risk in order to get the capital they need.

OPEN ORDERS

If you decide that a given stock is fairly priced at $20 a share, and at the moment the shares are selling for $24, you can place a bid with your broker and try to get the shares at a price which you think is fair. These are called "open orders" and can be arranged so they are good for a specified period, or good until cancelled. The advantage of open orders is that after making a study of a stock, when all the data are fresh in your mind, you make a decision on what price you will pay for it. If you then place an open order with your broker, the matter is finished for the next month. If you get the stock, fine; if you don't, you review it again for the next month to see if there have been any changes in the company's fortunes or prospects. The danger of open orders is that you might forget about them. Then, during a spectacular drop in the market, you find transaction slips coming into your office, and you don't have the money to pay them. We will discuss more complex ways of protecting paper profits later in the book.

FUNCTIONS OF THE BROKER

Treat the broker for what he is, an order-taker. If he does this job well, he has earned his commission, especially if he is a discount broker, consistently underbidding the so-called "full-service" brokers. Don't ask the broker for advice or support.

Brokerage house failures are very rare nowadays, but shotgun mergers are commonplace. The simplest way to carry a portfolio of stocks is to leave the actual certificates in the custody of your broker. This saves you the trouble of having them registered in your own name to put in your safety-deposit box. Stocks that are held by your broker can be sold by wire if you are away, since they do not have to be endorsed by you as owner. The brokerage house will give you a monthly statement of transactions, including all dividends paid into your account and all interest payments taken out. Most firms charge a small quarterly fee.

Don't get sentimental and forget that the brokerage house is in the business of buying and selling securities. The way the broker earns his living is through commissions on stocks that you buy and sell. Thus the broker has a pecuniary interest in having you buy one thing and sell another. It is not unknown in brokerage houses for the young and less-well-established junior members to sit down at the phone for a session of switching. This means that they phone their customers, suggesting that they sell one stock and buy another. This is how baby gets a new pair of shoes.

Allowing the broker to use his discretion on purchases and sales sounds plausible – after all, he is there each day, knows what is going on, and should be looking out for your success in order to keep you as a customer. However, here is a real and current instance of a broker-managed investment account (May 1985 to September 1986). The blow-by-blow details:

Money invested: $80,000 initially, plus $8,000 added
Expected portfolio promised by the broker: "Savings Bonds, Treasury Bills, Bank Shares, and a Mutual Fund"
(Sounds all right, doesn't it?)

Actual purchases: $14,000 Savings Bonds
500 shares of Royal Bank
$51,000 Treasury Bills

and, when the Treasury Bills came due,
$51,000 of the Bullock Dividend Fund

(So, what's wrong with that? *Plenty*.)

a) The Fund, sold without providing the legally required prospectus, netted a commission of over $2,000 to the broker, and after fifteen months of rising markets is worth $1,000 less than it cost.
b) The Royal Bank shares, purchased at $30.25, were sold at $30.75 and $30.875, for a loss of $246, after commissions to the broker of $528.
c) Subsequent purchases – Seagull Resources, Petrogold Resources, Cove Energy, Abaterra Energy, Magnetics International, Tee-Comm Electronics, and Orwell Resources (hardly household names) – generated gains totalling $5,100, losses of $18,600, and commissions to the broker of over $3,000.

Whose interests were being served? Would this investor have done this well by following the directions, principles, and clues of this book and/or natural human intelligence ("common sense") with *no* broker interference?

Answer: an unqualified Yes.

The investment dealer or investment banker can have an even more direct interest in whether you buy the stock he recommends. He makes part of his living as an underwriter, taking responsibility for placing a certain proportion of a new issue with the public at a fixed price.

New stock issues, even though floated by reputable houses, should ordinarily be avoided by the investor.

Remember, the issuing company thinks it's a good time to sell stock. We know that large amounts of money have been made on such issues, but the market tends to drop when the underwriting house withdraws its support. Then you are all alone in a big cruel world.

How To Interpret the Margin Account Data Your Broker Sends

You will get two kinds of information forms:

1. Confirmations

These will confirm either an unfilled order,

e.g. to buy 100 shares of Amalgamated Rubber Bands (ARB) at $12.50 a share or better, "good until cancelled". It is trading at $13, so you have to be patient.

or, an order that has been filled.

e.g. Sold 200 shares of Bedrock Memorial Stonework (BMS) at $8.75 less commission. Your account will be credited with the money in five business days.

2. Monthly statements

These statements (not usually issued at month end) list the transactions in your account.

1. You added $2,000 to open the account. A credit.
2. Your broker filled your ARB order at $12.25. Including commission, this makes a debit of $1,255.
3. You delivered to your account the 200 shares of Bedrock.
4. The broker sold the BMS for a credit of $1,720.
5. He bought 100 shares of Almayet Enterprises (ALE) at $33.75, commission $50, for a debit of $3,425.
6. Quarterly dividend was paid on ARB of .10 a share. Credit $10.
7. Broker charged you interest on outstanding debit balance for 8 days. Debit $3.

Finally, your security position is listed:

100 shares of ARB
100 shares of ALE
and your ending debit balance. . . $953

To know the approximate market value of your account, you need to get the prices of ARB and ALE from your newspaper or your broker, say $12 and $35. Then:

100 shares of ARB	@12	$1,200
100 shares of ALE	@35	3,500
Total value of securities		4,700
Less debt to broker		953
Equity in account		3,747

Subtract your original investment $2,000 cash and $1,720 securities	3,720
Your account shows a gain of	27

Another adjustment (for exchange) would be required if the securities were valued in a currency different from the money invested.

DISCOUNT BROKERS

In the United States there are now many discount brokers who will handle your orders at a price that deeply undercuts the commission rates of the old-fashioned "full-service" broker. Among the better-known names of discount brokers are: Fidelity U.S.A., Boston; Stockcross, Boston; Fidelity Brokerage Services, Dallas; Rose and Company, Chicago; Brown and Company, Boston; Charles Schwab, New York; Quick and Reilly, New York. In Canada there is now at least one discount broker, Marathon-Brown, with offices in Montreal, Toronto, Vancouver, Halifax, and Winnipeg. The Toronto Dominion Bank is opening up a service, but we haven't tried it. If you can find one, choose a discount broker who has been in business long enough to have survived at least one downside. We know this is difficult to do, but make the effort.

PART II: START WITH $1000

CHAPTER FOUR

How To Invest Without Having To Read or Think

The social object of skilled investment should be to defeat the dark forces of time and ignorance which envelop our future. The actual, private object of the most skilled investment today is to "beat the gun" as the Americans so well express it, to outwit the crowd. . . .
JOHN MAYNARD KEYNES (1883–1946)

If, after having read our credentials in the authors' note and brushed up on some basics, you want to trust us to show you how to go ahead right away, here is what you do. First, you determine where you are in your financial life, and sum it up in a realistic statement of your net worth. Second, you establish some priorities having to do with life insurance, tax considerations, and your rate of savings. Third, you open up an RRSP (Registered Retirement Savings Plan) at a trust company or broker's office, but you don't allow them to manage your money. You use the self-administered plan. Fourth, you open up a margin account with an investment broker, aiming for capital gains rather than income. By these means you commit yourself to a voluntary forced-savings program, even though this sounds like a contradiction in terms.

Your goal is very simple: to increase your net worth from $1,000 to $5,000 in the first year, and then to do at least as well every year thereafter. This is quite within the range of probability if you are earning $20,000 a year or more.

Now we will go over the five steps in detail.

1. Assessing where you are now.
2. Establishing financial priorities.
3. Starting a self-administered RRSP.
4. Opening a margin account at the broker.

1. ASSESSING WHERE YOU ARE NOW

Taking Stock

You need to make up a list of basic facts, including your gross and net (post-tax) income, your assets and their depreciation, your earning prospects for the future, your debts and obligations, your life insurance, your pension plans, your house or cottage, and so on. Then there is your investing experience. Try to connect with the investing experience you have already had (however bad) and learn something from it. Next, you must make a catalogue of your special personal fears. These are debilitating and must be faced. Are you a Depression baby? Are you terrified by borrowed money? Examine your psychoses and neuroses as best you can to see the kinds of investment you should avoid. Finally, there is the question of emotional preferences. Can you, in good conscience, invest in companies that sell products that injure or kill people? Many investors can. If you have qualms of this kind, you may have to avoid the securities of industries that produce liquor, cigarettes, automobiles, armaments, and permanent life-insurance policies.

The Answer

Looking for "the answer" is an emotional problem you will have to solve. If you believe in "the answer", your choices are restricted and usually wrong. Besides, after you have "the answer", you cannot help being very rigid from then on. The real situation is that we have multiple choices in an imperfect world. No single investment will ever satisfy all our criteria perfectly.

What It Feels Like To Invest

Don't feel ashamed of yourself for being prey to nameless fears. We all have those, and the act of investing is a heroic act of will. You are on a high-diving board, in the dark. You don't know for sure that there is a pool down there, or, if there is a pool, whether there is any water in it. But once you have gathered up all your courage, jumped in, gotten wet, and swum back to shore 'ou feel exhilarated. The first-time investor has a hard decision to make, and no one sneers at his timidity.

The Net-Worth Statement

This is the realistic statement (for you), not the optimistic one for your banker. The blank forms are the same, but the numbers are different. Make it out in detail, following the form in Figure 11.

FIGURE 11: **Net Worth Statement**

ASSETS (In thousands of dollars)	MARKET VALUE	LESS MORTGAGE	EQUITY TOTALS
1. REAL ESTATE			
Home	70	50	
Total			20
2. FINANCIAL ASSETS			
Cash	1		
Canada Savings Bonds	7		
Cash value of life-insurance policy	2		
Total			10
3. OTHER ASSETS			
Car	10		
Furnishings	10		
Total			20
Total assets			50
LIABILITIES			
Bank	7		
Family loans	3		
Total.			10
NET WORTH			40

The Exponential Nature of Finance

Nobody jumps from being an ordinary wage-earner to being a millionaire unless he has been stupid enough to buy a lottery ticket. This is why we advise against reading any book whose title contains the words "million" or "millionaire". In finance, if all goes well, your net worth goes up in jumps, but you have to touch each one of the steps. Is your net worth $100 ($10^2$) or $1,000 ($10^3$) or $10,000 ($10^4$) or $100,000 ($10^5$)? Place yourself on this exponential scale, and then resolve to reach the next higher step as soon as possible. Don't even think about the million until you have gone through the four steps before it.

The Stock Market Now

The little guy who bought this book in 1982, when the Dow Jones was under 1000, has had a marvellous five-year run. With the index now approaching 2000, he may look like a genius because he took our advice then. We now hope he is smart enough to listen to our advice again, because we think he is about to get shorn. It is now five years later, and all the indicators are different.

2. ESTABLISHING FINANCIAL PRIORITIES

A. Life Insurance

If you have been swindled into buying cash-value, or "permanent", life insurance, replace it at once with term insurance, and then cancel the old policy. Either buy group term insurance where you work, or buy term as an individual, paying not more than $2.00 a thousand, at age thirty-five. See Chapter 5 for details on how to do it. Do not buy any of the so-called "new products" being offered by all the life-insurance companies under dozens of names, such as Universal Life, Variable Life, Adjustable Life. Prudential of America calls them "innovative forms of life insurance", and they *are* new to The Rock. They carry out the first injunction I published away back in 1944: "Buy term and invest the difference." This simple rule has gotten me into endless trouble with all sorts of respectable people for forty years. But the new policies are all unacceptable because they violate the second basic rule of life-insurance protection, namely: you must have your insurance and your savings in separate contracts. If The Man is insuring your life, don't let him invest your savings.

B. Tax Considerations
These are important to sort out. What is your average tax bracket? your marginal tax bracket (the rate paid on the top slice of income)? How much did you pay in tax last year? on what taxable income? and on what gross income?

C. Savings
What percentage of your gross income did you put aside in savings last year? What percentage of your post-tax net income? Now is the time for a new high resolve about saving, with the goals of saving a higher percentage of your income, and also of working to increase the income. We want you to think about investment, allocating money, muscle, and mind to increase income and net worth. Whose mind? Yours. Don't trust other people with this job. If you have no savings and no money, do not despair. You have the other two. You have muscle you can hire out, and you have a mind you can use for management. If you save 10 per cent or 20 per cent of your salary, it doesn't take long to save the money needed for an investment program. Halfway through your first year of employment, even if you are not moonlighting, you will have saved the $1,000. While expanding your income you should make a real effort to live conservatively. Don't eat junk food, or fad food, or foods that are at the top of their annual price cycle, or fruits and vegetables that are out of season. Eat poor-people's food. It tastes just as good when you are hungry, and if you aren't hungry, why eat? Sell your car if public transportation exists. If it doesn't, learn how to buy cars second-hand and repair them yourself. Buy at garage sales rather than at department stores. Always let somebody else pay the sales tax, and the 30 per cent to 50 per cent immediate depreciation when a new object is taken out of a store.

Now that you have saved the $1,000 we can go on to give you specific steps showing how to invest it. There are two basic rules: 1. Do it *now*, don't delay. 2. Do it yourself. The answer to the plaintive cry "On whom can I depend?" is simple: "Yourself."

3. WHAT TO DO WITH THE FIRST $1,000

The best game in town now is the RRSP (Registered Retirement Savings Plan). To be eligible, you must have what the tax return calls "earned income".

What's good about an RRSP?
- The capital going in is tax free.
- The earnings of the capital are tax free.
- The money can be under your control.

There are some basic rules, such as:
- Be sure you establish a self-administered plan.
- Husband and wife can each have a plan.
- Contribute the maximum eligible amount as early in the year as practical (even though contributions are possible up to 60 days after the year end).
- Pay the administration fee of $100 with a separate cheque, thereby giving yourself an additional tax deduction.

Even if the RRSP has taken all your savings, the tax laws give you back some of it. J. Paul Getty used to say to interviewers who marvelled over his billions: "It's not how much money I *have* that's important, but what it is *doing*." It's what your $1,000 is *doing* that matters to you. It is now at work.

4. STARTING A SELF-ADMINISTERED RRSP

Go to a broker or a trust company and open a self-administered Registered Retirement Savings Plan (RRSP). This is a tax-deferral plan which now allows you to save $7,500 a year (or 18 per cent of your earned income, whichever is the lesser) and deduct it from your taxable income. Both the amounts saved and the year's income from previous contributions are free of tax as long as they stay in the plan. If you are already a member of a company plan, the maximum you may contribute to all plans tax free is $3,500. But by far the best part of the RRSP is the provision that you can do it yourself. As usual, the insurance companies, trust companies, banks, and mutual funds have guided the legislation so that they are cut in on the deal. They will all manage your RRSP for you, complete with front-end loads (administrative fees) that effectively remove most of the earnings for the first years. But you do not have to hire anyone to mismanage your money for you. The law permits you to choose a self-administered type of plan, in which you pay the trust company only for its custodial function.

We know that the Delaney Report expressed the view that it is too difficult for a beginner to self-administer his first RRSP.

This is to be expected. Any Canadian report is bound to present conclusions that are conservative, tried and true.

One disadvantage of the RRSP that is real is the requirement that 90 per cent of the funds be invested in Canadian securities. At times when the Canadian market is high and foreign markets are low, this is serious.

Here is how you calculate the amount of money you can put into the plan: Take your earned income as defined in the federal income-tax guide (available free at all income-tax offices and post offices) and subtract the cost of earning the income, including union or professional society dues and unemployment insurance premiums. You are now allowed to invest the lesser of 18 per cent of this sum or $7,500. If you are a member of a company pension plan, you are allowed a maximum contribution of $3,500, including the amount contributed to the company pension.

For example, if you earn $20,000 a year from an employer, you may put up to $3,500, less your contribution to the employer's pension plan, into your self-administered RRSP each year. If you put in only $2,000, starting at age twenty-five and retiring at sixty-five, at 8 per cent compounded you will accumulate $560,000. If you are already forty when you begin, the sum will be nearly $160,000. With your self-administered plan, you should expect to do much better than the present 8 per cent.

We see this as a growth vehicle over an extended period of time, such as twenty-five to forty years. This gives plenty of time to learn from your mistakes and develop expertise. Even if you are just as bad at investing as the trust company, you will still have a substantial sum available upon retirement.

You now borrow $2,000 from your bank or credit union, secured by your honest face and steady employment at $20,000 a year. In repaying the bank loan, count on the tax saving from the RRSP (thirty to thirty-five per cent of your $4,000 tax). This gives you a total of $100 a month, which should satisfy any but the most avaricious banker.

If you maintain this program for twenty-five years and do no better than the trust company, it will amount to $150,000 compounded. Pursued over forty years, even at the low rate of 8 per cent, it will amount to over half a million dollars. If you are close to retirement, $250,000 might be a more reasonable goal. Even after taxes, this will give you a larger income after retirement than before.

Steps in Picking Shares To Invest In

When you buy the RRSP with the borrowed $2,000 and particularly later when you set up your margin account with the broker, you have to tell the nice man what to buy. Most of the following chapters of this book address themselves to this problem. But you want to get started right away and then refine your investment choices as you learn more and more about how to do it. What we suggest at the very beginning is this: buy the shares of the company that employs you, or if this is impossible, the shares of the company that makes a product you use and admire. What you are trying to buy is the shares of a company that has intelligent management. They were smart enough to hire *you*, and the fact that you are reading this book proves that you are not just the run-of-the-mill Canadian. The same reasoning applies to consumer goods. Good products, fairly priced, do not happen by accident. They are the result of good management; hence the manufacturer of a good product, or the provider of a good service, is often a good bet for your original investment move.

Going into the problem of choice a little more deeply, here are the basic steps (more detail about all of these steps is in later chapters):

1. Go through Monday's *Globe and Mail* and circle all the shares that are selling for less than 10 times their earnings. This is called the P/E (price / earnings) ratio. This gives you a list of companies to be investigated. When we wrote the first edition of this book in 1982, the Dow Jones Index was at 800 and we told you to look for stocks selling at 3 to 4 times earnings. Today the Index has exceeded 1900, and even stocks selling at 9 to 10 times earnings are hard to find. But the basic rule is still true: Look for stocks with low multiples.

   The other possibility is to do the opposite: Find the stocks with the *highest* possible multiples and sell them short. Just now, with the basic economic indicators looking pretty bad, and the Dow Jones near the highest in its history, short selling must be considered. Another possibility is to get out of the market and stay out. Buy solid bonds and ride out the storm until the signals change. But both selling short and getting out are difficult for the average person to do. It takes more guts than most of us have. Retreating to bonds is seen as the coward's way out, and selling short is difficult psychologically. Even if you hedge by buying a call on the shorted stock at the same time, the risk is covered only for a limited time.

2. At your broker's, go through the *Standard and Poor's Stock Guide*, or the *Financial Post* Corporation Service cards to be found at a central urban library. These give, by company, many of the basic figures you need to make a decision. The ones we emphasize are: P/E (Price / Earnings) ratio, Price, Price range, Yield, Assets (Current), Liabilities (Current), Number of shares, Non-cash expenses, Earnings, Working capital per share, Debt per share, and Equity per share. These should be typed out as headings across a sheet of accounting paper, and the figures entered opposite the company name.
3. Having done this, you notice that some industries produce many companies with low P/E ratio or low debt per share. You want to study those industries, to see what is going on. Just at the moment you should be studying the airline industry, because it is being deregulated. Try to pick out the airline that will make the best recovery soonest.

Once you notice that steel, airlines, and cement are at low multiples, you go to the *Moody's Manuals* at the public library, or to the commerce library at any university, and consult the full data there. These books give you the company head-office address, so that you can write for an annual report of any company that really interests you. All the major factors can be seen in this reference book. You don't need to meet the management to know whether it exists. All you need are the numbers, plus the knowledge of how to use them in making investing decisions.

5. INVEST FOR CAPITAL GAINS AND BORROW TO DO IT

As soon as you have borrowed or saved another $2,000, go to your broker and establish a margin account. Order $3,500 worth of stocks, for which the broker provides $1,500 as a margin loan. His interest charge is slightly above the bank rate, but on the other hand he doesn't insist on capital repayment so long as sufficient equity is maintained. This is usually half the market value of the portfolio.

Why invest for capital gains? The answer is simple. Apart from the $1,000 exemption and the dividend tax credit applicable to the dividends of taxable Canadian corporations, income is all taxed. In the 35 per cent bracket you pay $350 tax on $1,000 profit and have $650 left. If you have $1,000 capital gain, none is taxed, unless you have exceeded the limit allowed, presently $50,000, eventually to be $500,000 accumulative.

Why borrow? Again simple arithmetic provides the answer. You may pay 12 per cent interest on the loan, but there is a tax saving of 3.6 per cent because your marginal tax bracket is 30 per cent. Therefore, the real interest rate is 8.4 per cent.

There is less restriction on this account than on the RRSP. For example, you may buy foreign securities if you want.

Voluntary Forced Savings Program

Suppose your initial instruction to the broker was to buy 100 shares of a U.S. stock selling for $25. With exchange and commission your account will be debited with nearly $3,500, leaving you in debt to the broker by nearly $1,500. You now send him your monthly savings cheques for $200 or $300 (from your initial plan for saving 10 to 20 per cent of your income), and in five to six months you own the shares outright.

Now it is time for another move. With your equity now at $3,500, you can buy another $3,500 worth of stock. You might buy more of the same stock, but there is a comforting feeling about having another horse in the stable, especially if the first is limping about in agony. So you order another 100 shares of something with good prospects. (It is best to buy in 100-share lots because, commissions being less, it is cheaper.) At the end of six months (a year from starting), your second debt is paid and you can buy another $3,000 worth of stock.

Your stock-taking at the end of the first year looks like this:

RRSP	$3,000	plus or minus stock movement and dividends
Margin account	7,000	plus or minus stock movement and dividends
	$10,000	

From a standing start at $1,000, you have put together in one year $10,000 of assets working for you. You owe the broker $2,000, and the banker a balance of $800 (remember, you have been paying him back at $100 a month out of your tax savings), so your net worth is $7,200, plus or minus stock-price changes during the year.

Do You Have Any Taxable Income Left?
If you have, don't stop now, but keep thinking. The principle is: don't pay taxes unless you have to. Look at these figures:

Income	$20,000
Deductions and exemptions	9,000
Leaves...	11,000
Less RRSP and deductible interest	3,000
Taxable income	$8,000

On this your tax liability is about $1,700, as against $2,600 tax without these efforts.

To save some more, if you are in a risk-taking mood, consider approved government-inspired tax shelters such as:
- oil and gas drilling ventures
- 100 per cent Canadian-made movies
- Canadian stock-purchase plan (Quebec and Alberta residents only–yet)
- MURBs (Multiple Unit Residential Buildings)

In some of these your deduction from taxable income may exceed your investment, but you will have to borrow more money from the bank to do it.

See Chapter 6 (Personal Income Tax) for specific examples, but by and large we feel you should be very cautious about trusting *any* of these government-inspired tax shelters. The government is not trying to save you money, but is trying to entice you into risking your money so it can achieve one of its political goals. More often than not, you trade a small tax benefit for a large capital loss.

For example, MURBs (Multiple Unit Residential Buildings) are now out as a new tax shelter because the government has allowed the legislation to die. However, keep your eyes open for a return on the part of both federal and provincial governments to some kind of encouragement to real-estate investors. When housing starts are very low, with threats of more unemployment and recession in materials industries and trucking, expect government intervention. Lack of available cheap housing annoys voters, and sooner or later governments will want to do something about it. Moreover, there was talk in mid 1980 of the federal government removing the indexing provision built into the income tax returns. If this is done, there will be great pressure to provide an alternative shelter for people willing to risk their savings in real estate. Nothing does this better than generous depreciation provisions, especially if the loss were allowed to be deducted from other income, as it was in the happy time prior to the 1971 income-tax act.

This chapter deals with what we would suggest you do to put your $1,000 to work for you right away. In a sense, the rest of the book expands on topics we have touched on here – such as life insurance and pensions, tax planning, and, of course, investing.

CHAPTER FIVE

Life Insurance and Pension Plans

Truth, Historical truth, never imposes itself independently. . . . This is perhaps what partly explains why falsehood everywhere has the upper hand and wins out so generally. It is also because falsehood is advantageous, flattering, pleasing (at least to the majority), whereas truth always embarrasses and hurts some in some way or other.
ANDRÉ GIDE (1869–1951)

If you have debts or financial dependants, no financial-security plan is complete without some kind of life insurance. But your long-term aim should be to become self-insured – that is, to have enough money saved to provide for your dependants when you are dead. When you are self-insured you can stop paying insurance premiums. But it takes years of conscientious saving to achieve this, and in the meantime you need protection.

The material that follows is very elementary, and will not be of much help to you when you try to change the insurance you already have into something that makes sense. The insurance salesman will run rings around you and leave you for dead. If it turns out that you have to change your policies, you had better read a whole book about it before braving the salesman. He gets 100 per cent of the first premium now, and 10 per cent of the next ten premiums, so he is not going to let you have a low-premium type of protection without a fight. As it happens, I wrote the book you should read. It is J. J. Brown, *Winning the Life Insurance Game: How You Can Get Good Protection and Still Save Money,* Macmillan of Canada, 1985. The basic thing you have to keep in mind is this: The premium you pay for "permanent" life insurance covers the cost of two services, protection for your dependants if you die, and protection for yourself if you live. You *pay* for both these services, but unless you have mastered the trick of being alive and dead at the same time, you can't possibly *receive* both services. If you die your heirs collect the death benefit, and if you live you can collect part of your savings: but in either case part of what you have paid for is never received.

All-life insurance policies belong in one of two classes:

1. A mixture of protection and investment
2. Pure protection

The life-insurance salesman is going to sell you the first, because it costs more and he makes a better commission. We want you to buy only the second, and to do your investing our way, not the life-insurance-company way.

Life-insurance policies of the second type (those that are all protection) are fairly simple. Pure life insurance is exactly like fire insurance on your house. You pay the premium of so much a year. If at the end of the year your house hasn't burned down, you lose your premium. Similarly, if you do not die during the policy year, your life insurance premiums for that year must be considered a total loss. There is no way of getting around this hard fact. All pure insurance is a service (like maid service), and once it has been rendered and paid for you have nothing to show for it except a year's peace of mind.

Most of us know we are going to die, but very few know exactly when the event will take place. If we can arrange to die early, our books will show a profit if we are heavily insured. But if we insure heavily and then have the misfortune to live, the resulting financial distress is appalling. Obviously, some sort of compromise must be made. Making this compromise is called making an insurance plan.

Since the reason for having life insurance is to protect dependants, as your dependants leave home you will require less insurance. It is often helpful to make a graph of your insurance needs (see Figure 12). (Chapter 2 should have helped you with this.)

Let the vertical lines be the time in years, the horizontal line be the total amount of insurance needed at any given time in dollars.

The life-insurance needs of the average married man are not constant but look something like the graph. He starts out with no insurance because he has no dependants, or creditors. But when he gets married at age twenty, he buys insurance to protect his wife. As children are born and substantial amounts of credit used, he buys more insurance to protect them. In his thirties, when he is carrying protection for creditors, spouse, and children, the line reaches its highest point on the graph. But in his forties the children start to leave home. Some of the debts are paid off. His assets increase.

FIGURE 12: **Life-Insurance Needs**

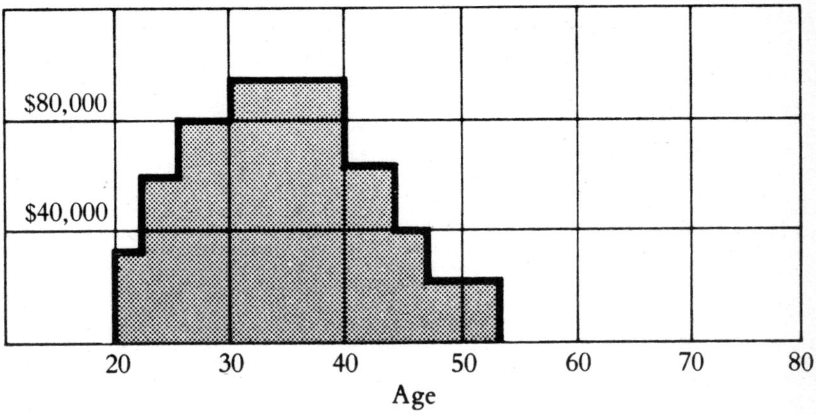

Hence, the amount of insurance protection he carries begins to drop. By the time he is fifty all the children have gone and his accumulated assets may be such that he can "afford to die".

On your own graph, any shaded space is going to cost you money because it represents the insurance on which you are paying premiums.

As mentioned earlier, one way you can eventually avoid having to pay any premiums at all is to develop your savings and investment program rapidly so that you become self-insured.

If you could get an insurance policy whose graph would be exactly the same as the graph of your insurance needs, it would be ideal. But in this world such things seldom happen. What you want to do is find the type of insurance whose graph looks most like the graph of your insurance needs. In general, life-insurance policies that are a mixture of protection and investment have protection graphs that look like the graph in Figure 13.

The pure-protection type of life-insurance policy has a graph that looks like the one in Figure 14 (although some companies will renew term-insurance policies until age eighty if you wish).

From the graphs you can see at once that term insurance fits your needs, while "permanent insurance" does not. Permanent insurance is so named by the industry because it is really temporary. The average life of a "permanent" policy is only seven years.

FIGURE 13: **"Permanent" or Investment-Type Insurance**

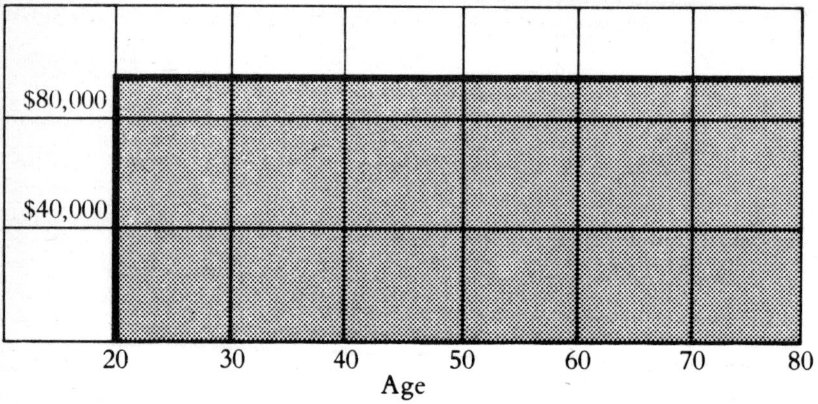

As an example, consider Sun Life policy number 6118827, taken out at age twenty-seven for a face amount of $3,000, at an annual premium of $59.19 until death do us part. Assuming this woman really needed insurance (she had no dependants or debts), the fair price for $3,000 protection is $1.60 a thousand, or a premium of $4.80 a year. The Sun Life price of $59.19 obviously includes some provision for upkeep of its block-long mausoleum in Montreal.

FIGURE 14: **Pure, or Term, Insurance**

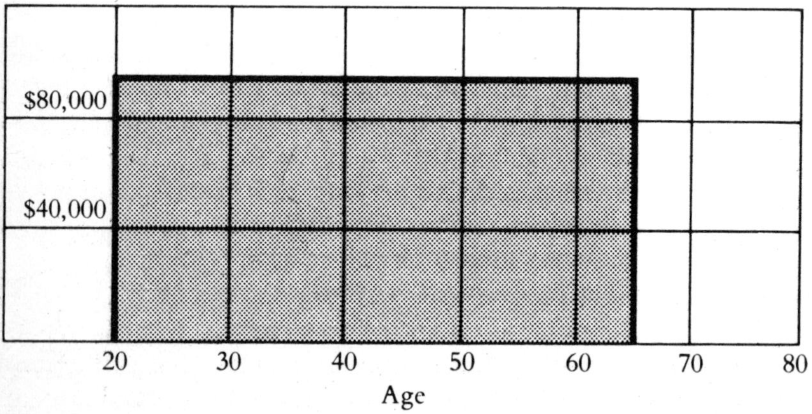

PENSION PLANS

Investments are designed to look after the future needs of dependants. One of your dependants is yourself. Sooner or later the time will come when you will be too old to compete efficiently on the labour market – or, even if you can compete, you will want to live a more leisurely life. When this time comes you will be dependent for your livelihood on the money you have put aside as savings, or in a pension. A pension or an annuity contract is simply somebody's promise to pay you a fixed amount of money each year until you die.

Say you have just sold your business and, at the age of forty-five, find yourself with $150,000 in cash. Your family is taken care of, and you want to arrange it so you get the maximum enjoyment from the money each year. Yet you want it to last until you have no further need of it, being dead. You might put the money into various securities, common shares, or mortgages, and live on the interest and some of the principal that is withdrawn each year. But this plan is not ideal because you don't know how soon you are going to die, hence you don't know how much of the principal to use.

To avoid these difficulties you can sign a contract with a company by which they promise to pay you so much every year until you die, in exchange for your giving them the $150,000 right now. Many people put a part of their savings into annuities or pension plans because these offer the safest fixed-dollar investment. Also, if you come of a long-lived family and watch out for trucks, you can take out much more than you pay in.

The trouble with annuities and all fixed-dollar-value pension plans is that since the Second World War we have had such chronic inflation that all investments that pay off in fixed dollars are highly suspect. You are investing dollars worth 50¢ and will probably be paid off in dollars worth 10¢. This is no bargain, no matter how safe and sure.

How To Retire on a Pension

Every fall the papers are full of advertisements showing contented elderly couples enjoying their retirement stretched out on Florida beaches, or fishing in the warm Gulf Stream. In a world where there is no free lunch, you can be certain that this idyllic picture will not come to pass without plenty of planning. Not many people have both health and the money to enjoy leisure at age sixty-five. It takes time to build up a pension fund. So, if you are serious in wanting to retire at age sixty-five, you must do some planning for it now.

Just now, because there are more people than jobs, you can retire early if you can afford it. Many companies are making it easy for you by offering a generous "golden handshake". You can, at age fifty-five or so, take a big cash settlement and get out of their hair. Air Canada recently offered such a golden handshake to some of its senior pilots, expecting perhaps twenty to accept. When the number reached ninety, they rushed to stop the applications. This will cost the company $45 million over the next few years, but it doesn't matter. It is taxpayers' money, not *real* money. What is serious is, if the expected shortage of experienced pilots develops in the next few years, the company will have to replace them at top competitive salaries.

In both the United States and Canada there are tax advantages in pension plans. In both countries the income earned by a pension fund does not have to be declared for tax purposes until you receive it, although some November 1981 federal budget provisions moved in a threatening direction. Moreover, your employer's contribution to your group retirement fund is not considered part of your income.

RRSP (*Registered Retirement Savings Plan*)

Since 1972, Canadian taxpayers have had a better break. In Chapter 4 we discussed RRSPs, the tax-deferral plan which allows you to save (for 1986) $7,500 a year (or 18 per cent of your earned income, whichever is the lesser) and deduct it from your taxable income.

You can contribute to your RRSP up to sixty days after the year end. This gives you time to pull yourself together and sort things out right after Christmas. You can borrow money to pay into the plan, but the interest is not deductible from your taxable income. On the payout side, you can buy an immediate annuity with the proceeds at age seventy-one, when the annual proceeds become taxable as income. Or you can get cash out gradually at any time before that by setting up a second plan, transferring the continuing fund to it, and collapsing the first plan.

We recommend that you start taking money out of the RRSP at age sixty-five or in the first year you have no employment income. If your RRSP amounts to $100,000, take out $10,000. That year your income tax will look like this:

Income: Old Age Security and Canada Pension			$5,200
Your RRSP pension			10,000
			$15,200
Less exemptions and deductions (1985 rates):			
Exemptions:	Personal	$4,140	
Deductions:	Age	2,590	
	Charity	270	
		7,000	7,000
Net taxable income			$8,200

The tax on this is about $1,800.

So, by paying a tax of $1,800, you get out $8,200 ($10,000–$1,800), which you can invest any way you want – in a mobile home, a foreign security, or even in a foreign country. Having some freed-up cash is always an advantage, especially if the country sinks into a major depression and cash becomes valuable again.

Pension-planning is difficult for an individual because there are at least thirty major classes of plans for accumulating the capital, and your pension upon retirement depends upon which system you choose. It also depends on how much you have paid into it each year, and how old you were when you started. If we take amounts ranging from $100 to $2,500 in hundred-dollar jumps as the possible annual premiums, and settle for forty starting ages from twenty to sixty-five, the number of different plans possible is thirty thousand. This is why you won't learn all there is to know about retirement plans and how they affect you from reading one chapter in a book. But if you get your feet down off the couch and read what follows carefully, you will know the advantages and disadvantages of the various plans offered, and be in a position to make a reasonably intelligent choice.

Plans Available

There are three major factors in planning a pension plan: government efforts, company pension plans, and individual plans. Since government Old Age Security and the Canada Pension Plan apply to all at age sixty-five, not much special planning can be done with them. You contribute, take what you get, and like it.

Many companies, especially the larger ones, have pension plans which function as a sort of fringe benefit received by employees in addition to their salaries. These are open to both hourly-paid and white-collar workers. According to the latest figures, nearly 70 per cent of industrial employees are covered by some sort of company pension plan. But of course industrial workers make up only a small part of the total labour force.

Company pension plans are of two kinds, contributory and non-contributory. In contributory plans the employee and the employer together pay the cost of the pension. A common system is to have the employee pay 6 per cent of his salary each year and the employer pay the balance of the premium cost. This balance is small when you are young, large when you are old.

In non-contributory plans the employer pays all costs, but the amount of the final pension is normally much smaller.

Even under a fairly generous contributory retirement plan, the amount of pension is not large. For example, a man earning $12,000 a year would retire after thirty years with the company on a pension of $488 a month. Figure 15 is a table of various income brackets, showing the total income from government plus a generous company pension that might be expected by an employee who retires at age sixty-five after thirty years' service.

FIGURE 15: **Proceeds of Retirement Income Plans**

Your monthly retirement income after thirty years' service would be:

If you have earned an average each year of:	From government (after age 65)	From your company pension plan (after age 65)	Total (after age 65)
$6,000	$354	$288	$642
8,000	354	384	738
10,000	354	480	834
16,000	354	816	1,170
24,000	354	1,180	1,534

If the amounts in the table seem too small, you can join an individual plan in addition to the company and government plans. Most insurance companies, trust companies, mutual funds, professional and trade associations, and investment-counsel firms are coming out with plans to separate the investor from some of his hard-earned dollars. Each of these plans has features that might conceivably fit the needs of a particular individual, but since each company, naturally enough, is selling its own plan and glossing over its unfavourable features, it is difficult for the consumer to get objective advice.

The Advantages of Joining a Plan

Beyond the tax relief, the only advantage of a pension plan is that you enjoy the moral support of the insurance company or trust company in carrying it out. As individuals we are weak and find saving difficult. When we tie ourselves up by a contract with a big institution, we can rely on them for a measure of arm-twisting.

Disadvantages of All Retirement Plans

The basic disadvantage is that the capital you accumulate is locked in, both before and after retirement. Under existing legislation, once you have put money into an approved plan it must stay there until you retire. You can't even use it as collateral for a bank loan. On the other hand, this "locked-in" feature may not always be a disadvantage, since the money is locked away from bad investment decisions by you or your advisers.

Even after you reach retirement age, the money must be used in just one way – to buy an immediate annuity at the rates in force at that time. If you want to spend the money some other way, for example on buying a small business to provide you with a new interest in life during retirement, the money will have to come from somewhere else. This does not apply to our suggested use of the RRSP.

Another major disadvantage is that the income-tax benefit is not clear gain. You are merely exchanging one tax benefit for another. To the extent that you place your savings in a retirement plan, you can't put your money into other investments that carry tax benefits (e.g., depreciable real estate or movie films).

Perhaps more important, in most plans managed by institutions you lose the advantage of possible capital gains. If you are a prudent investor or a lucky speculator, and buy stocks for $1,000 which you later sell for $10,000, it is possible to build up an estate after paying taxes on the capital gain. Once gained, this money can be employed any way you see fit. You can retire on it, paying tax only on the income portion and drawing on tax-paid capital for the balance.

Weighing Pros and Cons of Pension Plans

From the above, there may seem to be more disadvantages than advantages to joining a retirement plan. But this is not true. It looks that way because it takes longer to write out the disadvantages. They are more complicated.

How much weight you give to these various advantages and disadvantages depends on your personal circumstances and your goals.

The Costs of Joining a Plan

There are two costs involved when you join any retirement plan. The major cost is the savings you have to put aside each year to remain a member of the plan. These savings are in part involuntary (withheld by your employer as part of your pension plan) and in part voluntary (i.e., your RRSP).

The second item of cost in any plan is the cost of administration and management. Money management is a skill, like legal service, and when you need it you have to pay for it. In addition, trustees and insurance companies have fixed operating costs that must be covered. The fee charged for these services is normally small in relation to the amount of money at stake. Hence, you should not allow your decision to be swayed by small differences in charges. On the other hand, you should calculate how much of your savings will eventually come back to you, and how much will be swallowed up in costs of administration and front-end loads.

Since these figures are important, and since the rules of the RRSP game tend to change every year, you had better look at how well the companies are doing managing the investment portfolio, the charges and the loading of various plans, and alternative ways of terminating the RRSP. We like our plan much better, because it is flexible and allows you to retain control of your own money at a cost in taxes that is below the threshold of real pain.

Financing Your Mid-Life Crisis

Unlike most government programs, the RRSP can be a real friend in time of need. When in your forty-fifth year you realize you simply must get away from it all and spend a year or so as a beachcomber, you can slip the money you plan to leave in Canada into a new RRSP and collapse the old plan, releasing (after tax withheld) the required amount of cash to you. This should be done early in the calendar year following your departure, when your income is non-existent and your tax rate is lowest.

Contracting Your Services

The best possible deal is to have agreed with your employer to be an employee under contract. This allows you to carry on your own show and run your own RRSP the way it should be run. It also allows tax savings if you sell your services through an intervening company. This is easier to negotiate if you work for a small company rather than a large, and if you are a recognized hot-shot rather than a drone.

How To Plan Your Pension

A good pension plan is an individual thing, created specifically to suit the needs of one person. In order to get a plan that suits your needs and your pocketbook, you will first have to answer some questions. These, in order of increasing difficulty are:

1. How old are you? If you are young, trusteed plans, and especially those containing common stocks, may appeal because the long-term trend of the economy seems to be upward. If you are nearing retirement age, the certainty of the insured plan may have more appeal.
2. How much do you earn? The more you earn, the more risk you can afford.
3. How many dependants have you now?
4. How many dependants will you have later? Make an intelligent guess.
5. What will be your earning pattern over your working life? Some professions, like medicine and the law, show earnings that begin late in life and modestly, but climb to high levels later on and last beyond age seventy. Other occupations have high earnings early in life but drop off rapidly to zero. This obviously makes a difference in the kind of pension plan needed.

6. What kind of person are you? This is the most difficult question of all, since most of us don't know much about ourselves. For example:
   (a) What is your taste in risks?
   Some people can't sleep nights if they take risks. But risk is inescapable, no matter what you do with your money. So you have the choice between risks that show and risks that don't show. Do you prefer to lose money prudently, in a way that is acceptable to solid citizens, or to lose it in a speculative way? If you prefer to lose your money prudently, you will favour a trusteed plan that is guaranteed, or an insured plan.
   (b) How do you feel about inflation?
   The kinds of risk you assume in a pension plan depend on your views about inflation. People who bought annuities in the fifties using dollars worth 100 cents are unhappy today when they are being paid off in dollars worth 30 cents. In the next three decades, will the pendulum swing the other way? We don't think so.

These are difficult questions. Our view is that most people are best served by the most flexible type of plan. In other words, choose a plan in which you don't have to make all the major decisions right now. In general, trusteed plans are more flexible than insured plans, and the RRSP is the most flexible of all.

Conclusion

The income you will have to live on after retirement depends on three factors: the number of years you have contributed to your retirement fund, the amount in dollars you contributed each year, and the rate of return on the capital invested. To maximize the first factor, you should start building up a retirement fund at the earliest possible age. To improve the second factor, you should put aside from current income as much as you can conveniently spare, without actually impairing your present living standards for benefits that may be mythical. The importance of the third factor is shown in the table in Figure 16.

The choice of a retirement plan that is suitable for you, like many other financial decisions, is complicated by emotional factors that are to a large extent beyond your control. But by studying the various plans available and then choosing the one that is closest to your individual needs, you can maximize benefits and avoid major pitfalls.

FIGURE 16: **Pension Plan Totals at Different Rates**

If, at age 40, you put aside $2,000 a year for 25 years:

If your pension plan earned (capital appreciation plus interest) an average of:	the total at age 65 would be:	which amount would buy an annuity of: (1980 rates)
9%	$169,400	$15,931
11%	228,826	21,526
15%	425,586	40,000

A well-established farmer, one of Dr. Ackerman's clients, had bought the insurance and pension plans that enterprising salesmen had *sold* him, not the ones he needed. This is normal. What is not normal is he had the wit to consult an expert. The "whole life" plan that he had been sold at age twenty (when he didn't need insurance at all) and the twenty-year endowment he had been sold at age twenty-five, together with the $80,000 policy from his fraternal order, bought at age thirty-five, had together a cash value of $11,000 and a death benefit of $110,000. The fraternal policy gave him a monthly pension at age sixty-five. The whole mess was costing him $4,000 a year in premiums at age thirty-eight.

The sensible alternative was to buy term insurance for the protection needed for ten years, at which time he will be self-insured. This costs $400 a year for $110,000 protection. Since he was an experienced and successful farmer, he knew he could earn at least 10 per cent a year on any money invested in the farm. So, after the term insurance was in hand, he took the cash-surrender value of the old policies ($11,000) and invested it. Each year thereafter he invested the money he saved each year in premiums between the old and the new plan. This amounted to $4,000 less $400, or $3,600 a year. At his retirement age of sixty-five his plan will look like this:

Accumulated (compounded) value of $11,000 capital at 10% for 27 years	$149,435
Accumulated value of $3,600 annual savings in premiums	411,886
	$561,321

This amount at age sixty-five will buy an annuity of $50,000 at today's rates.

CHAPTER SIX

Personal Income Tax

He that forbears
To suit and serve his need
Deserves his load. GEORGE HERBERT (1593–1633)

The government gets money to finance its activities by levying taxes. Whether or not we approve of the activities, or of the methods used, we have to pay. Since taxes are a fact, we need to seek out creative responses to them, rather than the negative throwing up of hands, or even the dramatic throwing up. This chapter is about income taxes – how to think about them, and how to put off paying them as long as possible.

In 1971, Edgar Benson, then Minister of Finance, assured his television audience of anxious taxpayers that the new tax laws would be no more complex than the old. He scoffed at the suggestion that we would have to become a nation of bookkeepers. In spite of this solemn promise, we in fact *have* had to become a nation of bookkeepers. Better, even, we should be chartered accountants. The income-tax form now consists of twenty-five closely printed pages, and shows no signs of getting smaller. Quebec provides its taxpayers with sixty-seven pages.

The language of taxes has its gentilities. A guide to the semantics of tax language has not yet been published. However, if there were such a guide, it would say that "tax reform" means "tax increases", that "fair" means "unfair" (that is, favouring some more powerful class of taxpayer), while "exemplary provisions" are destined to become "loopholes", to be closed when "abused". Canadians don't use words like "evade" or even "avoid". The acceptable word is "defer". The government itself has its own favourite schemes for tax deferral, which it suggests to taxpayers because it thinks the economic results will help the government achieve some of its political goals. Usually it is wrong, but this has nothing to do with the morality of using the tax shelter offered.

ACKERMAN'S PRINCIPLE

"A tax dollar deferred is a tax dollar eliminated, if deferred long enough, and well enough invested in the meantime."

By putting $3,000 a year into an RRSP, the tax saving for someone in the 40 per cent bracket is $1,200. This $1,200 is available to save, invest, or repay borrowed money, thereby increasing equity by $100 a month.

A THOUSAND DOLLARS FROM THE GOVERNMENT!

In order to learn how important tax considerations are for your investment program, go to your local post office or tax office and pick up a copy of the current year's tax guide. The 1985 edition has twenty-six pages of instructions, plus a like number of the return itself and the necessary schedules in duplicate. Begin by roughing out pages one and two of the return. You will find it helpful to have a copy of what you filed last year. Then extract the following information:

Employment income	$24,500
Less employment expenses (maximum)	500
	24,000
Less deductions and exemptions	4,500
Taxable income	$19,500

Employee pension ($1,470) reduces taxable income to $18,030.
Individual RRSP ($2,030) reduces taxable income to $16,000.

Consult the tax table at the back of the guide to find out what taxes will be expected if you do nothing with your money. Depending on what province you live in, this will be about $6,000. If you are contributing 6 per cent of your salary to an employer pension plan, the additional $1,470 deduction will lower taxable income to $16,000 and taxes to about $4,894. Note that $527 ($5,421–$4,894) of the $1,470 saving has come from tax savings, leaving your net outlay at $973.

Tax Payable	No action:	After 6% pension:	After RRSP:
Example 1. Nova Scotia	$5,421	$4,894 Saving: $527 (36%)	$4,262 Saving: $1,159 (33%)
Example 2. Quebec	$6,981	$6,230 Saving: $751 (51%)	$5,400 Saving: $1,581 (45%)

Now, in line with the priorities you have established, you have put out the maximum amount eligible for RRSP ($3,500, less $1,470 for your pension plan, is $2,030, which you have borrowed from your friendly local banker). Now calculate the results of implementing these two steps.

Example 1. The employer's 6 per cent deduction of $1,470 brings the taxable income down to $18,030 and the tax to $4,894.

Example 2. Your individual, self-directed RRSP contribution lowers taxable income a further $2,030 to $16,000 and taxes to $4,262, saving $1,159 and making the net outlay $2,400 on the $3,500 paid.

OVERALL RESULTS: a $1,000 reduction in taxes, in return for your $3,500 sacrifice. Can you afford to ignore this large tax saving?

If you are a Quebec taxpayer, your incentive to save taxes by putting out the maximum allowed for company and individual RRSPs is much greater. Example 2 shows that, if you do nothing, you pay $6,981 on the same income. Your employee plan brings the tax down to $6,230, and your individual plan drops it to $5,400. That is to say, 45 per cent of your contribution is made up by the government.

Already your savings are at the 14 per cent level (as opposed to the Canadian average of 10 per cent). The $3,500 from your salary of $24,500 will go into the RRSP and the employer pension. Additional savings will be assigned to service the bank or credit-union debt for the RRSP, $100 or $150 a month.

If this is your first commitment to save, you will probably now feel like slowing down and letting your conservative nature adjust to the situation. Come April, you will be pleased with having lowered your taxable income by over 30 per cent, and thereby cut your tax bill by a third.

After one year, your net worth will have improved as follows:

Employer pension	$1,470	plus perhaps 7% income of $103 is	$1,573
RRSP	$2,130	plus perhaps 11% income of $234 is	$2,364
			$3,937
Less outstanding debt re the RRSP, perhaps			900
Showing your net worth to be			$3,037

Of this, about $1,159 came from tax savings.

In addition, you have established yourself as a responsible borrower, given yourself a voluntary forced savings plan, and found the incentive for studying Canadian equity investment opportunities in order to make use of the money in the self-administered RRSP.

SPOUSAL RRSP

The one-income family can achieve a modest tax-free income transfer by establishing a spousal RRSP for the husband or wife who has no earned income. The working spouse contributes all or part of his eligible contribution to the spousal plan. The spouse may remove these funds and the money they have earned after three years.

THE TWO-INCOME FAMILY

Perhaps you are part of a two-income household. Let's say your wife's income is $20,000 and yours is $15,000. Your two young children require $4,000 worth of child care. Your family tax calculations might look like this:

	Hers	His
Employment income	$20,000	$15,000
Less employment expenses	500	500
Net salary	$19,500	$14,500

Less deductions and exemptions (includes $4,000 child care)	9,500	4,500
Taxable income	$10,000	$10,000
Tax (approximate)	$ 2,500	$ 2,500

In summary, you have a $35,000 family income with about $20,000 taxable and about $5,000 of taxes. If family savings were $6,000, each spouse could still establish an RRSP and contribute $3,500 and $2,500 for a total of $6,000. A $500-per-month savings plan would have the following impact:

	Hers	His
Taxable income (after RRSP)	$6,500	$7,500
Original taxes on full income (approx.)	$2,500	$2,500
Tax on new taxable income	1,500	1,900
Tax savings	$1,000	$ 600

Required net outlay for RRSP: $6,000–$1,600 ($1,000 + $600) = $4,400.

The savings required to finance these two RRSPs:

Hers	$3,500
His	2,500
Total	$6,000
Less tax savings	1,600
Savings required	$4,400

The tax savings are sufficient to pay interest on a bank loan large enough to pay next year's RRSP in advance. Many people use their mid-year tax refund cheques to pay down their RRSP bank loans. A recent example of this is the following case from Dr. Ackerman's practice.

In January 1985 appeared two new clients, Rose and Ray. He was about to retire; she had another five years in her office job. Both are very conservative Canadians. Self-administered RRSPs were established with a brokerage firm. Each paid a $100 yearly administrative fee to a trust company.

Ray deposited the maximum for the year 1984 and an equal amount for 1985 (his last full year of employment), for a total of $4,400. As of March 1986, his account shows an equity of $4,900, 200 shares of Fruehauf Canada at $24 and $100 cash – a gain of about 11 per cent. This does not include his tax savings on the contribution of $4,400, approximately 40 per cent, or $1,800. If the latter were considered, by subtracting the tax savings from his RRSP contribution he has invested $4,400-$1,800, or $2,600. The $500 gain on that amount is over 19 per cent.

Rose has done even better. Her 1984 and 1985 RRSP contributions came to $6,300. One year later, since she will continue working, she contributed $3,200 for 1986. Her investments to date (Sept. 1986):

	Cost	*Market*
50 shares Fruehauf Canada	$1,100	$1,300
100 shares Goodyear Canada	3,800	4,500
400 shares Empire Company	3,800	8,400
100 shares Halifax Developments	800	1,600
	$9,500	$15,800

That is a gain of 66 per cent to date on the funds invested. On the invested net contribution after tax saving ($6,200) the gain is 102 per cent. She has become an enthusiastic investor.

CLOSING OUT THE RRSP

When Rose becomes sixty and before she reaches seventy-one she can transfer her RRSP accumulation tax-free into a Registered Retirement Investment Fund (RRIF), accepting each year until she is ninety a set fraction of the fund as income. The advantages of the RRIF over the insurance company monopoly on annuities are the following:

1. You can continue to manage your own money, and thus earn and receive the going rate.
2. If you die, your beneficiaries get your accumulated money, not the insurance company.
3. The amount received from your RRIF increases year by year. This helps you to believe you can afford to live.

An alternative plan for Rose is to take chunks of cash out by creating a second RRSP, transferring the funds she wants to it, and then collapsing plan 1.

Between the ages of sixty and sixty-five, she should take out chunks of cash each year. During this five-year period she will be in a lower tax bracket, since she has stopped work, but will not yet be receiving income from the Canada Pension Plan or old-age security.

The above strategy of shifting from plan 2 to plan 1 works well at earlier ages if you take a year off to travel or go back to school, or if you need to finance your mid-life crisis (see p. 87).

If you can possibly resist their high-powered salesmanship, avoid closing out your RRSP through an insurance company annuity. The insurance company does not manage your money in your interest, nor do they pay the going rate. Their annuity is a lifetime contract that ties you in forever at a rate of return substantially below today's current rates. Once you buy an annuity you have lost your freedom of choice. Normally, when you die, the rest of your money goes to the insurance company. You can prevent this by a last-survivor or a joint annuity, but either of these reduces your monthly income drastically. For example: a person of sixty-five would typically receive $600 a month on a straight annuity, $500 on a fifteen-year guarantee, and $400 on a last-survivor.

THE IMPORTANCE OF TIMING

How to invest money in such a way as to defer taxes ranks in importance with *where* to invest money. When these two considerations can be coupled with perfect timing, all is well. Here is an example from another of Dr. Ackerman's clients.

A farmer has an investment portfolio of $55,000. In November 1978 he decides to replace his combine with a new one costing $45,000. By signing the deal in December he can get a 1978 serial number for the machine and take delivery of it the following June, paying no interest in the meantime. Because the deal was made before year end, his 1978 tax is reduced by the investment tax credit of 10 per cent of the cost ($4,500). This is a direct deduction from his tax liability. The 1978 depreciation on the machine of 30 per cent of the full cost less the tax credit ($45,000–$4,500) gives him about $12,000. Since he is in the 40 per cent bracket, 40 per cent of this is $4,800, which, with the $4,500 investment tax credit, makes a total of $9,300 saved. During the first six months of 1979, a major holding in his portfolio, 1,800 shares of Wheeling-Pittsburgh Steel, increased 50 per cent in value, from $12 to $18 a share. After commissions but before capital-gains taxes (not due until the following April), his gain exceeded $10,500 U.S. This was a further substantial help in financing the combine. For 1979, depreciation of $8,400 (30 per cent on the now $28,000 machine) provided tax savings (40 per cent of $8,400 is $3,360) more than covering the tax on the capital gain (50 per cent of $12,000 Canadian × 40 per cent is $2,400).

By waiting until June 1979 to cash in his portfolio, the client saved a further $10,000. The difference between just cashing in and buying the needed combine, and doing it in a managed way, being alert to tax consequences and market trends, amounts to a total of nearly $20,000. While this level of tax saving and investment performance may seem extraordinary, it shows that tax savings are well worth taking into account, even if stock prices had not increased. But since this was a counselled account, the advice was that portfolio gains were worth waiting for, and this paid off handsomely by the time the combine had to be paid for in June.

Beware of attempting this same manoeuvre now, because tax laws have changed. Now investment tax credits are available only in selected provinces, such as the Maritimes. Moreover, the allowable depreciation (Capital Cost Allowance) has been cut to half the normal rate for the first year. History may repeat itself. Wheeling Steel may come out of Chapter 11 bankruptcy and move once more from its present price of $8 to $10.

WHATEVER HAPPENED TO RHOSPs?

In February of 1976 in line with the Trudeau government's idea that it alone knew how to manipulate the marbles, and all the taxpayer had to do was obey, the feds conceived and gave birth to the RHOSP program in a miraculous seven days. Its goal was supposed to be support of the housing industry by making it easy for people to save to buy a home. The rule in Canada is "Legislate in haste and repent at leisure." Every year since its inception the RHOSP rules were changed, until finally, in 1985, the whole scheme was abandoned in disgust. This happened only a couple of years after they had strangled MURBs, the government's only other attempt to improve the housing picture.

DOES IT HELP TO INCORPORATE?

The advantages of incorporation are very clear and immediate, while the problems make themselves apparent only after you are committed. Lawyers and accountants benefit from getting you set up in a company, hence their advice about the pros and cons is likely to be biased. Here are some of the main advantages:

1. If your company qualifies for the small-business deduction, you limit your upper tax liability. Up to $200,000 profit a year you pay only 27 per cent (varies slightly by province). This is a lot better than the 50 per cent paid by larger corporations, and by some individuals.
2. The company form is a big help in estate planning because you can transfer shares to heirs very easily, and common ownership of certain assets is easily arranged.
3. The company has a continuing life after you are dead, and can sometimes be arranged to continue some of your favourite projects.
4. The company can receive income without paying a withholding tax, even if one of its principals lives abroad.
5. With a company, you can pay travel and other business expenses, and pay your spouse a salary for working in the business.
6. With a company, a tax-loss carry-forward is more simply and easily arranged than with individuals.
7. With a company it is easier to get credit, you can buy cheaper (through a contractor's discount), and you can pay by cheque without special arrangements.
8. You can now be the only shareholder, director, and officer of your company. This makes for perfect communication among the officers, eases the problem of calling directors' meetings, and generally gets rid of much red tape.

The disadvantages, besides the difficulties in winding up a company if that should become necessary, have mostly to do with dealing with the civil servants of the federal and provincial governments.

In addition, there are certain classes and types of people who are now somewhat deterred from incorporating themselves, since they will not be allowed the small-business deduction. These include sports stars, medical doctors, and television performers. In any case, your plan should be examined by a tax accountant or a tax lawyer before you move in the corporate direction.

What You Can Do If Not Incorporated

You should become fully aware of what can be deducted from income. The costs of earning investment income, or the carrying charges – the safety-deposit-box rental, investment-counsel fees, some accounting fees, legal fees, etc. – are all deductible. The administration fee to the trust company should be paid by a separate cheque each year to make sure it is deductible. Be sure to designate your spouse as beneficiary of the RRSP in your will. This allows increased flexibility in deferring taxes after your death.

DIVIDEND TAX CREDIT AND OTHER DEDUCTIONS

Dividends from taxable Canadian corporations have the advantage that the first $1,000 of income is free from tax. This applies also to interest on bank accounts and fixed-income securities as long as they are Canadian. Dividends from taxable Canadian corporations provide you with a dividend tax credit. This is a traditional deduction from your taxes that was seriously reduced in the February 1986 budget. Also, the first $1,000 of employer pension income is free from tax when received under a pension plan as an annuity for life.

THE IMPORTANCE OF DEPRECIATION

If you are in a capital-intensive business for which machinery and equipment are essential, you probably understand that high rates of depreciation can be taken. These are 20 per cent, 30 per cent, or even 40 per cent a year for some classes of equipment. The depreciation allowed in the first year has now been reduced to half these figures. Many airlines lease their planes because it helps them if they are short of capital, while the high rate of depreciation makes it worth while for the investor to put up the capital required. Ships, trucks, railcars, and shipping containers all enjoy a high rate of depreciation.

Farmers claim that the railways are charging them too much to get their grain to export markets. The railways claim they *must* charge high prices because of the high capital cost of hopper cars.

One way to solve the controversy by government edict might be to allow such a high rate of depreciation on grain cars that many investors would buy them and rent them cheap to the railways. The depreciation taken against other income would save the car owner taxes, while the grain, with cheap cars available, would get moved.

TAX SHELTERS

The ideal tax shelter is one that takes otherwise taxable income and transforms it into something that delivers a capital gain upon its sale. While racehorses and exotic breeds of beef cattle appeal to the high-tax-bracket investor because of the total write-off of the cost of acquisition, many investors find that by the time they sell them the operating loss has removed most of the tax advantage. This is less likely to be true during the upward swing of the beef-cattle cycle.

One way to achieve the goal of transmuting taxable income into an eventual capital gain is to use "stripped" government bonds. This system is not as exotic as racehorses, but is more free of risk. These bonds are called Sentinels, and are stripped – that is, the interest coupons have been taken off. These bonds sell for low prices, because they don't pay any interest, but twenty years from now, when they fall due, the full face value will be paid, if Canada still exists as a country. You buy, say, $2,000 for your RRSP and forget about them. Twenty years later you get a cheque for $10,000, and the $8,000 profit is completely yours, free of any tax.

Of course, there have to be some disadvantages. The bond dealer takes a bit much up front, so your net cost is a bit higher than the bond quote. Also, the secondary market for these stripped bonds is so thin as to be invisible, so if you change your mind, and need the money badly before the bonds mature, you may have trouble selling.

Here is another procedure using Canadian government bonds that is a bit more scary, but a lot more lucrative. Say you are someone like a Canadian airline pilot, with a large income, but a sitting duck for income taxes. You earn lots of money, but, being in the 50 per cent tax bracket, you never seem to end up the year with much cash.

Remember, your goal is to convert your tax payments into a long-term capital gain.

You buy $1 million face-value of Canadian government 3 per cent bonds of 1996. To pay the $650,000 they cost, you deposit them at your bank, and promise the banker you will pay him interest on 95 per cent of the purchase price.

Cost of $1-million bonds	$650,000
Less 95% put up by bank @ 12%	617,500
Cash required	$32,500

You borrow the cash from another bank, secured by your general earning power. If you make this move in January 1986, your tax declaration for that year will look like this:

Interest paid to 2 banks	$78,000 ($74,100 + $3,900)
Interest received (bonds)	29,000 ($30,000 – $1,000 tax credit)
Net deduction from other income	$49,000

Line 222 of the tax form says that all interest paid for the purpose of earning taxable income is deductible.

So, if your income before this transaction was $70,000, afterward it will be $100,000 ($30,000 interest). But you subtract $78,000 in interest paid, which, together with other deductible expenses, will bring your taxable income down to about $20,000. You instruct the accounting department of the airline to send the tax money withheld from your salary each month to the banker instead of to Ottawa.

Result: After ten years the bonds are redeemed at par.

Tax-free profit	$350,000
Less bank loan	32,500
Net profit	$317,500

You don't make this kind of money tax-free without taking some risks. Among the major risks are:

1. If you lose your job for any reason, at a moment when interest rates are high and therefore bond prices are low, you are in trouble.
2. If your banker gets into a panic and calls the loan, you will have to sell the bonds.
3. If the government changes the law retroactively, you might find yourself pinned.

Tax evasion by failing to declare income is a way of life in some countries, but not in Canada. It is important to distinguish between tax evasion and tax avoidance. The first is a criminal act; the second has been praised by an English judge as the citizen's duty. Failing to declare your total world income under oath is an evasion, and we do not recommend it. Including arguable deductions is avoidance, and we do recommend it. You and the government tax man may disagree about the nature and extent of the deductions, but you have a perfect right to make your case in tax court if called upon.

GOVERNMENT-INSPIRED TAX SHELTERS

From time to time the government, in its idiocy, or following the suggestions of powerful lobbies, ventures into high finance. It allows investors to charge against income an amount larger than that invested. As mentioned earlier, here are two current examples:
- oil and gas drilling ventures
- 100 per cent Canadian-made movies

Each such venture must be approved by the government, and is marketed by the investment dealer or the film industry respectively. The characteristic they have in common is that, in addition to a small sum of original money, you are legally committed to invest a larger sum later on. Since costs during the first year of the investment usually exceed any income generated (drilling rig being set up, film shot but not edited or marketed), the investor's share of the loss will greatly exceed the initial investment. The total of such loss can be written off against that year's taxable income. The legally binding promissory note, due in a later year, sometimes requires the investor to throw good money after bad. However, if all goes in accordance with the sales pitch, sufficient revenue to pay the balance will have been generated in the second year and returned to the investor.

The conflict of interest inherent in having someone from the oil patch as your guide, philosopher, and friend is not to be ignored. Too often he is faced with the choice of putting a given oil play into your portfolio or into his own. The best prospect he has found in years may go into JR's company instead of yours.

For example, one film I know of was financed through units of $25,000. An investor put up $5,000 in 1979 and obligated himself to pay an additional $20,000 in 1983, plus the interest on the amount at 1 per cent over the bank prime rate. This contract allowed the investor to write off $25,000 against his 1979 taxable income.

Six years later, the film had been shown in theatres in different parts of the world, and on pay TV in North America, but any revenues generated were kept by the producers and promoters. The investors have not even received a financial report in the past three years, and it is years since they have heard anything from the people responsible for marketing the film. This is a good example of what happens when you let other people manage your money.

As for movies in general, in retrospect the government plan is a failure. The shysters and charlatans who flooded into the country to take advantage of the tax law either made off with the money, or produced garbage that had no market value. The exceptions are distressingly rare.

Two other financial triumphs of the government in this area are the Indexed Security Investment Plan (ISIP) and the Scientific Research Tax Credit. The first is as dead as the dodo. The second was introduced for the 1984 tax year. At year end your accountant probably had you buy shares in hitherto unknown Canadian companies set up for the sole purpose of taking advantage of a substantial tax benefit. Much of the money never did find its way to its anticipated use in scientific research. The taxpayer had his credit, but probably at the expense of a capital loss on the worthless shares. The government lost the revenue. Over the years we have been treated to a continuous parade of government inspirations, mostly moribund, some dead and hastily withdrawn. These represent a tremendous waste of time and money for everyone.

OVERALL

In taxes, every year it's a new ballgame. With the exception of 1973, the rules have been changed every year since 1971. Hence, it is impossible in a book such as this to keep the reader up to date. For this reason, no one knows what the law is. It takes several years for a tax case to go through the courts. Thus, the arguments about the 1972 law (which might well go against the government) have not yet been settled. Moreover, the government's IBs (Interpretation Bulletins) are not the law, and do not necessarily say what a tax court would rule. The IB simply gives the interpretation that the Minister of Finance would like to see prevail. This normally doesn't favour the taxpayer. There is no prospect of any improvement in this situation, either as to IBs or as to court cases, in the near future.

In theory, in advance of any transaction you can go to the tax office and get their opinion on your estimate of what the tax consequences will be. In due course the office will issue a ruling. This ruling may differ from the ruling that another taxpayer in similar circumstances has received. Hence, it is reasonable to expect an income-tax officer to delay or avoid providing you with a ruling. So you have to be persistent.

PART III: TYPES OF INVESTMENT

CHAPTER SEVEN

A Debate on Real Estate

Thou shalt not covet; but tradition
Approves all forms of competition. ARTHUR HUGH CLOUGH (1819–61)

The following ten pages are reprinted almost verbatim from the first edition of *Start with $100*, which I wrote in 1957. In spite of changes in the tax laws (1971) which made real estate less of a tax shelter, high interest and mortgage rates, and what seem to be ridiculous prices, I still think real estate is a good place for investment capital. My colleague, Dr. Ackerman, believes that in general real estate has priced itself out of sight, and is now highly vulnerable to catastrophic collapse. This slight difference of opinion between the two of us (both of whom have made considerable profits from real-estate investment) is dramatized in the organization of the following chapter. Following the ten pages from my earlier book, I bring my views up to date and cite examples of real-estate coups that have happened and can still happen. Then Dr. Ackerman follows with his very different views. Real-estate investment depends very much on what you think is going to happen to the economy. If it is going to bumble along in the same way for another decade, fine; but if a major depression is just around the corner, watch out. I happen to think that Canadians are an incurably conservative, not to say stolid, people, and that nothing very radical is ever going to happen here. I believe we are going to muddle along about the same, no matter what government is in power. I think it will be possible for us to maintain this balance for another decade or two, by our usual system of paying for our mistakes by selling off more of the heritage of our grandchildren.

Why Invest in Real Estate?: The Case *For*, by Dr. Brown

"Since the beginning of western civilization, prudent investors seeking safety, income, and capital growth have put a portion of their savings into real estate. In growing countries like Canada and the United States, where we have adequate stores of raw materials and land to support an increasing population, investment in real estate is particularly attractive.

Real estate has two major advantages over other types of investment: land is indestructible and buildings are semi-permanent; and the amount of land available in any one district is limited. These factors make real estate a good long-term investment in any sound economy.

The wide range of possible investments also makes real estate an attractive field for the investor. Alternatives range from speculative purchases of vacant land on margin, to the outright purchase of mortgages on stable revenue-producing properties. The type of real-estate investment you choose depends on your age and your investment aims. For the older person, interested chiefly in income, carefully chosen mortgages can provide good yields with safety. For the younger person, equity ownership can provide capital appreciation at the expense of greater risk.

REAL ESTATE AS A HEDGE AGAINST INFLATION

Some professional investors, men who manage millions of dollars for institutions, favour real-estate investments as a hedge against inflation. As the purchasing power of the dollar falls, rents rise in proportion; hence the actual yield of revenue-producing properties can remain about the same in good times and bad. The value of real estate can be decimated in a catastrophic depression, but this can also happen to any alternative investment.

In spite of the ups and downs of business activity, the general trend over the past four hundred years has been toward gentle inflation. Since the Second World War, inflation has been less gentle, with money losing its purchasing power at an average rate of about 3 per cent each year. But by 1995 the rate may well have averaged 3 per cent over the fifty-year period.

TAX BENEFITS

Another attractive feature of real estate for some investors is that in many cases it can constitute a tax-sheltered investment. All costs of running a building – mortgage interest, maintenance, depreciation, taxes, insurance – may be deducted from income from the property before payment of income tax. Under certain conditions, depreciation is subject to recapture for tax purposes if you sell the building, but usually depreciation allowances on several buildings can be pooled to minimize tax liability.

HOW TO INVEST IN REAL ESTATE

Should You Borrow or Lend?

The basic decision you must make about real-estate investing is whether you want to take up an equity or a debt position. That is, do you want to buy a property and assume all the risks as well as the benefits of ownership, or do you want simply to lend your money at a fixed rate of interest against the security of a mortgage? The equity holder not only puts up his own money, but borrows against a mortgage to pay the balance of the sale price. For a real-estate investment of given quality, the equity holder assumes more risk, in return for a higher expected rate in both income and appreciation of capital. The mortgage holder assumes less risk, but expects correspondingly lower income and no capital gain.

If you are young, or worried about the effects of inflation on the future purchasing power of the dollar, you may be more attracted to ownership. If you are older, and dependent on a stable source of income, you will probably tend to favour taking the lender's position, and will buy carefully chosen mortgages. These, if well managed, give you assured fixed income for a definite period of time.

The needs of some investors, particularly those in middle life, may best be met by a real-estate portfolio consisting of a mixture of well-selected equities and mortgages. A balanced portfolio of this type contains hedges against both inflation and deflation.

PROBLEMS OF REAL-ESTATE INVESTING

When you buy a share of common stock, you know that it sells for the same price, and has the same privileges attached, as all the other millions of common shares of the same company. In real estate, each property is unique. Whether you are lending on a mortgage or buying the property, you must inspect it carefully and compare its value with other properties being offered in the same price range. Not only is this time-consuming, but it requires a combination of long experience and intimate knowledge of real-estate markets.

Real estate also requires more attention after purchase than do common stocks. Dividends on sound common stocks will be paid without your taking any action beyond cashing the cheque. But with a revenue-producing property, if any net revenue is to be enjoyed, you must attend regularly to a long list of chores. These jobs must be done, even if business or pleasure takes you away from home or if you fall sick.

A traditional rule for investing in real estate is that you should buy only in the district where you live. This automatically rules out all investments by northerners in Florida real estate. It also allows you to watch building trends, and sell quickly if things change for the worse. Changes in street plans, or a new zoning law, can affect values very quickly. On the other hand, federal legislation, while benefiting the country as a whole, often works a hardship on particular regions, thus depressing real-estate values for long periods. If your home happens to be in such a district, the only thing you can do is trust your money to some reliable agent for investment elsewhere.

Another difficulty with real-estate investment is that you never actually own any piece of property. Land is held subject to taxes. Thus, in a sense land titles are really transferable leases from the state. Any property owner can be separated from his assets by the simple procedure of raising taxes and freezing rents. This has happened abroad, and some North American landlords claim that it happened here during and after the Second World War.

The owner of real estate, especially housing properties such as apartments and flats, is at the mercy of federal legislation in still another way. If, because of political pressure, the federal government makes available large sums of money at low interest rates to encourage home-building, prices of existing homes and apartments will fall. Every government is under strong pressure (from trade unions and manufacturers of raw materials used in building houses) to make mortgage money cheap and easy to get. Thus, the owner of an asset that provides housing is constantly threatened by government action that may reduce his income or wipe it out altogether.

A third difficulty is the constantly changing nature of a city. Within one man's lifetime, a district can be successively an exclusive residential district, a crowded slum, and a cheap manufacturing area of lofts and small shops. These changes can cause drastic fluctuations in property values.

THE VARIETIES OF REAL-ESTATE INVESTMENT

A large variety of real-estate commitments is available to the investor who looks about him. Each one of these investments can be made on either a debt or an equity basis. That is, you can buy a vacant lot outright for cash and become the equity owner, or you can lend someone else the money to buy the vacant lot and become the holder of debt. Real estate, particularly in a country whose population is growing and which is expanding industrially, is a good hedge against inflation. It must be said also that any kind of real estate is a very bad investment at times of deflation and depression. The best kind of real-estate ownership for the small investor is for him to own the place where he lives. Whether times are good or bad, you must always have a place to live. If a proportion of your savings is tied up in a home, you can guard it to some extent by keeping the home in good repair.

You often hear people say it's always cheaper to own your home than to pay rent. Like most common sayings, this is quite wrong. The way people arrive at this comforting conclusion is that in figuring out how much their home is costing them, they neglect the interest on their own money (their equity) invested in the house.

If your own money could be earning 6 per cent interest if invested elsewhere, you must include this amount as one of the costs of owning the home. When you do this, it will give you pause. On the other hand, if you can rent a house cheaper than you can buy it, why should anyone ever want to be a landlord?

The truth about home renting versus buying is that either can be cheaper than the other, depending on the trends of the market – that is, on the demand for housing. If there are more houses than people, landlords will rent at a loss rather than have their houses empty. Under these circumstances, it is cheaper to rent. If there are more people than houses, landlords can get higher rents. Then it becomes cheaper to buy your own house and pay off the mortgage in the form of rent. If the government is passing through a phase in which it is taking all steps to encourage home ownership, home owning can be much better than renting. On balance, in a growing country, the odds would seem to favour home owning over the longer term. Home owning, like other forms of savings, can be good or bad, depending on how carefully you have studied the various factors involved in each particular case. But since the value of all real property rises and falls with the changing purchasing power of the dollar, this type of investment should be considered for at least a part of your savings program.

Duplexes and Triplexes

My favourite real-estate investment for a young couple is a duplex or a triplex. This is a happy combination of an income property and a home in which to live. The beauty of the duplex is that, since you live in the upper or the lower half, you can keep a close eye on your tenant and on the general maintenance of the property. Normally, in a well-managed duplex, bought at, say, seven times the revenue, the rent your tenant pays covers all expenses of the property, and you live rent-free. It should be said, however, that this means rent-free only in the sense that you don't put out any money each month. You pay in the form of considerable bother countering complaints, or complaining in your turn about the tenant's excessive use of hot water and his opening of windows in sub-zero weather.

Normally, the profit margin in a multiple-unit dwelling becomes larger as the number of units increases. By this I mean that it is very difficult to make any money out of a detached dwelling by buying it and renting it. Duplexes and triplexes can be successful investments, but six-, eight-, and twelve-unit cold flats and sixteen-unit apartments are much more likely to be good revenue-producers.

Cold Flats

Flats in which the landlord supplies only the bare building and the tenant provides his own heat, electricity, and hot water can be excellent investments in parts of the country where a solid middle-class group of citizens is accustomed to living in them. If in your part of the country cold flats are inhabited by the type of people who beat their wives and fight with broken beer bottles, avoid this type of investment, because collecting the rent is a full-time job. In areas where cold flats are respectable, their great advantage is that the landlord is selling a minimum and highly predictable service. He knows how much the building costs to buy, he knows the taxes, he knows the rate at which the building is depreciating, and he knows the cost of annual repairs. Since the basic factors are known, the investment can be very carefully calculated.

Apartments

Apartment houses, where the landlord supplies not only bare rooms, but heat, light, electricity, and hot water, are much more difficult to calculate. Apartment tenants are notorious for throwing windows open in the dead of winter because the place seems stuffy. They have also been known to have all the hot-water taps running continuously in order to improve the relative humidity of the air. In spite of these difficulties, apartments can be good investments if carefully chosen and closely watched. Here the number of units is very important. In a sixteen-unit apartment house you will likely have some people who are away a lot, and therefore use little hot water, to act as a counterbalance to the family using a hundred gallons a day. Thus, in a larger apartment house you can be reasonably sure of striking an average cross-section of humanity. In a smaller apartment house you are less sure.

Another important point in investing in an apartment house is its location in relation to the income level of the people you are trying to attract. Other things being equal, it is better to own real estate that caters to the largest segment of the population in your city. I know that large fortunes have been made out of luxury apartments renting at $600 to $1,000 a month, but unless your city has a large group of people with incomes of $50,000 a year, investment in such an apartment would seem to me ill-advised. Another type of apartment investment I consider dangerous is the bachelor apartment consisting of large numbers of furnished 1½-room suites. In my experience, I have found bachelors notoriously footloose. They tend to pack all their belongings into a kitbag and leave without paying the rent. Moreover, in my opinion young unmarried people of both sexes have less sense of responsibility about other people's property, and about such matters as paying their debts, than has a well-established, conservative family man. Money can be made out of bachelor apartments, but only if you have an excellent manager who is on the premises twenty-four hours a day and who is not himself a thief. Such managers are hard to find.

Other Opportunities in City Real Estate

Vacant lots in a growing city or community can be an excellent investment, but everything depends on timing. Say you pay $1 a foot for 5,000 square feet of vacant land. The capital you invest is $5,000. As sidewalks, sewers, city water, and other improvements go in, your annual taxes might vary – let's say $400 a year. To this we have to add the interest that your $5,000 could have been earning if you hadn't put it into this vacant lot. Let's say that this is 12 per cent, so that you are losing $600 a year in interest. This $1,000 of taxes and interest a year, mounting up for ten years at 12 per cent interest, amounts to about $21,700 compounded. Say now that you were lucky enough to sell your property at twice what you paid for it, namely $2 a square foot. Your proceeds from the sale would be $10,000. But the actual cost of the property to you at the end of the ten-year period would be your original $5,000 plus $21,700 of accumulated operating costs. Thus, on this particular investment, if you had to wait ten years before selling it at double your cost, with correct bookkeeping you would show a loss of $16,700, rather than a profit.

Of course, if you bought the same piece of real estate last year for $2 a foot and sold it this year for $4, you would show an immediate profit of nearly $10,000. Thus, the trick in investing in vacant lots is to show either a spectacular per-foot increase (such as twenty times) over a relatively long period, or a nominal increase (such as twice) over a short period.

Land Speculation

Large sums have been made by real-estate promoters by buying up extensive farmlands on the edge of developing communities and then subdividing them into small lots for houses. I believe this area should be avoided by the amateur investor. Subdividing takes large amounts of capital, good political connections, and other assets and skills not normally possessed by the individual investor.

One exception to the statement that vacant lots are dead property until they are resold is if you can rent out your vacant lot as a site for billboards or as a parking lot. Some elegant real-estate speculations have hinged on buying a condemned downtown property at a low price, demolishing the building on it, and then operating the lot as a place to park cars in a crowded downtown area. After a period of years, varying from two to twenty, this vacant lot is resold as the site of a new skyscraper. This is nice work if you can get it, but it takes exquisite timing. In addition, operating a parking lot is not as simple as it looks, and unless you are willing to spend a good part of your own time supervising the car jockey and setting up financial control on the operations, you had better leave this type of investment to the experts.

The basic requirement for successful speculation in vacant lots is the ability to predict the direction in which a city will grow. This is not easy. While there are some rational rules for approaching this problem, they are often more than counterbalanced by population moves that take place for irrational, imponderable, or political reasons.

Farms

Farmland can still be bought fairly cheap quite close to large cities. For some who are willing to spend the time and effort required to learn about the unique economics of farmland, this can be an excellent investment, but there are many hazards for the city slicker. If you buy a farm and then rent it out to your neighbours for cultivation or pasture, you are likely to end up with a desert produced by underfertilization and overcropping. You have to find a good tenant, and then keep him up to scratch by periodic soil analyses and frequent visits.

In times of inflation, the cost of food goes up. Hence a farm, which is basically a food-producing machine, becomes more valuable. But it must be a food-producing machine, not a ragweed waste. Perhaps a simpler way to get operating expenses out of a farm is by means of a government-sponsored pond containing fish, or by means of a woodlot. In many provinces the governments will sell trees for next to nothing if you are interested in reforestation. Revenue from fishing rights and from lumber can sometimes be made to pay all the expenses of the investment, including taxes and interest on the invested capital. Then, if in twenty years the value of the land has quadrupled, you have an excellent capital gain.

Real-Estate Securities

In most American cities today there are still properties selling at 1929 prices. This is particularly true in the downtown areas and districts that somehow escaped renovation. It is obvious that if these areas were bought at a dollar a foot and then the whole area was rebuilt on modern lines so that the land could command $100 a foot, an immense fortune could be made. This is the procedure used by William Zeckendorf, the well-known New York City real-estate speculator who was responsible for putting together the present site of the United Nations Building. By buying a very large acreage of land and buildings and demolishing the slaughterhouses that had polluted the site, he was able to convert cheap land into an expensive mid-city location suitable for large office buildings. But this sort of coup can be carried out normally only by those who can buy very large blocks. True, you can join a syndicate, where the individual contributions of a few hundred investors are pooled and used to buy some large block of property. But this involves many difficulties. A more practical solution is likely to be found in real-estate securities.

In a depression, real estate, far from being an asset, is a distinct liability, because the taxes and operating costs must be paid whether or not there is any revenue. For this reason, real-estate values drop during a depression and real-estate securities drop correspondingly. In the thirties, when prices hit bottom, real-estate stocks could be bought at prices that ranged from 1/10 to 1/100 of their value today. This fluctuation is roughly four times as great as that of the stock-market averages during the same period. The canny buyer of real-estate securities, if he can hit the bottom of a depression, is certain of spectacular gains."

Thirty years after writing the above I am still basically in agreement. True, several important factors have changed for the worse. In 1971, the income-tax law was changed, introducing the capital-gains tax and rescinding the wonderful rule that depreciation on real estate could be used to decrease taxable income from a profession or salary. Bad luck. It is true that interest rates have risen from 6 per cent to 13 per cent to over 20 per cent, but for a person in the 40 per cent marginal tax bracket, 15 per cent interest becomes 9 per cent (40 per cent of 15 per cent), because interest paid on some money invested is tax deductible. So the cost of money could be worse.

One hazard of real estate that I have learned about only recently turns out to be tucked away in the tax laws. In real life your capital gain or capital loss on any transaction will be figured out on a completely arbitrary basis by junior civil servants who know nothing about real estate. They are in the business of collecting taxes, not of following the tax law or trying to achieve abstract justice, hence you may well find that you get no credit for tax losses and are forced to pay capital-gains tax on investments where you lost money.

Here (I am sorry to say) is a specific case from my own portfolio. In 1968 I paid $13 a foot for a property on St. Catherine Street East in Montreal, planning to build a river-view apartment house on it. But the planned financing collapsed, as sometimes happens, and I was forced to cover the taxes by renting it out as a vacant lot. On Valuation Day (December 31, 1971), the income was stabilized by a lease, but rent was hard to collect. Two years later I got a firm offer, with a certified-cheque deposit, of $8.18 a foot. This I refused, because, in the meantime, two huge government office buildings had gone up near by, Radio Québec head office was just across the street, and I thought the property might again be a good candidate for a high-rise apartment. But time dragged on, I had to go to court to collect back rent from the tenants, and finally, in 1983, I was glad to get the property off my back by selling to an Arab for $6.90 a foot. The loss was $6.10 a foot for 11,000 feet, or $67,000. I owned about half the property, so I claimed a capital loss of $35,000 on my 1984 income tax.

The tax department, after a two-year debate, disallowed the entire capital loss, and maintained that I had actually enjoyed a capital *gain* of $18,000 on the transaction. So there is a difference of $53,000 between our calculations. I reached *my* figure by adding up the cancelled cheques I had paid for the property, and subtracting the amount of the cheque I received when I sold.

The tax department reached its very different figure by positing a deep drop in real-estate prices in that district just in time for Valuation Day. From $13 a foot the price dropped in three years to $2.20 a foot on Valuation Day, and then climbed rapidly to the offered figure of $8.18 in 1975. Real-estate men, professional appraisers, and accountants all laugh hysterically when I show them this graph, with its caption saying this rapid dip in price must be unique in the entire sweep of economic history. But the tax department is so far unmoved, and I have paid the extra tax (a few thousand dollars) on capital gains I never made.

Another point I want to make is that no ten-page summary of real-estate investing can avoid being simplistic. For a more adequate treatment of the subject, see my *The Intelligent Investor's Guide to Real Estate*, New York, Putnam, 1964. I still agree with all the major views there expressed – in spite of the changes in tax law.

What happened between 1957 and 1981, as everyone knows, was a spectacular rise in real-estate prices almost everywhere. A house in Montreal which I thought I was very smart to sell at $25,000 in 1957 (having paid $9,000 for it in 1948) sold recently for $80,000. This is 12 per cent a year compounded. True, the young couples that buy the $80,000 houses will have to devote a large part of their disposable income to this one investment, but the psychological dividends of home-owning may well justify the expense. Some people are in the nest-building business. Spouses who neglect to take this into consideration do so at their peril. In Toronto they are renting single apartments by the month until the builder can find a buyer for them, as part of a condominium. This means that, soon after you are settled in your new apartment, you get a registered letter saying you have to be out at the end of the next month. Your spouse is furious, and some of this displeasure focuses itself on you. After this has happened two or three times, you may look with more favour on buying a house, even at today's prices. Then, emotions calmed and fear assuaged, all you have to worry about is paying the taxes and the mortgage. This means living a relatively simple life.

Real-Estate Investing Now: The Case *Against*, by Dr. Ackerman

1. Real estate is not liquid. Properties that attracted daily interest from investors at their peak prices (when you bought) are now languishing month after month, awaiting the phone call and serious inspection that never seem to come. You have your commitments elsewhere – the job out West, the family that has already moved – but the real-estate market is insensitive to your needs. Or, consider the small apartment block that you are ready to sell. With vacancies higher than usual, and government legislation (rent control or tenant rights or whatever) promised and pending, your fancy profit seems to be melting like April snow.

   Even the wilderness dream, "back forty" or cottage lot, may be difficult to unload when other dreams like food and clothes for the kids take priority. Ask your banker about the value of your recreational real estate. Instead of its loan value he'll prefer to discuss fishing, swimming, and how good it is to get away from the city. Your best bet in trying to recoup your costs is to sell it to him for his own use.

   Mortgages, you may find, are usually even less liquid. Who wants to take over from you the challenge of investigating the property owner and his current financial prospects, much less the agonizing step-by-step procedures of foreclosing when he doesn't pay? Besides, interest rates have increased, and that of itself makes your mortgage worth less.
2. As with a fur coat, the initial cost is one thing, the annual upkeep another. While the small down payment may appear easily arranged, remember the DIRTI FIVE costs of owning real estate: *D*epreciation, *I*nterest, *R*epairs, *T*axes, and *I*nsurance. These are worse yet when they have to be paid out of after-tax income. Before you rush to buy the $80,000 bungalow with the imaginary roses, calculate the DIRTI FIVE thorns:

Interest (12% on $80,000, including down payment):	$9,600
Depreciation and Repairs (2% at least):	1,600
Taxes (at least 1%):	800
Insurance:	100
Annual fixed costs	$12,100

The costs of ownership are over $1,000 per month. Could you not rent something as satisfactory for a lot less?

In the summer of 1979, I had extended difficulty in finding someone to rent a dream mansion amid the trees along the river in the centre of Winnipeg for $1,000 a month (and its value would be at least three times as great). So don't believe for a moment that landlords always have it easy.

Deductibility of mortgage interest payments would assist mightily ($200 to $300 per month tax savings), but at the time of writing this hasn't yet happened in Canada. My perhaps cynical view is that as the government giveth here, the government taketh away somewhere else.

3. Real-estate properties do not look after themselves. Management is essential, scarce, and expensive.

   It has taken twelve years of collecting camping fees for me to recover just the annual upkeep and improvement expenditures on Lake Six (the "old swimming hole" I purchased in 1966). As a sentimental winter dream it fills a need of mine. But as an investment, it's not liquid, it's unusable as bank security, and it's subject to the ravages of beaver-flooding, porcupine destruction, and invasion by hunters and hoodlums who bark trees, shoot up signs, and pollute the lake with their garbage.
4. Another cost of real estate is acquisition and disposition. You pay an agent six to ten per cent on every transaction. This fee comes immediately off the top and explains in large part real-estate firms' motivation for phony ads that suggest that "paying rent is like throwing away a fur coat every year."

   If you postpone owning a house, you can likely afford a fur coat to keep you warm in the meantime. And you'll be free to move to another part of the city or even another city when your current lease expires.
5. One of the strongest negatives on real-estate investing is that others are there first. I don't mean other virgin or amateur

investors, I mean "pros" – those that know what you don't and can do what you can't.

Some of these persons are realtors who list the property and lawyers who see the mortgage first. Others are city councillors directly or indirectly involved in real-estate usage decisions. Still others are powerful real-estate organizations known to run roughshod over majority local views, as with the parking garage at Portage and Main in Winnipeg or the Halifax buildings that, contrary to city bylaw, obstruct the view of the harbour.

Let me cite some examples of clients of mine who profited by delaying their real-estate purchases and financing everything through other investments.

CLIENT EXAMPLE NO. 1

In June 1962 a professional couple fresh from graduate school chose to rent a modest home and invest their equity in the stock market with professional guidance. Here is their investment experience from the beginning until they sold out in 1970 in order to pay for the major share of their custom-designed dream house on the river with all the exotic and expensive furnishings:

The initial investment of $2,500 reached a total of $5,932 through systematic small additions by August 1963. The carefully selected securities were:

1. The Getty Oil companies – Getty Oil, Tidewater, Mission Corp.
2. Northwest Airlines, purchased at 25, 32, 54, and 68
3. Kaiser Industries
4. Pittsburgh Coke and Chemical
5. Great-West Life
6. National General
7. Red Owl Stores
8. Rapid American (convertible debentures)
9. C. F. & I. Steel (convertible debentures)
10. Ling Temco Vought. Sold at $15 because the client disliked it. The stock later reached $165.

Had the entire account been cashed in at the market peak of December 1968, the total equity would have been over $100,000. As it was, money was gradually withdrawn to pay for the new house and its furnishings. The total of the withdrawals was $48,700, leaving an equity of $10,000 in the account.

These are spectacular results from a modest beginning with less than $6,000 cash. This could not have been achieved with any real-estate investment in Winnipeg during the sixties, nor even in the seventies, when the real-estate boom was well under way. Note, however, that these results were achieved before the tax authorities began to share in capital gains.

CLIENT EXAMPLE NO. 2

Another early client of mine was a single, business-career professional with extensive territory to service that required considerable travel. This client had an especially satisfactory apartment in a quite-liveable section of Toronto and was trying to decide whether to buy a house or an away-from-it-all retreat. Maintaining a property while away was a problem, but sharing it was undesirable.

Finally – action. Just two blocks away there was an exquisite townhouse with private backyard, flowers, and trees exactly to her liking. Financing was no problem because she had invested well – sell these debentures, these shares, and borrow on the rest. Negotiate a cash purchase (at a considerably lower price) and still maintain an investment portfolio to which is added (through a "voluntary forced savings program") $400 per month that would otherwise have gone to service the house mortgage.

She was very glad that she had gotten into stocks *before* buying a home.

INVESTING IN FARMLAND

Thought I'd try farming, the only pursuit that is sure.
"Acres of Clams", folksong

Aesthetically, a farm is a perfect investment – an inflation hedge because farmland prices seem to be always on the rise, a tax shelter even when you spend money foolishly, and in times of deflation, unemployment, and destitution, "you can always grow your own food." Add in, if you will, the running stream, the wildflowers, visions of apple-picking and maple-syrup-making, bountiful gardens, and ideal play-places for children, complete with horse, cow, pigs, chickens, dog, and kittens and all suffused with the heady smell of new-mown clover hay. No wonder so many of us become entranced with the notion of owning a farm.

In practice, only a few of us are suited to farming, and then only for brief parts of the year. Mud, snow, pests, insects, power failures, stuck cars, decaying buildings, burdocks, thistles, and dandelions – along with just plain thankless work – often offer more challenge than the soft city family cares to endure.

"But I want to anyway."

Well, for a nominal amount the neighbouring farmer may rent your crop-land and may keep an eye on the place for you. This avoids the embarrassment of your own attempts at farming and may hasten your acceptance as a sensible community member.

"We loved the view."

You could improve the financial outcome of your farm investment if you were to pay attention to the soil and what is being grown *before* you purchase. Land that is cheap per acre is usually quite overpriced, whereas the very best cultivated land – suitable for fruit, vegetables, even irrigation – is more likely to continue to rise in price over the longer haul. Nearness to urban centres is important, but often involves a speculation component that baffles the uninitiated.

"And so we bought it, and hung on."

My own purchase of farmland (1964) was designed to lend some verisimilitude to my work in the area as a farm-management consultant. Whether or not this objective was accomplished is perhaps for my neighbours to conclude. I do remember some traumas associated with new practices, new crops (rapeseed, fava beans), hailstorms, weather worries, storage problems, and marketing frustrations. But I also remember the soft spring breeze and the fresh scents of each phase of crop growth. I learned how bright, fresh, and vigorous is prairie sunshine, how responsive those seedlings are to the eighteen-hour days, what tension comes from the uncertainties, what joy follows a satisfying harvest, and how rich and comforting are the neighbourly expectations for a better year next year. All of which has little to do with producing an adequate return on the money invested.

Manitoba land prices peaked in 1967 and sank unmercifully

through 1971 because only small quantities of grain could be marketed. With the sellout to the Russians of the entire U.S. grain surplus in August 1972, markets opened rapidly, grain prices increased sharply, and all retiring farmers who didn't sell in the late sixties found ready buyers.

With so many new young entrants, the average age of farmers declined for the first time. Advances in technology and management know-how emphasized the advantages of larger farms. I bought the land of my immediate neighbour and soon negotiated a better lease than had been possible heretofore.

Through this rare period of bonanza conditions of prices rising faster than costs, prairie farmers cleared debts, bought new machinery, and bid up the price of land.

Then the provincial government got into the act. It began with an ill-informed attack on non-resident owners of farms. This was followed with legislated restrictions and a purchase-and-lease program. Now, with a change in government, the purchase-and-lease program has been dropped and other restrictions have been lifted (except for rules against foreign purchases – these have been tightened).

"And did you make any money?"

Results: an approximate quadrupling in price per cultivated acre over a seventeen-year period. But it would not have been mine if I had sold between 1968 and 1973, instead of in July 1981.

"Will farming be for me?"

Probably not, unless:

a. You understand the physical and technical aspects *and* the operational and timeliness aspects *and* the financial dimensions and risks.
b. You can gain market access for what you want to produce: e.g., milk, eggs, poultry are sold through marketing boards, and entry is not automatic.
c. You can enjoy coping with the sociology of rural communities at a time of shifting values.
d. You can bear up under increasing governmental regulation.
e. You love work for its own sake and are prepared to forgo immediate returns on your investment of mind, muscle, and money.

Otherwise, the onrushing years will bring increasing disillusionment and a sense of failure. You will need other outlets for your creative ingenuity to maintain your self-respect.

A NON-DEBATED NOTE

While both Dr. Ackerman and myself are aware of exceptions, we do share the conviction that being offered a good deal in real estate is at least as unlikely as being offered a truly good used car.

The best investments are those you seek out. Do not rely on any sales agent. In real estate, this is the rule, not the exception.

CHAPTER EIGHT

Commodities

If you can look into the seeds of time
And say which grain will grow and which will not
Speak then to me. MACBETH, Act I, scene 3

In the sixties a prominent U.K. economist, Nicholas Kaldor, proposed an international monetary unit based on thirty useful commodities – rice, wheat, coconuts, etc. What a spendid idea! What a contrast to usual thinking to choose something that can be used by human beings, rather than a unit artificially fixed on a single ornamental commodity, such as gold, or the currency of one of the world's trading nations. And how perceptive to give the second-, third-, and fourth-world countries the opportunity of improving their terms of trade by producing more of the commodities.

But, on the other hand, how naïve, in view of the political power-block realities of today's world.

A country's currency has value as long as it is well-managed by the central bank. This is accomplished by keeping the supply of it in line with, but not ahead of, the nation's production, refusing to accommodate massive expenditures by the government in power, seeing that shifts in the balance of payments are moderate, and acting quickly to restrict the money supply when inflationary pressures build. That is the theory. In practice, central banks are seldom free from political pressures from the government of the day. When there is insufficient commodity and production backing for the currency the rules get changed, so that those in power get to do as they propose: go to the moon, start a war, or undertake something equally uneconomic.

GOLD

Gold was called upon to cure the depression in the United States when, in 1934, its price was raised to $35 an ounce. Though the action was not a success, proponents of the gold standard saw the price as disciplinary in nature. By the late sixties, pressures for a cheap war and an interplanetary excursion took priority over a valuable and well-managed currency. The great grain sale of 1972 to the Soviet Union was financed by the United States just a few months ahead of the breakout rise of imported oil prices. Gold was freed from the $35 price tag, and the discipline designed to maintain the value of the currency vanished at the stroke of a pen.

At long last, the world's gold investors, who had been wrong in their judgments for thirty-five years, came into their own. Since then, they have increasingly held sway, with the price of gold spiralling upward to $875 an ounce. Several books and many international investment organizations have been created to encourage and service the expanding demand for gold ownership.

Is gold your best investment now? We think not. Before you buy, consider these points about gold ownership:

1. It has no reproductive characteristics.
2. It has little industrial use beyond ornamentation and dental work.
3. It provides imperfect protection against loss of purchasing power.
4. It is expensive to store and protect from thieves.
5. There is no assured marketability at any price.
6. Its purchase does nothing to enhance the wealth, comfort, or productivity of the human race.

WHAT ABOUT OTHER COMMODITIES?

Silver is cheaper per ounce and has significant industrial uses besides jewellery and coinage, and its annual rate of use exceeds new production. But, on the other hand, caution is needed, because the U.S. government and the Hunt brothers of Texas have combined forces to make a mess of the market. Late in 1978 and in early 1979, refined nickel, at less than $2 a pound, was selling well below the cost of production. The major mine and its union shut down business while the world surplus was gradually sold off. Then a 50 per cent price increase could be announced, justified by the world shortage. This would have been a good buy, if you had had a place to store a few tons. The ingot is too heavy to steal, your building could burn down without hurting it, and you knew that a good industrial market would exist at a much higher price.

In 1975, I began buying cement for a building project. I sent a big truck to Montreal, loaded it up with bags at $1.19 each, and stockpiled it at the building site. I knew that cement was a good inflation hedge – I had praised it in the 1960 edition of one of my books. I knew that inflation was with us and was going to get worse, and I was warning my readers in every book. I had the money, the truck for transportation, and the barn for dry storage space. Why didn't I buy many carloads of cement at $1.19 and then sell it at today's price of $4.30? I considered it, but was deterred by the danger of total loss. If the barn had burned down, the cement, which had already been calcined once, would be ruined. If the barn roof leaked, the cement would be destroyed, and it is hard to get insurance coverage in the country.

This illustrates one major difficulty of commodities – you have to transport, store, and insure the holding, and many commodities are bulky. Nobody wants a living-room full of sowbellies. But the developing commodity market has made it possible for you to buy contracts or futures, so all you hold is a piece of paper, and you never see the actual commodity. Today you can buy futures in metals (gold, silver, copper, nickel), petroleum, grains, oilseeds, livestock, fibres, wood, foods, and even money.

One of the undertakings made possible by the International Monetary Market in Chicago is betting on or betting against the Canadian dollar. The contracts are for $100,000, and brokers require a margin (initial deposit) of $1,500 to $3,000. Thus a one-cent change in the value of the Canadian in relation to the U.S. dollar means a $1,000 gain or loss on an equity of $1,500 or $3,000, a 60 or 30 per cent return after commission. What with a dumb boondoggle like the F-18 fighter plane, an already adverse balance of payments getting worse because of fewer tourists and rising oil prices, a money supply without forceful ıanagement control, and an astounding percentage national deficit, you may have agreed with Dr. Ackerman that the Canadian dollar was overvalued at 85¢ U.S. and deserved to decline to its present level of 72¢ U.S. Over a period of years, almost all world currencies will present from time to time striking opportunities for going either long or short. The stock indices themselves can now be used as commodities. You can go short or long on options to buy or sell an index at a fixed price. This is a clean way of expressing your views on the market as a whole.

With the combination of rapid price changes and the leverage inherent in commodity-futures trading, you could be wealthy by Wednesday and forgotten again by Friday. An exciting way to go, but remember you are competing with specialists, hedgers, and knowledgeable professionals. The novice investor is likely to be caught and cleaned before he knows enough to understand why.

A slower-paced and more predictable outcome awaits the investor who buys the shares of companies making his favourite commodity – be they gold-mining companies, oil producers, forest-product manufacturers, or food processors. Such companies often have inventories and contract positions that produce windfall earnings when prices increase. When you can predict a price decline that these company managements are ignoring, selling the shares short can provide you with significant if not superb profits.

CHAPTER NINE

Securities Issued by Governments

I don't make jokes: I just watch the Government and report the facts. WILL ROGERS (1879–1935)

In the 1960 edition of *Start With $100* (written about 1957), complaining about the government's lack of imagination and flair in marketing bonds and specifically about the lack in Canada of the lottery bonds common in Europe, I wrote:

> My own view is that the reason why lottery bonds have not been tried in the United States and Canada is not financial at all, but is attributable to our Anglo-Saxon hypocrisy. Because of our predominantly middle-class Protestant upbringing, we have an uneasy feeling that any speculation is morally wrong. It would make us quite uncomfortable to have our government encourage such speculation openly.

What can I say now? Without going through the intermediate stage of lottery bonds, the federal government and most of the provincial governments have gone directly into lotteries. This is a most despicable method of stealing from the poor and ignorant. Its use by any government is immoral, and calls into question the government's right to regulate any business when it is itself engaged in such activity. Lotteries appeal to the worst instincts of human beings, encouraging them to lust after something for nothing, instead of inculcating the virtues of honest labour, virtue, and thrift. In a word, it is a tax on ignorance, and on unfortunates who, through no fault of their own, have suffered a deficient upbringing. We Canadians have never had much sense of noblesse oblige, but this going out of our way to punish innocent people is something new. In Canada we have been moving in this general downhill direction for some time, but never before have we made such a sudden and concerted leap over the cliff. Quite apart from its effect on individuals and their government, lotteries develop a national market for numbers games, bookmaking, and casino operations in which the Mafia is the major force all over the world. Thus, a country that already has trouble with its police forces, and boasts one of the largest per-capita prison budgets in the world, deliberately encourages businesses which attract criminals.

The government in the lottery business seems to legitimatize blind chance-taking. This type of gambling, where no amount of mental energy can affect the outcome, is degrading. It brings out the worst in people, particularly those who can't defend themselves because of lack of education. It also brings out the worst in civil servants, as scandals in the administration of provincial lotteries go to prove.

Not only do lotteries corrupt the governments who tout them, and rot the minds of the citizens who buy them, but they have the further effect of corrupting the business community. Now, instead of giving us lower-priced gasoline as the result of lower world prices for crude, the oil companies give us "free" coupons and a chance to win a lottery. Canada Trust now attracts new savings accounts by offering a million-dollar lottery; the Bank of Montreal uses a lottery prize to get new home mortgage business; the Bank of Nova Scotia will make you eligible for a lottery prize if you bring your new-car financing to them.

GOVERNMENT BONDS

Besides helping companies get started by lending them your money for working capital, you can lend your money to the various levels of the government. Securities issued by federal, provincial, and municipal governments are invariably in the form of bonds rather than common stock. For the speculator, however, they have certain advantages from time to time.

The first thing to remember about government bonds is that, in spite of what everybody says, they can drop drastically in price, and even become worthless. Except for savings bonds, governments almost never guarantee even the face value of the bonds they issue. They put them on the market like any other product, and if there are more sellers than buyers the price of the issue will drop. Government bonds have a high degree of respectability as investments because most people think that the face value of the bond is guaranteed. But this is true only in a very limited sense. If a government issues a 9 per cent bond due in 1996, all the government is promising is that if all goes well and they are still in business in 1996, they promise to pay back a thousand dollars for every thousand-dollar bond. In the meantime, they promise to pay interest of $90 a year. But between now and 1996 many things can happen. The bottom may drop out of the bond market as more people fear inflation and refuse to buy bonds. When this happens, the price that you can get for your bond, if you have to sell before 1996, may be very low. From time to time in the last few years, U.S. and Canadian bonds have sold as low as $320 for each $1,000 bond. What this means is that a government bond, even when issued by a government of the highest integrity and excellent long-term prospects, is "guaranteed" only in the sense that the principal amount will be paid at maturity. What happens between the time you buy it and the time the bond matures is uncertain.

The price of government bonds may drop after you buy them at the issue price, or the market price may go up if interest rates decline. In addition, bonds are subject to another danger. When you get your thousand dollars back at maturity date, the thousand dollars will have less purchasing power than it did when you bought the bond. The depreciation of money in the U.S. in the twenty years between 1940 and 1959 was 51.6 per cent. Between 1960 and 1978 the rate of decline was about the same, 54.8 per cent. This means that the 1960 dollar, twenty years later, was worth 45¢ in terms of actual buying power. Thus, if ten years ago you purchased a thousand-dollar bond that yielded 3.4 per cent and were fortunate enough to be able to reinvest all the income from the bond at the same rate as soon as the income was received, you would just break even. But, of course, bonds are fully taxable, so you would be in the position of paying taxes on income you did not actually get, in return for the privilege of risking your capital.

Billions of dollars' worth of government bonds are sold to small investors who have been persuaded to buy through expensive advertising campaigns. They buy partly because they think the bonds are a good investment, and partly because they think it is a patriotic thing to help the country finance its affairs. The small bondholder's reward for these services has, in the past forty years at least, been a net loss of working capital. By having to pay income tax on the alleged income from bonds, the small investor has been forced to pay tax on a profit he has not received. Moreover, because of inflation, the small investor lost a good proportion of his capital.

For these and other reasons we believe that, for the small investor, buying new issues of government bonds of any type is a sucker's game. What we are against is buying bonds when they first come out. This is exactly like buying a new issue of stock, and often just as risky. Never do it. Wait until the artificially pumped-up enthusiasm has subsided a bit. But there is always an exception. See the story of the 19½ per cent of 1981 below.

CANADA SAVINGS BONDS

In order to finance the ever-expanding deficit brought on by the interest cost of an increasing national debt, brought on in turn by the drunken-sailor spending policies of whichever political party is in power, Canada's central bank sells Canada Savings Bonds every November. The combination of a multi-million-dollar advertising campaign, a ¾ per cent commission to the financial community, and payroll-deduction possibilities provides an aura of respectability, comfort, and sound conservatism far exceeding the prospective Christmas trip to the shopping centre. But the results may be somewhat similar.

In January you return to the department store with the toys and gadgets that fail to work properly, arguing that you deserve "value given for value received". Good luck. When you return the savings bonds to your local bank, somehow avoiding the manager's questioning stare, you receive less purchasing power than you gave when you bought them. Meanwhile, you have received income at less than the going rate and paid your top marginal tax rate on it!

The astuteness of the pricing decision (setting the interest rate to the public) provides harmless amusement for bystanders. In both 1978 and 1979, in order to make the savings bonds acceptable, the interest rate was changed twice. For 1981 the same people overshot, setting the first-year rate at 19½ per cent just as money demand slackened and rates began to fall. If you had purchased the maximum of $15,000 and borrowed on them to buy fifteen other government bonds (such as the 4½ per cent issue of 1983), it would have given you an excellent capital gain on the latter, as well as an above-market rate of interest on the former for the first year. Thus the exception proved the rule. As soon as legally possible, the Bank cut off sales, but not before those Canadians sensible enough to ignore the Governor's October 8 commentary (about interest rates needing to stay high due to continuing inflation) purchased over eleven billion dollars' worth of Canada Savings Bonds!

Nearly a quarter of Canadian government financing is done through savings bonds, with a 1 per cent cost to taxpayers every time there is a rollover (old savings bonds being exchanged for newer ones with higher interest rates). This is the most expensive means of government-bond financing, considering the net cost of the new money.

In December, once the patriotic small fish have all been fried, a cheaper method of government financing usually appears. This provides higher interest and earlier maturity for serious investors. The issue is marketed wholesale to institutions and large investors who can put up substantial sums. There is an established continuing market for these bonds.

That bonds move up and down in price is difficult to understand because it runs counter to everything that has been implied in millions of dollars' worth of advertising. Nevertheless, it is true. Bond prices are charted in two different ways. The most common way in financial circles is to chart, not the actual price of the bond, but its effective yield. That is, if a 3 per cent bond is selling at 80 (i.e., $80 for each $100) on the market, its effective yield is not 3 per cent but 3¾ per cent. This is because, for the purchaser who buys the bond at 80, the $3-a-year interest is $3.75 on each $100 invested, or 3¾ per cent.

The chart in Figure 17 shows the trend of bond prices from 1963 to 1973. Over this period, yields have ranged between 3 per cent and 8½ per cent. For a bond yield to change from 3 to 6 per cent, its price must drop in half. That is, if a 3 per cent bond drops to 50, it will then be yielding 6 per cent. This chart, then, is designed to impress upon you the fact that government bond prices are anything but fixed. They fluctuate like any other security. Bond prices swing up and down according to changes in supply and demand.

FIGURE 17: **Graph of Bond Yields**

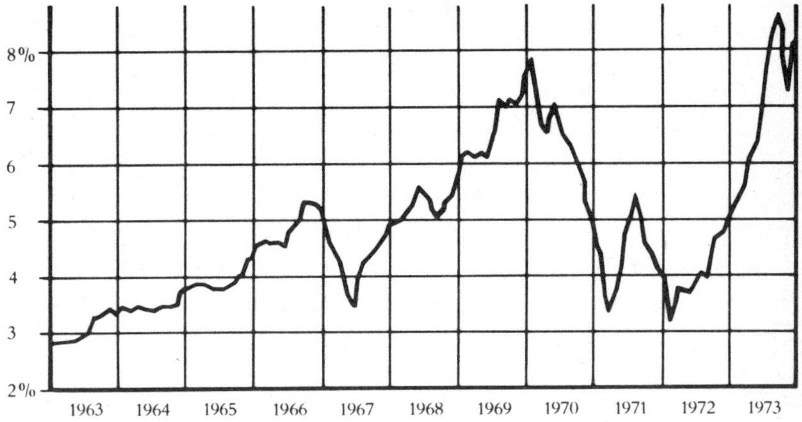

If federal government bonds are selling at a price that yields 9 per cent income, provincial bonds may well yield about 10 per cent, and bonds issued by municipal authorities 10 to 11 per cent.

These different rates reflect the greater degree of risk you are taking when you buy a bond issued by a smaller government unit. Presumably, if the Canadian government cannot meet its obligations as they fall due, every investment is dead. This is partly because the federal authorities control the entire credit structure, and partly because companies and banks often keep their liquid capital in the form of government bonds. If these suddenly become worthless, the liquidity of every enterprise is threatened.

We know that millions of innocent victims have been taken in by government advertising and have lost a portion of their capital by buying government bonds. But this is a hidden loss, hidden in fact for the most part even from its victims. To come out and admit that our previous system of bond financing was a swindle requires more courage than financial people are ever likely to muster.

FOREIGN BONDS AT A DISCOUNT

The greater the degree of risk in any security, the more likely you are to be able to buy it at a discount. Foreign bonds are generally speaking more risky than domestic, for two reasons.

First, you know your own government and conditions in your own country better than you know foreign affairs. At least domestic problems are in the newspapers, and you read about them every day. Second, there is the exchange problem. You can make a very successful investment or speculation in foreign bonds, yet find yourself coming up with a loss because the exchange rate is temporarily against you. By the same token, however, you can pyramid profits from a foreign bond speculation by making the commitment when the exchange rate favours you, selling at the proper time, and then bringing the money back to your own country under a favourable rate of exchange. But this takes skill or luck in three different speculations rather than just one. Hence, in order to pyramid the gains, you have to pyramid the risks.

Some quite respectable foreign bonds can often be bought at a large discount. If, for example, you believed that Germans are very hard workers and that West Germany, therefore, would make a quick recovery after the war, you could have made a lot of money speculating in German bonds. As late as 1953, the Dawes Loan 7/49 (that is, yielding 7 per cent and due in 1949) were selling for 70, and Young Loans 5½/65 were selling for 64. As West Germany recovered and got back its foreign trade, all the government-guaranteed bonds moved back toward par.

An investment in German bonds, made after careful study of German prospects of recovery after the Second World War, might be classed as an investment. Purchase of Russian Imperial bonds, even at the spectacularly low price of 26¢ for each $100 bond, must be classed as a speculation. It seemed highly unlikely that the White Russians would come back into power. And even if they did, it was even more unlikely that they would redeem their defaulted bonds. Nevertheless, it must be said that some people made very large profits by buying Imperial Russian bonds at 26¢ per $100 and selling them following the surprise announcement in July 1986 that the Soviets would redeem them for a percentage of the original purchase price.

In investing in foreign bonds, you have to find a situation in which everybody thinks that a given country is entering a period of economic decline. You, because of your studies and special knowledge of the situation, are pretty sure that, far from going into a decline, the particular country is going to come out of its current difficulties and be a big success. That is, in investing in foreign bonds, as in every kind of investing, you buy the securities nobody wants and hold them until they regain their popularity.

FANCY BONDS

Every government has noticed that immense sums of money are gambled away each year on such things as dog races, numbers rackets, and football pools. This money is spent in a way that benefits neither the country nor the people who put up the money. In Europe and the Near East some governments are trying to do something about it. They are putting out a new class of bond that has been nicknamed a "bingo" bond. This is a mixture of gambling with investment, in which the buyer of each bond has a chance to make a very large tax-free capital gain as a result of a drawing. If, as is usual, he doesn't win anything in the draw, he at least has the bond.

This is not exactly a new idea, the first nation-wide bond lottery having been issued in Sweden in 1918. In Italy and England, bingo bonds are a standard way of raising funds for the government. There, and in many other countries, it has been proved conclusively that a government bond issue can be made attractive to small purchasers by adding a dash of gambling. One difficulty with the Italian issues is that large banks and insurance companies have been known to buy up the entire issue of a lottery bond. By doing this, they are sure of getting not only the interest but all the prizes, which might total as much as $100,000 on every $2 million worth of bonds. This spoils the fun for the small investor, but is a lovely windfall for the company.

One beauty of most European bingo bonds is that they are issued in very small denominations, such as $10 and $20. This means that small-businessmen and other small investors who have a bit of gambling urge and a little money put aside can use their surplus funds in a way that is respectable and, at the same time, have a chance of winning very large sums of money. In England the Archbishop of Canterbury has denounced the idea of bingo bonds as "debasing the spiritual coinage of the nation", but the government has nevertheless gone ahead with a premium bond issue that pays 4 per cent interest and gives each buyer a chance at valuable prizes. In a country where football pools are a major industry, the government probably figured that any harm to the national moral tone had long since been done.

GUARANTEED-PURCHASING-POWER BONDS

As mentioned above, a major objection to buying any type of bond is that, in times of inflation, you get back less effective dollars than you put in. That is, in times of inflation, a bond has a guaranteed negative interest rate.

In Finland, France, and Austria, there have been issues of "inflation-proof" bonds. The prices at which such bonds are paid off are tied to some sort of cost-of-living index. In Israel, for example, the purchaser of a bond has a choice of being paid off either in money or in orange groves. The theory is that the orange groves in times of inflation will increase in price at a rate equal to the cost of living. Another Israeli commercial bond is tied to the selling-price of the company's product. Both the interest rate and the final repayment of capital are tied to the rising price of cement. Another series of bonds issued by the same company gives the bondholder the right to have his capital investment paid off in actual bags of cement. A U.S. oil company has recently come out with a bond based on the price of crude oil. Thus, no matter how frantic the inflation at the time the bond matures, the investor will have something he can sell. On the other hand, bags of cement are awkward to carry about.

The idea of attracting capital into the marketplace, where it could do some good by means of guaranteeing the purchasing power of bonds, is not new. Economists such as Alfred Marshall were writing about the idea in the 1880s. John Maynard Keynes wrote in 1924 that the British government should issue bonds whose interest and capital payments would be tied to a commodity index. The objections to this type of financing are heard chiefly from accountants, who are stuck with the headache of trying to figure what the assets and liabilities of a business are at any given time. In addition to admittedly serious problems of bookkeeping and administration, another difficulty is that the inflation hedge chosen sometimes turns sour. For example, if you have a bond issue whose redemption price is tied to the price of apartment houses in a certain district, and if that district, contrary to expectations, goes downhill instead of up, then your bond is no longer inflation-proof.

Two relatively new bond ideas should be mentioned. The first is the "floating rate" bond, which answers the problem of inflation by changing its interest rate in line with LIBOR (London Interbank Offering Rate) every six months. Thus, when interest rates are going up for everybody else, they will follow suit for you after a slight delay. The same is true on the down-side, but then you will appreciate the delay. This is a good way of protecting at least some of your income from the ravages of inflation.

A more recent attempt to build guaranteed purchasing power into a bond is the proposed bond of the Sunshine Mining Company that is payable in the company's product, silver. This is another good idea; hence, it may have trouble getting approval from the Securities Exchange Commission.

You should look at any old bonds you hold to see if by any chance the issuing company made a mistake and guaranteed to redeem the bonds in something besides dollars. If so, you are in, or at least you have a good case in court. In the early 1980s, in Montreal, a group of bondholders sued Canadian Pacific Railway, trying to get them to redeem one of the company issues in gold. (This is what it says on the document itself.) CPR won in court.

STRIPPED BONDS

People in high-income brackets want capital gains, not income, and are prepared to wait. They can buy bonds that have had their interest coupons removed and have been sold to people who want regular income. The stripped bonds sell at a discount, so they yield a capital gain at the end of their term.

CHAPTER TEN

Types of Company Securities

When it is a question of money, everyone is of the same religion. VOLTAIRE (1694–1778)

THE FEATURES OF VARIOUS INVESTMENTS

There are hundreds of ways to save money, and thousands of ways to lose it. In an imperfect world there is no such thing as a perfect investment. Every way of putting money aside for future use has certain advantages and certain disadvantages. Saving can take hundreds of forms, each of which can be rated in terms of four characteristics: safety, liquidity, income, and growth. Safety means the amount of risk there is of losing your money. Liquidity has to do with how easy it is to turn the investment into quick cash if you need it. Income means the amount of payment you get each year as a reward for lending your money to someone else. Growth has to do with the chances that the thing you buy for $10 today may be sold for $200 five years from now.

THE DIFFERENCE BETWEEN SAVINGS AND INVESTMENT

In savings, you simply buy a ready-made product that someone else sells. It is like buying a suit off the rack. This could be a bank savings account, a certificate of deposit, a trust company certificate, or a savings bond. Investment, on the other hand, consists of two elements, your capital and your mind, or at least your focused attention. Because of the mental input associated with investment, you expect much more from it. You expect the results to cover at least taxes and inflation, and preferably a bit more to pay you for your work.

There are some financial operations that are neither savings nor investment. These are best dismissed as "get rich quick" schemes. In terms of results, they are just ways of getting rid of unwanted money quickly. The lottery is the classic example.

When you are young, begin your black book recording your financial history. It is perfect if you can start learning about investment before you get hooked into endless consumer debt for cars, television sets, and vacations. If, when young, you have learned how to take investment risks, when you reach middle age you will have understanding. You will also have capital. Then you can afford all sorts of costly luxuries. Perhaps one of your grandchildren is richly endowed in musical skills. The world does not pay for developing skills of this kind. Think of the satisfaction that will be yours if, without straining your resources, you can give the child $20,000 for a musical education.

Every person tries to use his money in such a way as to get a maximum amount of satisfaction out of it either now or in the future. How a person spends his money is really no one else's business. In this book, we are not trying to tell you how to use money, but are trying to describe the field of investment, so that when you use your money in a certain way you will know what you are doing. Thousands of people have put their hard-earned savings into what they thought were conservative investments and then lost every penny.

We have no quarrel with any way of using money so long as the user is aware of what he is doing. Some people enjoy the thrill and excitement of wild speculations. Instead of spending their recreation money on bowling, movies, or ice-cream sundaes, they spend it this other way. There is a man in New York City who gets an immense amount of fun trying to sell five-dollar bills to canny passers-by for $1. He loses $4 on each successful sale, but this activity is his idea of fun, and he may be right.

If, after we have finished laughing at the man in New York, each one of us were to take a look at investments made in the past few years, we would probably find we had paid $5 for things that are now worth only $1. The difference is that we thought we were hard-headed and conservative when we made our investments. The man in New York is not kidding himself.

When you put aside money as savings, your capital is always at risk, because no one knows what will happen in the future. There is always a chance of losing all or part of the money you have put aside. If you invest, your capital and your mind have a chance to use the system to stay ahead.

However, before you can decide about investing in bonds or stocks, you must have some understanding of the elements of company organization.

HOW A COMPANY GETS STARTED WITH COMMON SHARES

Businesses, like babies, start out small. Usually one man takes his savings and uses them for buying the equipment needed to make a product he thinks will sell. If he is right, he has a business. If he is wrong, he has lost his savings. Sometimes, even at the beginning, more money is required than can be found in the savings of one person. In this case two men will form a partnership, or several persons will pool their money in a syndicate. Most of the older businesses got their start this way.

But today business is so complicated, and the machinery required for a new business so expensive, that a different way of starting or expanding a business is often needed. This way is to share the ownership of the business with a large number of people called shareholders. To raise, say, $100,000, one finds fifty people who are willing to risk an average of $2,000 each. These shareholders, in exchange for their money, receive a share certificate which indicates the proportion of the business they own. If the business is successful and makes a profit, each share owner receives a share of the yearly profits exactly proportional to the part of the company he owns. This is called a "dividend".

If profits are good, dividends can be good. The value of each share then rises, because more people want to own a share in a successful company. If, on the other hand, for any one of a multitude of reasons, the company does not make any profit, the value of each share tends to decrease. Finally, the company may go bankrupt, and all the shareholders lose their money.

Many companies fall between these two extremes. Companies, like people, have their ups and downs. In some years a company's prospects look extremely bright. More people want to buy the shares, and their price goes up; in other years the company may seem to be doing badly, people want to sell their shares, and the price goes down. This continuous change in the price of shares can't be helped, because it is caused not only by the changing prospects of the business, but by the changing opinions of the thousands of people who buy and sell shares. If enough people get the idea that a certain stock is good, its price will go up whether or not the shares are really worth owning. Similarly, if enough people get the idea that a company's stock is bad, the price of the shares on the free market will fall, even if the company itself is having the most profitable year in its history.

If we look at the history of a successful company over a period of years, we see that the average market price of its shares has an upward trend – that is, just about every year the shares sell on the average for more than they did the year before. Thus, the people who bought a share in a company for $10 might be able to sell the same share ten years later (if the company were successful) for $50. It is only fair that the people who buy shares after the company has demonstrated its usefulness should pay more than did those who took the major risk at the very beginning. People who put their savings into an entirely new business deserve to be well paid if the business is a success, because the risks they run are very large. The company doesn't know whether they can make the product, and if they do succeed in making it, they have no sure way of knowing if it can be sold. People who buy shares in the business in later years, after these two questions have been answered, expect to pay more for their shares, because the risk involved is considerably less. In most cases, the longer a business has been running, the less risk there is in buying its shares. This applies, of course, only if the factory's product is one we are still using. No one would buy shares in a buggy-whip factory today.

BONDS AND OTHER EVIDENCES OF DEBT

If a new company's product is well received, after a short time the company will have to increase production in order to meet growing demand. This means it must buy more machinery and perhaps build and move into a larger plant. All this takes money which the young company does not have, since all of the money put up by the original stockholders has been spent getting the company into operation. Under these circumstances the company has four possible ways of raising more money. The manager of the company can go to a bank and try to get a commercial loan on the basis of the company's successful history and unfilled orders. Or the company can issue bonds and sell them to the investing public.

Bonds differ from stocks in that they have a fixed face value (usually $1,000) and carry a fixed rate of interest. A bond is what is called a "senior security" of a company because the interest on it must be paid before the holders of common shares can receive any dividends. A bond is a fixed debt of the company and is usually backed by specific assets, such as plant. Both the instalment payments on the principal amount and the fixed amount of interest must be paid at specific times. Most shares, on the other hand, have no fixed face value and no fixed rate of interest. They represent, as their name implies, actual share ownership of the business.

Another alternative way of raising money is for the company to borrow against a mortgage on its property. If the company has machinery, tools, and a building worth several thousand dollars, the company can often arrange a cash loan by putting up these assets as collateral. The final alternative is for the company to issue debentures. A debenture is a long-term debt that is backed by the general credit of the company. It is like a mortgage, except that the mortgage names specific units of real property such as machines or a building which can be sold by the lender if the debt is not paid. A debenture names no particular real property as security but is nevertheless a senior obligation of the company, like a bond.

Within limits, it is a healthy sign that a company has been able to borrow from public and private sources by means of bonds, debentures, mortgages, or bank loans. Such borrowing, if the company continues on a successful course, obviously works to the benefit of both the common-share owner and the bond lender.

CAPITALIZATION

A description of where a company has obtained its money is called its "debt structure" or "capitalization". When companies obtain their charters from the government, they are given permission to issue a certain number of shares. Not all of these shares may be issued in the early years of the company. Some may be held in reserve and sold at a higher price after the company has established its position.

PREFERRED SHARES

A company's charter often gives it permission to issue a special type of share, known as the preferred. These are the securities which combine some properties of both bonds and shares. They are like shares in that they represent actual ownership in the company, but they are privileged issues in that they bear a fixed rate of interest (dividends) which must be paid each year before any dividends are paid on the common shares.

Preferred shares can be cumulative or noncumulative. If the dividend is noncumulative, each year of the company's operations is considered by itself. That is, if the company has a bad year and is unable to pay dividends on either the preferred or the common stock, the owners of both classes do without. The following year, if things are a little better, the holders of the preferred shares get their dividend. Only if there is something left over do the common shareholders get paid. If, however, the preferred stock is cumulative, the arrears of dividends owing on the preferred stock from previous bad years have to be paid in full before the common shares can receive any dividend for the current year. Obviously, cumulative shares are safer than noncumulative, if the risk is comparable in other respects.

There is still some dividend tax advantages in owning preferred shares of Canadian companies, but this advantage must be weighed against faults. Preferred shares from the investor's standpoint are not a growth vehicle. Compared with a bond or debenture the income is often higher, but it is less dependable. If the company has not earned enough to declare the dividend, you may be faced with a capital loss. By and large, we don't recommend them except in special circumstances.

CONVERTIBLE BONDS

Sometimes it is difficult to entice the investing public into buying bonds. One reason might be a general fear of inflation and a consequent rush to common stocks. Another might be the special risks of a new industry such as uranium, or of an industry with a bad financial history. When such a company comes on the market with an issue of bonds, the public is understandably reluctant to buy.

To make a straight bond more palatable, the bonds are often issued either with a conversion privilege, or with warrants attached. If the bonds have a conversion privilege, or have warrants attached, the owner can exchange his bonds for the common shares of the company at a fixed price, up to a certain time. Normally, this fixed price is such that if the company is successful, the purchaser of the bond will get a bonus. Conversion rights usually run for several years, and, of course, the longer they run, the more chance you have of making a profit on them.

In convertible bonds, you have to give up your bonds in order to convert into the common stock. For example, you might exchange each $1,000 bond for forty shares of stock. If you paid $1,000 for the bond and at some time during its conversion period you were able to convert into forty shares of stock worth $30 a share, you would end up with $1,200, or a profit of $200 on the transaction, in addition to your bond interest. The beauty of convertible bonds is that if the issue is a sound one, you have a sure interest return, and the risk to your capital is relatively small because you have bought a bond. But at the same time you have the possibility of substantial capital gain.

Other investors will bid up the price of your bond because of the substantial rise in the underlying common stock.

HOW TO DOUBLE YOUR DOLLARS IN DEBENTURES

Early in 1968 Dr. Ackerman put some of his clients into a thoroughly discounted debenture, the Bramalea Consolidated Development (BCD) 6½/1973 at 80. The case for buying it at this time was:

- attractive interest rate (at the time)
- early maturity
- less than $4 million of the bond issue outstanding
- principal and interest in $U.S.
- if new financing were required, these debentures would be "in the way" and therefore likely to be redeemed (at par) on 30 days' notice.

– the company was making good progress. Assets of \$42 million, 1967 sales up 50 per cent, earnings up nearly 100 per cent.

The Investment Arithmetic

For 10 BCD (face value \$10,000) debentures:		Bond interest paid: (subject to 15% non-resident withholding tax)	\$650.00
Purchase price 80 (\$800) × 10	= \$8,000	Interest out	
Borrow 90%	= 7,200	(9% on \$7,200):	\$648.00
Invest	\$ 800		

Capital gain when the bond is redeemed at 100 in 1973: \$2,000 (100–80 = 20 × 100)
Duration of investment: 5 years.
Therefore gain is \$400 a year on a cash investment of \$800, or 50%.

So: Debenture pays its way and assures a capital gain of 50 per cent / year.
The worst: Interest costs could increase past 9 per cent.

What actually happened was that in October 1968 the company redeemed the debentures at 100 (that is, they paid the full price of \$1000 for each \$1000 bond). The capital gain in the transaction came to 250 per cent in less than a year (they sold at \$10,000 and cost \$8,000, meaning a gain of \$2,000 on a cash investment of \$800).

This looked like a pretty good investment vehicle, so in September 1969 Dr. Ackerman sent the following to his clients:

Thresher Investment note

For discounted bonds – Happiness is:

1. A large discount from face value. Face value for most bonds is \$1,000. Although bonds are traded in thousands, ten bonds being a usual unit of trading, the prices are quoted in hundreds; therefore a quotation of 80 means that the \$1,000-face-value bond is in fact selling for \$800, or 80 per cent of face value.
2. A high-interest coupon. This is the assured annual amount of return that the company has agreed to pay the creditor who holds the bond or debenture. Incidentally, debentures are similar to but

subordinate to bonds. Instead of being secured by a particular asset of the company, they are in effect a floating charge on the company.

3. Early maturity. In today's market, this is perhaps ten years or less. Medium maturity could be considered to be ten or twenty years and long maturity to be bonds that do not mature until after 1990.
4. A small issue of bonds outstanding.
5. A sinking fund that ensures the redemption of most of the bonds in advance of maturity. Sinking funds are pretty much relics in today's financing; however, there are still some bonds that do have this feature. Its importance is that it requires the company to set aside money in the later years of the bond's life, so that redemption on schedule is assured.
6. Convertibility. Ideally the bond or debenture will be convertible into a large number of common shares. For this, the company must be an attractive investment, showing high assets and high prospective earnings relative to the present price. As a rough guide to what is a large number of common shares and therefore a highly leveraged debenture, I would suggest something more than 50 shares of common stock per $1,000 bond.
7. Solid working-capital backup. Calculate the working capital (current assets less current liabilities) per share. Multiply by the number of shares the debenture converts to, and compare it to the price you pay.
8. You need a broker or banker who will lend you a high percentage of the cost of the bonds. This should be 70 per cent to 90 per cent of its market value in order to add still more leverage to the investment. If the market price is under $50, the banker will probably not lend you more than 50 per cent on it.

Theory is all very well, but the practical problem was to find the bond that fitted these points. These opportunities do not arise every day. But another was found, and here is how it worked out.

Happiness is. . . a Discounted Debenture
Thresher Client Example No. 2
Tokyo Shibaura Electric Co. Ltd. (Toshiba) 6⅜ per cent 1978 selling at 80 to 100 between late 1967 and early 1969

The Case

- attractive interest rate

- early maturity
- \$20 million outstanding, but sinking fund beginning 1971. (That is, in 1971 the company has to start redeeming the bonds on a lottery basis.)
- interest and principal in \$U.S.
- convertible into 74 common shares (American Depository Receipts (ADRs) equal to 50 Japanese shares). Prevailing price \$9.50 each. With ADRs going to \$13.50, debenture would be worth its weight (\$1,000) in shares.
- The company is Japan's General Electric – \$1,447 million assets, \$300 million equity, \$1,000 million sales, 1967 earnings \$28.9 million, up from \$9.5 million in 1966.

The Investment Arithmetic

For 10 Toshiba debentures:

Purchase price		
80 (\$800) × 10	=	\$8,000
Borrow 90%	=	7,200
Invest		\$ 800

Capital gain

(a) by 1978: \$2,000

Debenture interest in:	\$637.50
Interest to pay (9% on \$7,200):	\$648.00
Net current interest return:	\$10.50 / yr

$$\frac{\text{Annual average}}{\text{Investment}} = \frac{\$200}{800} = 25 \text{ per cent / year}$$

(b) by 1973, if called for sinking fund: \$2,000

$$\frac{\text{Annual average}}{\text{Investment}} = \frac{\$400}{800} = 50 \text{ per cent / year}$$

(c) by 19XX, if ADRs increase from 9.50 in 1968:

to 13.50 $\frac{\$2{,}000}{800} = 250\%$

to 19.00 $\frac{\$6{,}000}{800} = 750\%$

The worst: Broker could refuse to lend against a foreign security. Interest-equalization tax of 11.25 per cent applies unless sold to a non-American.

Interest costs could increase past 9 per cent.

The best: ADRs went to 24, company offered one new share per 4 old at about $7.

Resulting price of ADRs: 17, of debentures: 120 (i.e. $1,200 for a debenture purchased for $800).

Another good opportunity to make money in discounted debentures occurred in 1970, when a Crane Company issue dropped to 80. The company was solid, so a purchase of the debentures with 70 per cent borrowed money seemed reasonable. The price rose quickly to 140, at which time the client got out with his money doubled. The bonds continued to rise, because of the convertible feature, and reached 200.

BONDS WITH WARRANTS

Some bond issues have warrants attached. This is another method of making a given bond issue more palatable to the investor. As mentioned earlier, these warrants give you the right to buy common stock of the company at a fixed price. In this case the investor can hold on to the bond and put up more money to buy the common stock if such a move is indicated. Warrants are an elegant medium for capital-gains speculation, especially for the businessman who can assume a high degree of risk. It is precisely because the company is not particularly solvent that it has been forced to attach warrants to each bond in order to find buyers. But in spite of this, the amateur investor who can devote very little time to his portfolio often does better on convertible bonds or bonds with warrants attached than on any other class of security. This is because the bonds provide some degree of insurance if things go badly, and the attached warrants provide substantial capital gains if things go well.

But you have to watch the time and respect the deadline when the warrants or rights expire. Don't expect your broker or anyone else to do this job for you. It's your money.

If the common share goes up 20 per cent, a warrant might go up 100 per cent in the same period. By the same token, however, in a declining market warrants can fall much faster than common shares.

RIGHTS ISSUES

From time to time companies will offer their shareholders the right to buy shares at below market prices. This right usually lasts only a few weeks. If this paper is offered to the company shareholders, it is usually called a "rights issue". Say you own 100 shares of the Canadian Imperial Bank of Commerce and the bank wants to cash in on investor interest in the stock. It has had a good year which the annual report did not underplay, but the management thinks the results will not be equalled next year. So now is the hour. The bank will send you rights to buy 100 shares at the discount price of $25 a share. If 5 rights are required to buy one share of stock, and the shares are currently selling at $30 a share, each right would be worth $1 on the market (since you can make $5 on each share). You need only to sell your rights before they expire, on the open market, to get a capital gain. Moreover, if you buy the shares, you are given time to pay. A feature of the Bank Act requires the banks to allow shareholders exercising rights to pay for the shares in 10 monthly instalments. No interest is charged, but you get only partial dividends until the stock is paid up.

If you are not already a shareholder and want to become one, you can buy rights on the open market and then use them to purchase the shares. The value of rights on the market rises and falls with the fluctuation of the underlying common shares. Short-term speculations can be made by buying rights in the hope that they will become more popular and you can sell them at a higher price before they expire. Since most rights expire, however, within a few weeks, you have to watch such a speculation very closely.

CHAPTER ELEVEN

Reasons for Investing in Common Shares

The universal regard for money is the one hopeful fact in our civilization. Money is the most important thing in the world. It represents health, strength, honour, generosity and beauty. . . .Not the least of its virtues is that it destroys base people as certainly as it fortifies and dignifies noble people. GEORGE BERNARD SHAW (1856–1950)

This chapter is not designed to tell you specifically what to do about your investments, but rather to make you generally knowledgeable about the subject. What it is seeking to demonstrate is: when you are investing via the stock market, even on a "random walk" basis, you are on a strong wicket. One of our goals is to make you more self-confident as an investor. One way to do this is to convince you that, even if you make bad mistakes in choosing your shares, the long-term trend of the market is basically with you rather than against you. The key word in this sentence is "long-term". We are not forecasters, and prefer to invest without use of the crystal ball, but just now we are looking for a sharp extended decline in the stock market.

The main reasons why we think you should use common shares in preference to other vehicles of saving and investment are these:

1. Movement:
There is a large enough price change each year to give you profit and excitement. The safe blue-chip stocks in the Dow Jones Industrial Average (the name given to the average price of thirty good common stocks selected from representative branches of the manufacturing industry of the United States) have provided only 5 per cent change in the past decade. This is not enough. Most stocks on the exchange move up or down 50 per cent to 100 per cent

within a year. This will give you worthwhile gains if you can call the direction of the move. For example, in the first nine months of 1986, Alcan ranged from 23 to 34, while Bethlehem Steel went from 22 to 7, Bank of America from 18 to 10, American Airlines from 38 to 60, and Kellogg from 49 to 58.

2. Liquidity:
You can get instant cash five days a week if you have to sell out, or you can borrow, using the shares as collateral.

3. Morally clean:
The investment is upbeat and creative. Money put into shares indirectly assists an actual business which employs people and makes products and services people use; it strengthens the country's gross national product, and makes for more investment opportunities. It is not like gold, which sits sterile in a vault, or a bond, which lacks youthfulness and optimism. Weight may be given to your emotional preferences by allowing you to avoid those companies that make addictive or dangerous products like cigarettes, liquor, and armaments.

4. Never a dull moment:
At any time there are opportunities presented by individual shares moving either up or down. Even in a dull market, *some* companies are doing something interesting, and their shares are moving as a consequence.

5. Plenty of choice:
There are literally thousands of companies on the listed and unlisted markets; hence you have plenty of alternatives in companies and industries. There are 1,575 companies on the New York Stock Exchange and 789 on the Toronto exchange, and lists of their names are available at all brokerage offices and banks.

6. Sell-now buy-later option:
Most investments require that you buy first and then sell later. Shares are unique in that they can be sold first (if you think the price is too high) and bought later when the price is lower (this will be discussed in more detail later). It can be done in stocks without

incurring the tight time restrictions of commodity futures. (See pp. 250-2 on puts and calls.)

7. Convenience:
There is no storage, insurance, or security-guard cost. A registered share certificate representing $1 million can be framed and kept on your living-room wall. Even if it is lost, stolen, or burned, you don't lose your money.

8. Availability of information:
The basic data you need to make up your mind is freely available. The "battle for investment survival", well named forty years ago by Loeb, the famous financial writer, is one of the few fair fights in our society.

9. Alternative to commodity speculation:
Rather than buying a commodity and paying for storing it, you can take a position in copper or gold by buying the shares of companies that produce the commodity. They have an inventory aboveground and ore reserves underground which may together produce higher profits if the price of the commodity rises.

10. Education:
Buying stocks is educational. You become knowledgeable about the company you buy and about its industry. You learn to judge the quality of management decisions and understand what makes a company go. The novice investor who bought gold in January 1980 because everyone was doing it is as stupid after the purchase as before.

11. Ownership:
In theory and to some extent in practice you are a co-owner of the company when you buy the shares. You can go to the annual meeting and ask the questions *you* think important. You can get answers. Management may even be interested in your views.

12. Income:
When you bought your shares you were looking for rapid growth, and got it. Later the company was successful and was able to pay out

a good proportion of its earnings as dividends, so you get an income too.

13. Built-in financing:
With the broker's system of margin accounts you can choose the level of risk you want to assume. "Borrow up to the stimulation point" or "sell down to the sleeping point".

14. Speaks to both hope and fear:
Bernard Baruch (who made several fortunes through investing, and therefore could prove he was worth listening to) had a unique way of classifying investment aims. He said that people invest in common stocks for two entirely opposite reasons. One large group invest because of hope. They are optimistic about the future of the country in general, and about the future of business in particular. Hence they invest in order to get their share of what they think will be a juicy melon. Those who hope invest in common stocks with the general aim of achieving financial security through participation in the long-term growth of the country.

The other large group invest in common stocks because of fear. They fear that their capital will be lost because of inflation; that their insurance policies, annuities, and pension plans, into which they are putting their dollars today, will be worthless when the time comes to enjoy them. This group sees common stocks as a hedge against the threat of inflation, as a way of investing that pays off, not in assets of fixed-dollar value, but in sums that may be tied to the actual cost of living at the moment they are paid.

With two such differently motivated groups operating in the market, it is no wonder, as Baruch points out, that the market shows contradictory tendencies from time to time, and reacts to domestic and world events in ways that are sometimes surprising.

15. Limited liability:
Being part-owner of a business is a pleasant experience in good times when the business is making a profit and you are getting your fair share. When the downturn comes, however, ownership becomes a liability. Years ago, when times were bad and a business failed, the owners of the common shares could be called upon to make up the debts owed by the bankrupt company. Today most

companies are of the "limited liability" type. This means that the common shareholder cannot be called upon to make good the debts. He can lose all the money he has put in, as the common shares gradually lose their value, but he doesn't have to put up anything more.

The concept of limited liability was one of the main factors encouraging risk-taking by investors in the late nineteenth and early twentieth centuries, and led to the highest levels of innovation, production, and employment the world has ever known. Now, however, the trend is in the opposite direction. The Province of Ontario has new corporation laws that make the directors personally responsible for everything that goes on in a company. Don't become a director of your brother-in-law's Ontario company. If anything went wrong it could cost you everything you own.

16. Inflation hedge or deflation hedge:
Carefully chosen common stocks have a part to play in most programs for financial security. Although not as safe as bonds or annuities, common stocks are valuable because their capital worth and the interest they earn tend to change in such a way as to counteract the unfavourable effects of inflation. Their value depends to some extent on how carefully the common stocks are chosen, yet several independent studies, made at different times and taking in different periods of business activity, bear out the assertion that even fairly uncritical and mechanical stock-buying can, over the years, work out successfully for the investor.

Two University of Michigan professors, Eiteman and Smith, published a study of mechanical stock-buying covering the period 1937–50. Their conclusion was: "If you were to invest a fixed sum of money every year for a period of years in a cross-section of common stocks, and if you reinvested all dividends, the return you could expect would be the equivalent of 12.2 per cent compound interest on your money."

The controls established for this study were such that a completely objective result was assured. The period chosen was long enough (fourteen years) to justify the words "long term", yet this period was not one in which the market was rising spectacularly. In fact, the level of the Dow Jones Industrial Average was exactly the same at the beginning and the end of the period.

Their method of selecting stocks was equally objective. They took every issue traded on the New York Stock Exchange in a volume of one million or more shares during 1936. It might be argued that stocks popular with investors in a year like 1936 would necessarily be blue-chip, and that these stocks would rise more than the averages when times improved. But an examination of the list shows that it is indeed a representative cross-section of the market, including good, bad, and indifferent issues in twenty-seven industries, ranging in quality from speculative to blue-chip.

Timing, too, was completely mechanical. On January 15 of each year, the authors assumed for each stock an investment of $1,000, together with the dividends paid in the year previous. In some of the years, stocks were near their high on this date; in other years they were near their low. Over the period, this factor seemed to average out.

The capital gain of 135 per cent over the period is somewhat exaggerated because of the policy of reinvesting gross dividends. In real life, the dividends would be subject to taxation, so that only the net dividends after taxes would be available for reinvestment.

On the other hand, to balance this, the period chosen contained the six years of the Second World War, a disastrous period for stock prices.

The results of this program are shown in tabular form in Figure 18.

A study covering the period 1929–69 done by the Center for Research in Security Prices at the University of Chicago came up with similar results. A random cross-section of stocks listed on the New York Stock Exchange, taken over the forty-year period, produced a pre-tax average return of 9.3 per cent a year compounded annually. That is, a single investment of $1,000 would have grown to $35,000.

We have not been able to find a strictly comparable random-choice study containing the period of the great bull market, 1949 to 1956, or the market boom ending in 1968. There is a study reported in the *Wall Street Journal* (October 8, 1979, page 40) which confirms in the most striking way the view that common stocks are a great hedge against inflation. The Institute for Econometric Research, of Fort Lauderdale, Florida, whose findings are reported, does studies from time to time showing the total return (dividends plus market

FIGURE 18: **Random-Selection Stock-Market Results**

Year	What was paid in	Market value of stocks
1937	$ 92,000	$ 92,000
1938	184,000	149,514
1939	276,000	255,589
1940	368,000	326,386
1941	460,000	412,083
1942	552,000	486,074
1943	644,000	690,273
1944	736,000	1,074,540
1945	828,000	1,580,878
1946	920,000	2,724,886
1947	1,012,000	2,169,708
1948	1,104,000	2,363,253
1949	1,196,000	2,525,266
1950	1,288,000	3,028,855

rise) of *all* the stocks listed on the New York Stock Exchange. You don't have to pick the best. Starting at the market low of September 13, 1974, the "total return index" by September 1979 hit 263 per cent, an annual rate of nearly 30 per cent for the five-year period. Compared to this, inflation is almost negligible: according to the Consumer Price Index, it was 44 per cent for the same period, or an annual rate of 7.6 per cent.

The total return index for all the stocks on the American Exchange was even better. It was 400 per cent for the period, an annual rate of 48 per cent, which is about five times the inflation rate for the period.

DESPAIR OF THE FUTURE; FEAR OF INFLATION

The group that invests, not because it sees an unlimited future for the country, but because it fears that the government will continue to foster controlled inflation, justifies its investment decision in a somewhat different way. These people harp on inflation, and what it does to the small saver.

Inflation is an economic fact, and both economic and political facts can be brought to bear on it. Yet we must remember that deflation, too, is an economic fact. Periods of inflation and deflation have alternated throughout history.

Perhaps the only way to be sure is to be, like Senator Snort in the comics, "a fearless foe of flation".

Inflation is the name given to the condition where too much money is chasing too few goods. Thus, prices of goods and services rise, and each dollar buys less than it did before. This is called "demand pull". When the price of oil in Canada is allowed to rise to the world price, every business will pass the increase on to consumers, and the inflation rate will rise.

Deflation is the opposite condition – where money is scarce and goods and services are plentiful. Hence prices fall, and each dollar buys more and more each day.

DOLLAR VALUE *vs.* VALUE OF THE DOLLAR

In a risky life, we at least have the consolation of enjoying a *variety* of risks.

RISK 1: Lose your dollars.

RISK 2: Lose the *value* of your dollars (their purchasing power).

These two kinds of risks are quite different. Yet to the individual investor the effect of one is as bad as the other. If your capital has been eroded, it doesn't matter to you whether it has been eroded through change in dollar value or through a change in the value of the dollar. You are poorer than you used to be.

For example, say in 1940 you had saved $1,000 to buy a car. But with a war on you decided that you might not need a car for some time, so you invested the money instead. Your first alternative was to buy a fixed-value investment such as a bond. If you had done this and then come back ten years later and cashed the bond, you would find that although you got the full $1,000 face value on selling, the $1,000 was no longer enough to buy the car. In 1940 you could have bought a new Ford with your $1,000, but in 1950 the same $1,000 was only a little over half the amount required; in 1960 it was only about one-third, in 1970 only about one-quarter, in 1980 only about one-seventh, and in 1986 only about one-tenth.

Anti-Inflation Measures Must Be Weighed Against Risk

We can all look back and see how we could be wealthy today if only we had taken this or that action in the past. For example, in 1941 I was much impressed by a book by E. C. Riegel called *Dollar Doomsday*. His thesis, in a word, was that economic and political factors both pointed to a period of unprecedented inflation. He gave some specific rules for living in an era of money inflation which, if followed to the letter, would have made anyone wealthy. I only hope he had the wit to take his own advice and is now enjoying his reward.

His rules, in summary, were to stretch your credit to the breaking point to accumulate any kind of useful property – land, buildings, and common stocks representing actual ownership of going enterprises. Such a policy, of course, would have paid off handsomely in the postwar period.

Yet the risk of following this advice is too great for most of us. Most people my age were brought up in the Great Depression, and we have an almost pathological fear of debt. So perhaps it comes back to the old financial-district saying: "Some people would rather sleep than eat." If you want to have peace of mind that allows you to sleep well at night, maybe you have to keep out of debt, and thus miss the high standard of living enjoyed by shrewd debtors in times of inflation.

What Inflation Does to Stock Prices

Most of the thirty major industry groups react to inflationary pressures by increasing in market value, and to deflationary pressures by decreasing in value. Certain industries, however, will consistently buck the trends. And, of course, many individual stocks within any industry will run counter to the trends because of special circumstances in their management or market situation. This accounts for the plaintive cry often heard on Bay Street: "Everybody's stocks are going up but mine."

The graph in Figure 19 shows how share values change. As mentioned before, the Dow Jones Industrial Average is the name given to the average price of thirty good common stocks selected from representative branches of the manufacturing industry of the United States. If the horizontal lines represent the prices of the stocks, and the vertical lines the years since 1910 – that is, plot dollar value against time – the graph plots the Dow Jones Average for those years.

In theory, in 1940 you might have bought common shares, which on the average might have undergone the same changes as the Dow Jones Average. In 1940 this Average stood at 130 and in 1950 it had climbed (after several disconcerting ups and downs) to 235. Getting back to that car, if you had chosen your stocks well, the $1,000 invested in 1940 would have amounted to nearly $2,000 in 1950, and you would have been able to buy about the same new car you had wanted in the first place.

The Consumer Price Index is a number representing the cost of those items commonly used by the average family. As you can easily see from the graph in Figure 20, this index has been rising fairly continuously ever since the end of the war. If we place this graph beside one showing the average yield of common shares for the same period, we can see that the trend of the two lines (in spite of various irregularities) is roughly the same.

From this, many people have drawn the conclusion that the buying of common stocks is a good hedge against inflation, because

FIGURE 19: **Dow Jones Industrial Average, 1910–1980**

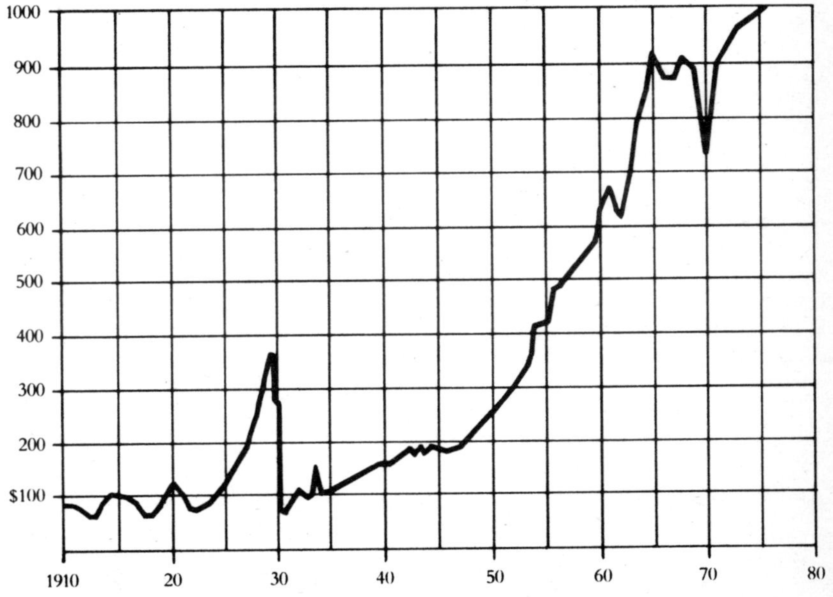

the rising income from the shares more or less parallels the rise in the cost of living. This is true, over the long term at least, provided you choose your stocks wisely. How well a company gets along depends on many factors, such as industry trends, good times, management skills, and markets. You must assess all of the factors before making a choice.

A good case can be made for this use of stocks, based on both their performance in the past and their potential for the future.

In the University of Michigan study cited on pages 156-7, the common stocks earned 12.2 per cent compound interest over the period. This is 72 per cent higher than the increase in the cost of living over the same period.

FIGURE 20: **Purchasing Power of the Dollar, U.S. (solid line) / Consumer Price Index, Canada (dotted line)**

1967 = $1

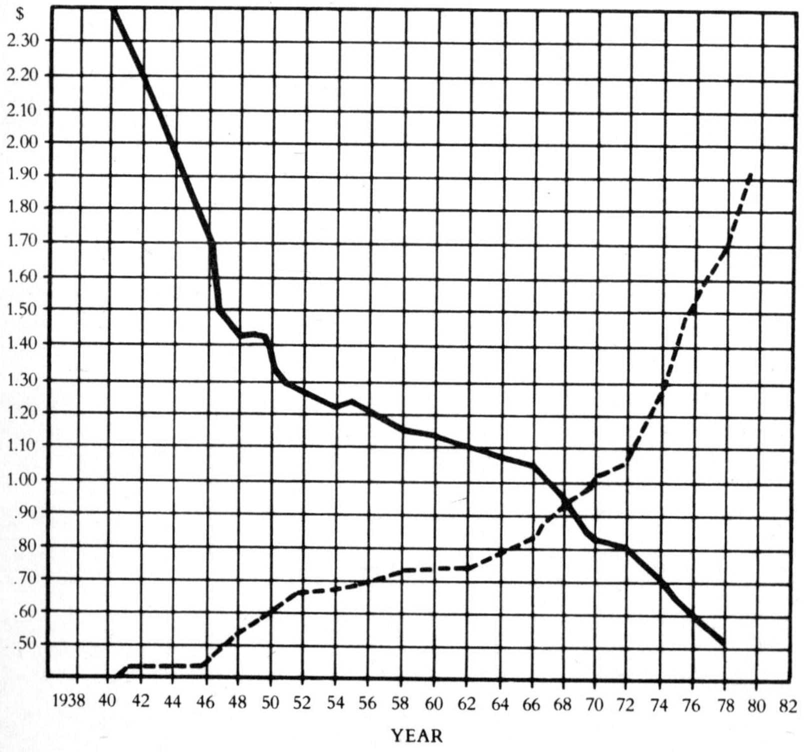

The graph of the Dow Jones industrials (Figure 19) shows even more favourable results. In the entire period covered by the graph, market prices have moved up at an average rate of 3.18 per cent a year. This is substantially better than the average rate of decline of the purchasing power of the dollar over the same period.

But as a practical matter, you can't buy the Dow Jones Average or the entire list used in the University of Michigan study. You have to choose individual stocks.

PRODUCTIVITY

One factor offsetting the effects of inflation to some extent is the increasing productivity of industry. Modern plants turn out better products using fewer man-hours of work than ever before. Thus, the twenty-five-cent dollar sometimes buys more than the old hundred-cent dollar, because of the intervention of machines. But, on the other hand, productivity in the United States and Canada has been falling and is now increasing by only 1 per cent a year.

PART IV: INVESTMENT ANALYSIS AND PLANNING

CHAPTER TWELVE

The Sources of Financial Information

There is nothing so fallacious as facts – except figures.
GEORGE CANNING (1770–1827)

The purpose of this chapter is to acquaint you with the various sources of investment information, and to assess them from the point of view of expertness and possible bias. In a later chapter we are going to talk about the kinds of economic forces, and their possible effect on market prices. Here we want to discuss the raw materials at hand for following the changes of the economic and political forces that affect market prices.

One point to make at once is that these factors are changing all the time. The most-used phrase in the profession of security analysis should be "as of today". Tomorrow or next week it could all be different. This means you must stay alert.

POINTS ABOUT FINANCIAL INFORMATION IN GENERAL

The field of finance is unique in that it has few disinterested students. We study finance partly because of the fascination of mastering its mechanics, but mostly because we want to make money. The objective is clear, so we mobilize all our faculties to reach it.

Just about everyone in the financial world has some kind of stake in what you decide to do with your money. Hence, it is extremely difficult to obtain wholly unbiased advice. Even if, as is the case with a newspaper, your source of information has no interest in what you do with your money, it often consciously or unconciously has an axe of its own to grind. This leads it to choose those statistics that prove its point and neglect the others. Therefore, if you read uncritically, you are misled.

There are two basic kinds of financial information, the bare facts and figures, and some fellow's comment on the facts and figures as he reads them.

DANGERS IN BARE FACTS

As Canning pointed out in the quotation at the beginning of this chapter, the facts and figures are misleading enough. This may be hard for you to believe. To make it sink in, perhaps I should let down my hair to the extent of telling how I was taken in by some figures. These were annual-income figures for the whole population, compiled by a moderately impeccable source, the United States Census Bureau. They showed unmistakably that wealth in the United States was gradually becoming more widely disseminated; the very rich are becoming less numerous in relation to the total population, and so are the very poor. The statistics were compiled from reports of the Internal Revenue Service. These trends are palatable to any liberal-minded person, so I accepted without challenge not only the figures but a mass of editorials based on them.

But the late C. Wright Mills, a Columbia professor and no lover of businessmen, pointed out that the income figures, since they were based on income-tax declarations made by individuals, can't possibly be accurate. Moreover, since very wealthy people have more income to hide from the tax collector, and more money with which to hire expert lawyers and accountants to help with tax-avoidance projects, the figures are probably most inaccurate precisely in those areas where all our conclusions were based. This was a lesson to me, and I hope it will be to you.

Rows of figures look completely unbiased, and sometimes they are. We should always remember, however, that the tables of figures before us are somebody's selection of data from a much larger mass. The key question then is: On what basis were these particular figures selected, and is this basis sound?

DANGERS IN COMMENT

In assessing other people's comments on figures, you can learn only by experience. You have to let yourself be exposed to different views. Then gradually your own increasing knowledge of the field will tell you who is worth reading and who is not.

However, it may be helpful to set down some criteria for judging. The first question, and perhaps the most important, is: Who is the writer? The average newspaperman who goes to work as a reporter after graduation from high school, and who drifts to the financial page because he happens to be not greatly interested in sports, is not likely to be a brilliant market commentator. The average newspaper financial page is worth little because the people who write it simply do not have the background of either education or experience required to do the job well. Morever, they are not likely to print anything but the obvious. Also, strict libel laws are very inhibiting for an author even if he knows the truth.

There are, however, some notable exceptions. Money talks; hence the best financial writers will, sooner or later, work for the paper that pays the most in money and prestige. This means that you should look for enlightening comment, not in the *Mudville Weekly Clarion*, but in the *New York Times*, the *Wall Street Journal,* or the Toronto *Globe and Mail*.

FINDING GENERAL ECONOMIC STATISTICS

Factual data on such general economic indicators as the gross national product, the current price of money, and so on can best be obtained in the United States from the Department of Commerce or the Federal Reserve Bank, in Canada from Statistics Canada, and for the rest of the world from the economic statistics issued by the United Nations Organization.

The Department of Commerce is making continual studies, in both the United States and Canada, of manufacturing industries, extractive industries, and merchandising, to name only a few. Its research results are published in numerous periodicals. All major government departments publish extensively, and can dredge up an astonishing wealth of statistical and interpretative material.

There are several companies who provide up-to-date economic and monetary statistics for businessmen for a yearly fee. Some of these services are excellent, and provide vast amounts of usable material. But the yearly subscription is expensive, and could be justified only by a larger company.

Such non-profit foundations as the Brookings Institution spend large sums each year on economic research, have no obvious axe to grind, and make their findings available to the public in excellent research papers. Major reports of the foundations are usually indexed by subject in reference books found in all large libraries.

A source of business information much neglected by businessmen is the flood of M.A. and PH.D. theses generated in the universities and the schools of business administration. Nobody collects data with as much enthusiasm as an eager degree candidate. While sometimes, because of the graduate student's inexperience, the interpretation of the data leaves something to be desired, the figures themselves are very useful. You can often let the student do all the donkeywork of collecting the data while you reap fame and even fortune by understanding the trends and patterns in it.

Every major industry has its trade journal, which is a basic specialized source of information about that industry. Examples are *Oil News*, *Iron Age*, *Chemical and Process Industries*, *Supermarket News*, and so on. In these papers you get not only the specific information about events in a particular industry, but an insight into how matters of wider significance, such as new government policy, are viewed by that industry.

FINDING SPECIFIC STATISTICS ON THE MARKET AND ON COMPANIES

Newpapers

Forget the text and editorials in daily newspapers, but read the daily price quotations. The *Financial Times of Canada* is rather thin in coverage but sometimes good. The best paper in Canada is the *Globe and Mail* "Report on Business". But, if you are going to be serious about securities, perhaps your best single investment is $150 a year for the *Wall Street Journal*. This is a fundamental trade paper of the financial world. It is a wealthy paper and can therefore afford to hire good financial writers and subscribe to all the press services. Try to read the *Journal* through every day. This is how you get the feel of the market – how you gradually develop a sensitivity to trends.

In the course of a year, the *Journal* alone will publish a good deal of fundamental statistical material you need. For example, every month they publish the complete "short interest" list. This is the list of stocks that people have sold without owning them, because they think their market quotation will fall and they may be bought later at lower prices. The list of "short interest" stocks is a good indicator of what other people think of a particular security at a particular time. Note, however, that the absolute figures given in the *Journal* are meaningless by themselves. You have to perform a simple arithmetical operation on them before they mean anything. This is a good example of the need for figuring in per cent. In this case, you have to divide the short-interest figure by the total number of shares outstanding to get the per cent that the short interest is of the total. The reason? On August 15, 1956, Chicago and Northwestern Railway and Standard Oil of New Jersey each had a short interest of around 32,000 shares. Does this mean that investors are equally bearish about the two companies? Not at all. Only a negligible proportion of Standard Oil's 196 million shares are involved in short sales, while 4 per cent of the railway's 815,000 shares have been sold short. This substantial proportion means that whether the speculators are right or wrong, their activities are going to affect the price of the railway shares much more than they will that of Standard Oil. Short selling is often an indication that something is going on in the company. Your job is to find out what it is. Such selling will force the market price of the stock down temporarily, but eventually it strengthens the market because all the short-sellers have to buy in order to cover what they have sold.

Statistics on particular industries are carried in the *Journal* at frequent intervals. If you clip those relating to the industries you are following, over a period you will have a valuable file of source material on which to base your judgment of trends and potential in that industry.

The same can be said of the articles and news items about particular companies. While there is no substitute for the annual report, the clippings from the *Journal* dealing with the companies whose stock you own will serve to keep you up to date on company activities between reports. As always, you must read between the lines.

Weeklies

Barrons is probably the best known of the financial weeklies. Each week it has at least one article, and sometimes two, on some topic of interest to investors. Moreover, it contains complete data on the weekly range of quotations of all securities traded.

The lead editorial by Alan Abelson each week is alone worth the price of admission. Not many financial writers can be witty and cheerful once, let alone week after week.

Company Publications: Prospectus, Annual 10K

These are the basic sources of information about any specific security you may think of buying. A prospectus is issued each time the company makes an offer of securities to the public, and also when it is listed on the New York Stock Exchange for the first time. A company that files a prospectus with the Securities Exchange Commission (SEC) as a condition of offering securities on the U.S. market has had to come clean about nearly everything. This includes such normally secret matters as executive salaries and bonuses and the extent to which advantageous stock-option agreements have been entered into with company officers. Your broker can usually get hold of a prospectus on any company that interests you, particularly if there has been a recent offer of securities to the public. The company will send you their 10K form (required by the U.S. government) on request.

Company Publications: Annual and Interim Reports

This is the normal continuing source of information about a company. Many companies give plenty of data, including earnings statements going back ten years. You should remember, however, that the annual report is, to a considerable extent, a public-relations device. You may therefore expect the company's phrasing in its annual report to minimize unfavourable factors.

Nevertheless, you are wise to judge a company to some extent by the frankness of its disclosures in the annual report, and the extent to which the company makes it easy for you to make long-term comparisons. A company that makes such comparisons easy should be commended from the share-owners' point of view. At the other extreme, a management that goes more than twelve months without issuing a report is not taking very seriously its responsibility to the share-owners.

A classic example of nineteenth-century company manners was shown at Premier Trust during the reign of Thomas B. Holmes.

Scarcity of published information about the company's business was as consistent as the tiny dividends and management's rebuffing of any questions from shareholders at annual meetings. Such questions were: What valuation methods were used for the major assets of the company? What is the present market value of the company's premises? Does management really receive twice as much pay as the shareholders receive in dividends? What happened to the $5 million item in last year's balance sheet that is not apparent in this year's statement? How could the same auditor verify both last year's and this year's financial statements when the net assets for last year were now valued some 40 per cent higher, and the net income increased accordingly? Is the auditor present?

Although the shareholders asking the questions were experienced investment counsellors, fully aware of their legal rights to such information, the only question answered by Mr. Holmes was the final question. "No, the auditor is *not* present."

The point of this story is not to take a gratuitous swipe at a minor trust company but to underline the critical importance of access to information. Dr. Ackerman and I are unabashed capitalists. We believe that the capitalist system, with all its faults, is the only system that can provide both the physical necessities of life and the freedom for the spirit that most men and women require. But the capitalist system is threatened from both inside and out. The inside threats, provided by unenlightened businessmen themselves, include secretiveness, evasion of the "full disclosure" laws, lobbying for unfair advantage, and so on. Every serious capitalist owes it to the community to expose and fight the abuses of the free-enterprise system. Only in this way can the system survive and prosper. We have spent years suggesting reforms that would make the Canadian life-insurance industry less of a racket, and we are not going to stop now.

Share prices in the market are determined not so much by what has happened in the past as by what people think is going to happen in the future. Of course, no one knows what is going to happen, so the best you can do is try to keep your information about past results as up to date as possible.

One way to do this is by careful reading of interim reports covering quarterly and half-yearly periods. Unfortunately, not all companies issue such reports, but the list is growing. Most large

U.S. companies now issue regular quarterly reports. Canadian companies are beginning the practice, and the trend is all in favour of the investor.

FINANCIAL SERVICES

At any given time there are about two hundred commercial financial services in the United States and Canada, all willing to tell you (for a fee) how to make your fortune. These range from the venerable *Moody's* to the fly-by-night fast-buck operator who for ten dollars offers to give you the name of a stock that will quadruple in two weeks.

There are three main types of financial service: the factual, the digested, and the interpretative.

Factual Services

Moody's and *Standard and Poor's* are the basic factual reference books of the financial world.

Moody's Manuals – including *Industrials*, *Over the Counter Industrials*, *Transportation*, *Public Utilities International*, and *Banks and Finance* – are too expensive to be bought by individuals but can be seen at public libraries in large cities and at most university libraries.

For Canadian securities, somewhat the same function is carried out by the *Financial Post* cards.

While *Moody's* does give ratings of bonds, the above services are basically non-interpretative. They give you the facts as reported by the companies, in a standard form that is convenient to use. The *Financial Post* cards, for example, simply tell you what the company says about its operations. Little or no attempt is made to dig deeper, to find out whether or not what the company says is true.

Digested Services

What we call "digested" services carry their help to the investor one step further. They attempt not only to select the most important statistics out of the mass of material available, but to digest the statistics in various ways. One way is to reduce the statistics of, say, "cash flow" to a standard basis that is the same for each company, no matter what the individual company's practice has been. This makes for easy comparison between companies within an industry, and between industries. Another example: companies use different methods of paying the cost of employee pension plans, some taking the money for funding out of current income, others taking it from reserves. Obviously, it is going to make a big difference to a company's income statement if the large sums needed to fund a modern pension plan are taken from gross income.

A final example: the handling of accelerated depreciation, investment tax credit, and deferred income tax. In some industries the government taxing authorities have permitted companies to write off the cost of new plant and equipment at faster-than-normal rates, because the country needed development of that particular industry. But no matter how a company takes depreciation, it can be taken only once. What accelerated depreciation does is allow a company to charge the cost of a new factory against this year's income instead of the income of ten years from now. At least one service follows the practice of treating accelerated depreciation as a loan from the government, and adding it to long-term debt. The reasoning behind this is that to the extent that accelerated depreciation is taken, present earnings are understated. These items are a kind of deferred income tax, a non-interest-bearing loan from the government.

Digested services can obviously be of more value to the investor than those that merely reprint the company's handouts, but their value depends entirely on who does the digesting. If it is done incorrectly, or on an unsound basis, the statistics can be misleading. Hence, the first thing to ask about a service that claims to digest statistics is: What are the qualifications of the person doing the digesting? If the person doing it is an expert, the statistics will be comprehensive and will stress essentials.

Value Line is probably the best-known example of this type of service. The graphs showing the price history of each company's shares are useful. It is best to ignore the share-price projections.

Interpretative Services

Interpretative services carry the work one step further. They not only digest the data into various convenient forms, but come up with definite buy, sell, or hold recommendations based on their interpretation of the data. Here again the value of the service depends entirely on who is doing the work. Some well-known services have mediocre records; some almost unknown services have a remarkable record of hits. There is no easy way to decide which services are valuable and which are a waste of time and money. No one has written a history of interpretative services from which we could derive their track records. The best solution is to learn to walk for yourself, so that you don't need such crutches.

PUBLICATIONS OF BROKERS AND INVESTMENT BANKERS

Some of the larger brokerage houses, especially those in Montreal and Toronto, maintain large research staffs to keep up a constant study of securities. They publish some of the results of this research in monthly letters and special industry and company reports.

These letters, if issued by a reputable house, will not contain any egregious errors or obvious misrepresentations; however, since human beings are fallible, they may well contain errors of interpretation.

Research from the big brokerage houses is not likely to tell you much that is useful. The key phrase, as usual, is "do it yourself". Brokers' recommendations, whether on xeroxed sheets or in hundred-page glossy booklets in full colour, are usually a waste of time. Very often the broker has an axe to grind – or perhaps a major customer with a large block of stock to get rid of. Any broker who is owned by or associated with a conglomerate is likely to be peddling shares that the holding company wants to shed: conversely, the broker will persuade you to sell shares the holding company is in the process of accumulating. Recent Ontario, Quebec, and Ottawa legislation accelerates this risk by allowing banks and life-insurance companies to own brokerage houses. Beware!

As mentioned earlier, in New York there are discount brokers whose commissions are much less than the old "full service" brokers'. Canada now has discount brokers in several provinces, and the Toronto Dominion Bank is starting to develop this service, which in due course will cover every province. We recommend that you use discount brokers, as we do ourselves. There is a list in Chapter 3.

OFFICIAL STOCK-MARKET PUBLICATIONS

For accurate information on what stocks have actually sold for on a particular market, you need the official daily news-sheet of the stock exchange. Most large-city exchanges publish such a sheet, which can be seen in banks, in brokers' offices, or at the exchange itself. Besides closing quotations on all stocks traded that day, the New York Stock Exchange sheet gives a record of dividend declarations and company notices, as well as stocks paying a dividend that day and the day following.

Some exchanges also publish a monthly bulletin giving data on all stocks traded that month. The *Montreal Exchange Review* gives price range and volume for the month, and for the year up to that month; it also gives the current dividend rate and past dividend history.

BOOKS ON HOW TO GET RICH

The important thing is to know what *not* to read, so you don't waste your time. Avoid any book with the word "million" or "millionaire" in the title because the author is clearly not aware of the exponential nature of finance. Remember, you go from $100 to $1,000 in net worth, and from there to $10,000 and $100,000. Only after you reach the $100,000 stage does the goal of a million apply. Not many people have saved this amount, particularly in their early years. If you haven't already reached the $100,000 level you are not in the market for advice on how to make the next step. So avoid all the million-syndrome books written by fast finance experts. What they are financing is themselves. Avoid, too, all the billion-syndrome books. For our part, we are dealing with the lower rungs of this hierarchy, talking to people who aren't yet even millionaires.

The trillion-syndrome books are yet to come, but be warned now. Inflation in this branch of the publishing industry is such that they are on their way.

Books by Salesmen

A real salesman can sell anything, good or bad. Therefore, he can't tell you anything useful unless you are yourself a salesman and have the same motivations. Salesmen in the life-insurance, real-estate, and investment fields normally know little about the products they sell, and usually are accustomed to lying about their products. This is not what you want, so keep away from them.

Books by Hirelings

The author who gets his salary from a life-insurance company or mutual fund is not likely to tell you the truth about his industry. He wants to continue eating for the rest of his natural life. Also, don't expect your bank manager to tell you that cheques are free at the credit union next door.

Books by People Without Practical Experience

Avoid all books by people who are commenting from outside, on a world they have never entered. The college professor of real estate who has never owned his own home, the amateur look at business from the man who has never owned a business, advice on finance from people who have never borrowed, lent, or invested. The results of investing, good or bad, are easy to see. This is not like medicine. If the author of the book can't verify his contentions with personal net worth statements and provide a past record of achievement, forget him. He has nothing of value to say to you.

Books by Apocalyptists

These men are promoters who specialize in a single commodity, such as gold. The man who bought gold at $100 and sees it now at $350 views himself as a financial genius. He is now beyond teaching, and cannot even learn by further experience. Nevertheless, with all his money in gold he is in an exposed and fragile position. Anything can happen, most of it bad. Buying gold reflects disillusionment with the idea that central governments *will* take action to maintain the value of the currency. But some day governments will awake from their coma and take drastic action, as did the United States from 1979 to 1985 with Paul Volcker managing Federal Reserve decisions. The operative question to a gold bug is: "What do you expect to happen, and when?" The gold investor at $350 today obviously expects gold to go to $500 or $700 (the 50 per cent to 100 per cent rule). The solid industrial demand for gold is meagre at best, and there are all sorts of fierce political risks.

Books Telling How To Make Money on the Stock Market

Typical of this class of book is Lempeneau's *How To Take a Fortune Out of Wall Street*. Before you go spending your hard-earned cash on this type of reading matter, look with a sceptical eye at the author's motivations.

Now, one elementary rule about authorship is that before writing a book you must have performed the actual operations you describe. If you are writing a book on how to build boats, the least your readers expect is that you have actually built a few boats yourself. If you write a book called *How To Take a Fortune Out of Wall Street*, you should have already taken out the fortune.

All books on investing are subject to this caveat to a greater or less degree. By rights, every author of a "how to do it" book on finance should be obliged to make a clear disclosure to his readers of his own financial position, and how he reached it. And it is not enough to attach a banker's statement to the preface saying that the net worth of the author is now $100,000. He might have inherited it.

Here is a simple arithmetical proof that all commercial advice on how to make money on the stock market should be looked at with a cold eye. Assume for the sake of argument that our advertiser can really do what he claims to do, namely pick stocks that increase in market value ten times in a year. Assume further that his credit is good for $10,000. He borrows this amount, invests it according to his advertised system, and at the end of the year has a net worth of $90,000 ($100,000–$10,000). He invests again, and at the end of the second year is worth nearly a million dollars. Why does he need the pitiful fifteen or so that you pay for his book?

The basic question about financial books is: Who is the author? If, like Loeb, who wrote *The Battle for Investment Survival*, he is a well-known partner of a big brokerage house, and enjoys expensive hobbies like yachting and antique cars, you can be pretty sure that he is a "prestige" author, a man who is writing, not for money, but for the pleasure of seeing his name in print, or because he feels he has something to contribute. In the case of Loeb, you get a book that is full of practical and sound advice, from a man who was in the field for over thirty years.

Allen's *Profits Without Forecasting* is another book of this type, although it is very short. The author was a partner of a brokerage house and knew what he was talking about, although he made no attempt to cover the whole field. He took one piece of good advice – "Cut off losses, let profits run" – and rang all the changes on it. But sound investing covers more ground than this.

Van Caspel's *The New Money Dynamics* is an up-to-date and sensible approach to investing. The pace is such that no reader is going to burn out any bearings in his brain, but what is said is true and well-illustrated. She tells the truth about the life-insurance racket, and is familiar with the activities of the major financial institutions. She is very good on her coverage of mutual funds, although some might say a shade partial. Her book provides a telling statistic: in the United States, the richest country in the world, 90 per cent of the people ready to retire at age sixty-five are flat broke.

THE MEMBERS OF THE FINANCIAL COMMUNITY AND THEIR BUILT-IN BIAS

Men who devote their lives to the various aspects of finance are a good source of financial information. But each area of the financial community has its built-in bias. There is competition for your investment dollar. If most people put their money into life insurance, the agents live high but bankers and brokers have to economize. Every segment of the financial community is out after a larger share of the consumer's investment dollar. Thus, you should not expect to hear much good about banks from a real-estate man, or much good about brokers from a life-insurance agent.

Until recently, the insurance industry was united in ignoring inflation and in pushing its fixed-dollar investment, the so-called "cash-surrender value" of the standard life-insurance policy. If you pointed out to anyone in the insurance business that your nest-egg of $1,000, put away in 1960 at compound interest in a paid-up endowment, although it has a face value of $1,400 today, actually buys only $350 worth of goods, you were answered calmly to the effect that "the economy has been through periods of inflation and deflation, and fixed-value investments over the long run have worked out best for the small investor."

The broker, although he lives on commissions from your purchases like the insurance agent, has an entirely different attitude. The large conservative brokerage houses, the ones that enjoy an established business, talk mostly about income. They say: "Why let your money moulder in a bank at 6 per cent or in an insurance policy at 3 per cent? We can put you on to a stock that pays 9 per cent and hasn't missed a dividend in fifty years."

The smaller or less well-known brokerage houses talk mostly of capital appreciation. They tell about stocks that jumped from thirty-seven cents to fifty cents in a week, thus appealing to the lust for unearned increment that resides in every human breast.

The two groups of brokers have one thing in common. They always find that it never hurts to work either for a profit allegedly available in some other stock, or to improve income. Trading results in commissions.

Do not deal with any broker who will not tell you what his personal interest or his firm's interest is in any particular security he suggests. Is he short or long in it, and if so, is his interest large or small? He is "long" if he owns the stock, and "short" if he has sold it without owning it. One large New York house makes this disclosure as a matter of policy. Any reputable broker should be willing to do the same in writing.

The promoter, the man who telephones long-distance at night and tells you that 1,000 shares have been reserved in your name, makes an unabashed appeal to your basest instincts. The fact that he can afford to spend thousands of dollars on telephone calls proves that the product he is selling (namely, baseless hope) is a useful product, one that fills a real need in society.

The banker, although he is perforce a fixed-dollar man like the insurance seller, takes an even more conservative view. If he suggests any investment at all, it will be government bonds, or, in a pinch, industrial or municipal bonds backed by the resources of the government. If he recommends common stocks at all, it will be from an approved list of the bluest of blue chips.

Remember, everybody has a set of horrible examples that he uses to prove what he wants to prove. These cases, even if true, are naturally selected from a larger number of cases, some of which prove the opposite.

A trust officer normally is not the best man to talk to about stocks. The banker has been trained as a money-lender. There is no reason why he should be a judge of stocks; rather the contrary. He is usually a person of little formal education who went directly from high school into a business that demands the virtues of perseverance, attention to detail, and accuracy. His training has developed solidity, rather than the imagination and flair required for investment in common stocks.

The investment counsellor is different. True, there are many well-born incompetents who happened to inherit money and then drifted into the business. But if he is the genuine article, he will be a person with either considerable formal education in finance or long years of varied experience in the business and financial worlds. His strong point is that, unlike the broker, the banker, or the insurance agent, he has no pecuniary interest in what you do. He gets no commission on sales, nor does his firm. He is in the position of selling advice for a fee, and if your portfolio is large enough to justify the fee, this is often the best way to handle the problems of investing. In Basel or Boston, both old investment communities, the investment counsellor plays an important role.

But even the independent investment counsellor has an axe to grind. It is in his interest to make investing look as complicated as possible. Then more people will throw up their hands, saying "This is too deep for me," and take their business to investment counsel. For this reason the publications of investment counsellors are often academic, not to say obscurantist, in tone.

Lawyers, trustees, and trust companies are normally fixed-dollar-value advisers. They are required by both law and custom to return to widows and orphans the same number of dollars entrusted to them originally. Therefore, the fiduciary fraternity tends to bury its talents, lest its members be accused of speculating with other people's money. Their advice is excellent in the areas they cover, but you must recognize their limitations.

The investment dealer or financial house can be a good source of investment advice, because many solid underwriting houses maintain large staffs of security analysts who study investments every working day. But the financial house is like an overstocked wholesaler. He has an inventory of shares piled up on his shelves. He is a member of various underwriting groups, and has been a member of them for a long time. Historically, the rule is that the individual house must take all the shares assigned to it by the other members of the underwriting syndicate. If the house refuses its share of a particular underwriting, it can legitimately be cut off from the syndicate's next operation. The house serves three interests: its own, the company's, and yours, in that order.

Thus it may happen that the salesmen for a particular investment house are selling their customers (namely you) a security that their research department has examined and found wanting. The underwriter usually recommends new securities which he is underwriting. The history of new stock issues as a whole has been dismal.

Hence, any person, be he broker, bond salesman, insurance agent, promoter, or banker, who is paid by way of a commission on the transaction he suggests, has to some extent a vested interest in the advice he gives, and so must be under a degree of suspicion as an adviser. The general rule, as with all other sources of investment information, is to figure out in advance what each one of your advisers stands to make out of you.

SHAREHOLDER PROTECTION FROM YOUR LOCAL SECURITIES COMMISSION

Perhaps, being naïve, you have assumed that minority shareholders in a public company need not fear tyranny in their company's management – that when the interests of management and shareholders were not being equally well served, you could achieve justice by appealing to an official government body established for that purpose. The laws would currently seem to be on your side. For example, in Ontario it is illegal for one company to take over another with a sweet deal for the controlling shareholders and a sour one for everybody else.

If you expect provincial or federal security commissions to protect you, forget it. In addition to being understaffed and overworked, they are hamstrung by inadequate legislation that is less than uniform in the different jurisdictions. This allows slick operators from inside or outside the company (sometimes both) to take advantage of unsuspecting investors.

During the takeover of one manufacturing company, the top insiders received $24 a share cash while those shareholders who failed to sell at the market peak of $18 received quite another deal. The intervention of the provincial Securities Commission, determined as it was, did not achieve equivalent treatment for the minority shareholders. Some year earlier that same company management distributed two new A shares (non-voting) for each common share held, allowing them to sell off their A shares while keeping voting control. The shares then dropped from $17 to under $3.

A more recent example of *major* shareholder protection occurred when the top officer of a major Canadian company got a bank loan to acquire a million shares for a family company and over 50,000 shares for himself. When a takeover offer was announced a few days later he was quoted in the paper as saying "not high enough". A later offer proved to be sufficient to separate him and his family from the shares. This three-week investment produced a gain for him and his family of some thirteen million dollars.

When asked about the propriety of these transactions, one provincial securities commission sent newspaper clippings from the *Globe and Mail*, saying it was "satisfied that none of the officials purchased stock on the basis of confidential information." This is small consolation to loyal shareholders who had hung on for years and then sold to the chief executive of the company at the pre-takeover price.

Canadian federal and provincial agencies cannot require the equivalent full disclosure of a sworn 10K statement in the United States. The tendency of executives to keep facts to themselves, and to play cards close to their chests, does not make for investor understanding. This is changing now with the new generation of managers and security analysts, but we are still far behind the United States.

CHAPTER THIRTEEN

Some Kinds of Investment Analysis

It is hard for an outsider to realize how perfect is the monopoly of commonplace, and to comprehend how fatal a stumbling-stone that man sets in the way of his own advancement who dares to think for himself, or who knows more or who does more than the mob of gentlemen-employees who know very little and do even less. SIR RICHARD BURTON (1821–89)

It's mid 1979. George, your buddy, office mate, rich relation, stockbroker, or friendly neighbour, tells you that he has gained 20 per cent on his investment in the shares of this company, having bought at $40, and is holding at $50. And the best is yet to come.

In blind faith, or because George has never been wrong, or because you happen to have enough money in your RRSP for it, you buy fifty shares at $50. But you say, "What if...?"

Exactly. What if the shares aren't worth $50? What if the economy goes into a recession? What if there comes a stock-market crash? These questions bring you to an appreciation of the need for investment analysis of two kinds:

1. intrinsic value
2. macro-economic-financial (macro means seeing the *big* picture)

INTRINSIC-VALUE ANALYSIS

First, unless you have decided to let George do it, it's important to examine the published financial statements of the company (making some adjustments), in order to assure yourself that the share value is more than the price you paid. Is the equity per share at least equal to your acquisition price? Second, are the demonstrated earnings per share a substantial fraction of what you paid? Specifically, are they enough to cover both taxes and inflation?

In the case of Gulf Canada, the shareholder's equity at the end of 1978 was $1,419 million, or $31.19 a share (dividing by 45.5 million shares). Two kinds of adjustments are called for. One is to take into account the likely replacement cost of fixed assets such as refineries, tank trucks, service stations, etc. – a gross value of $2,479 million, on which a total of $921 million of depreciation has been written off. If these assets are worth their original cost, an adjustment of $20.24 a share ($921 million divided by 45.5 million shares) is called for. Note that this adjustment applies only to oil companies.

A second adjustment tries to bring into account the oil and gas reserves. These are literally the lifeblood of the company, but traditionally they do not appear on any balance sheet. These were 256 million barrels of crude oil and 2,150 billion cubic feet of natural gas. Values to be assigned to these will depend on assumptions as to selling price, royalty rates, and future operating and capital costs, as well as future technology and the rate of inflation. If we use an estimated value of $5 a barrel of oil and 50¢ a thousand cubic feet of gas, the adjustment will be $1,280 million plus $1,075 million, for a total of $2,355 million. On a per-share basis, the figure is $51.76.

Adding up:	Stated equity	$31.19
	Fixed-asset write-off added back	20.24
	Oil and gas reserves	51.76
we arrive at an *adjusted equity* figure of		$103.19 a share

Maybe George is right again.

Now let's look at earnings per share. These were shown as $4.07 and $4.02 for 1977 and 1978. But during these years a substantial amount of cash flow was generated by write-offs (depreciation, depletion, and amortization), and by deferring income taxes. This amounted to $146 million in 1977 ($3.21 a share) and $160 million in 1978 ($3.52 a share). So the *adjusted earnings* per share amount to $7.28 and $7.54. Relating these demonstrated earnings to the $50 share price, we get 14 per cent to 15 per cent. This is enough to cover taxes and inflation.

Even with hindsight, George is a hero. The price of Gulf Canada shares doubled (from 50 to 100 on the old stock, 10 to 20 on the split shares), and the reasoning used was correct. It's called being right for the right reasons.

However, by 1986 this investment has matured. The company has sold off its gas stations and has come under entirely new direction. The partial ownership of East Coast offshore oil finds has little to do with the market price of its shares, now that the world oil price has declined fifty per cent, making offshore development impractical.

MACRO-ECONOMIC FINANCIAL ANALYSIS

The anticipated recession of the eighties has occurred, to a considerable extent. Recovery has been partial at best, with many businesses – indeed, many countries – reeling under the weight of subdued demand, high costs, and continued high interest rates.

The inflation psychosis which opened the decade has subsided, due in large part to the steady efforts of Paul Volcker and the U.S. Federal Reserve Board to restrict money expansion. Not that the risk of increasingly higher prices has disappeared or that government deficits have diminished. Quite the contrary. It rather seems that we have gotten tired of worrying over the consequences of such developments, and have begun to take annual inflation rates of 3 or 4 per cent as "normal". Ditto for 7 to 11 per cent unemployment.

The central bank in the United States has been busy rescuing the casualties of unwise lending practices of the early eighties – in large part loans based on the yet-to-happen energy- and land-price increases. Consequently, severe tightening of the money supply and its accompanying painful experiences have been at least postponed, if not indefinitely deferred.

Investment opportunities have been seized upon, and the scope of investments now available at anything approaching bargain prices is extremely limited. Extortion, or "greenmail" as it became known on Wall Street, has been used to enrich a few at the expense of the continuing shareholders. Leveraged buy-outs were invented to further insulate and entrench company managements. The expected synergy of companies merging became replaced by the enhanced values expected from asset deployment (selling off assets at prices totalling more than the company's total market value).

The task of investment analysts – to locate unrecognized or unexploited value – has become more difficult as more attention has been paid by investors to the opportunities available. Mutual funds found their sales records expanding as stock-market averages reached new highs.

Commodity prices are at low levels and the industries supplying them (agriculture, mining, energy, etc.) are, for the most part, suffering accordingly. Will there be special opportunities for the survivors in these industries? Undoubtedly.

If the risks of major financial collapse and panic can be circumvented (not at all a certainty), today's distress industries contain the seeds that will grow and blossom in the nineties.

CHAPTER FOURTEEN

Intrinsic-Value Analysis – The Study of Company Reports

What we hope ever to do with ease, we must first learn to do with diligence. SAMUEL JOHNSON (1709–84)

THE BUSINESS MODEL

What are the key elements of a business? We see a chain of assets which produce revenue – revenue large enough that, after all costs are paid, there are earnings. These earnings give an indication of share value. The rate of growth of assets, revenues, and earnings is important, even if it has not yet produced the required rise in share value on the market. The roles of management are:

1. To be entrepreneurial enough to assemble enough assets.
2. To have the production, management, and sales skills to make the assets produce enough revenue.
3. To have costs controlled so that sufficient net earnings appear.
4. To deal responsibly with human relationships – employees, shareholders, customers, and the general public.

INTRODUCTION TO FINANCIAL STATEMENTS

Why have a financial statement at all? The main reasons are four. The government demands them for tax purposes; the bank needs them to see if the company deserves credit; management needs them for intelligent decision-making; and the investor needs them for his analysis. These four entities have different needs; it is therefore not surprising that financial statements are required in different forms by different groups. What the investor has to do is pick out of the balance sheet and the profit-and-loss statement the figures that are germane to his particular needs.

When looking for a stock in which to invest our money, love, and attention, we seek management, assets, earnings, and growth. The quality of management is reflected in everything having to do with the company. Assets must be redefined from the investor's point of view, namely, do they make for earnings? We want to buy the assets at a discount, so we look for hidden assets, assets not being properly used, land available for development, and so on. Earnings, too, must be redefined from the investor's point of view. Finance companies and cement companies expect very different earnings, and cannot be compared without making several adjustments to both. Again we want to buy at a discount, and we look for hidden earnings, and for hidden losses. The flow of funds (source and application of funds statement) contains important clues. Finally we look at the internal growth of the company (that is, its progress in developing its own products) and study its effect on share price. This kind of growth we try to keep separate from the more conventional external growth that comes from acquisitions.

If a company's management is not reasonably honest, you will not want to buy its securities under any circumstances. If the management is honest, it will make a full disclosure of the company's financial condition in each annual report. The key, then, to intrinsic-value analysis is a close and careful study of successive annual reports of the company. The kinds of information usually found in an annual report are three:

1. The *balance sheet*, which contains the answer to the question "Is my capital going to be safe?"
2. The *income statement*, which answers the question "Is the company making money?"
3. The *dividend-rate record*, which tells you whether or not the company pays out profits to its shareholders.

From the above, it is clear that the nub of intrinsic-value analysis is the ability to read an annual report. This is not simple, and whole books have been written on the art of reading and comparing annual reports in such a way as to derive the information they contain. This is a subtle problem, because as much information is contained between the lines of annual reports as in them. Obviously, in a single chapter we can do no more than outline the essentials of annual-report study. If you develop an interest in this particular approach to investments, you can get other books that treat the subject more fully, beginning with the classic Graham, et al., *Security Analysis*, 4th ed., New York, 1962.

HOW TO READ A BALANCE SHEET

The balance sheet answers many questions concerned with risk and quality. The basic question is: If I put my money into this security, will the capital be safe? Another question that the balance sheet answers quickly has to do with adjusted equity. When you pay $50 for a stock, you are paying the market price, and this price may be either more or less than the net asset value or adjusted equity. The adjusted equity tells you what tangible resources you are actually buying when you buy one share of stock. These resources may be in the form of cash in the till or, more usually, in the form of plant and machinery that would probably have to be sold at a fraction of their real value if the company went bankrupt. However, at least the adjusted-equity figures give you some indication of what you are buying with your investment funds.

The average balance sheet of a large corporation is a confusing document because it has to use all kinds of special terminology to satisfy legislation and to suit the needs of specialists like accountants and lawyers. However, normal balance-sheet terminology can be translated into simple English, and this we have tried to do in the sample balance sheet in Figure 21.

Balance sheets are usually issued at the end of the company's fiscal year. A balance sheet is a static document that shows the situation at one point in time. It is divided into two halves: on the left-hand side is a statement of the assets of the company (what it owns), and on the right-hand side is a statement of the company's liabilities (what it owes).

The Assets Side

Taking the assets side of the balance sheet first, you will notice that this particular company has four types of assets. The first type is current assets, such as cash in the bank and money owed to the company by its customers (receivables). The next kind of asset is that represented by deferred charges. This means any money that

FIGURE 21: **Crane Company Balance Sheet**

CRANE COMPANY
Balance Sheet at December 31, 1979

	Assets (*what we owned*)		(Millions)
1. Current assets	Cash in banks and on hand to pay wages and taxes, to buy materials, supplies, etc.		$ 31.36
	Marketable securities, short-term investments at lower of cost or market		70.53
	Money owed to us by customers for products sold to them but for which they have not paid	178.58	
	Less safety factor, in case they don't pay	3.47	175.11
	Money tied up in raw materials, supplies, and products not yet sold		176.87
	Total current assets (those which can be quickly turned into cash in the normal operation of the business)		$ 453.89
2. Deferred charges, etc.	Money paid in advance for insurance, taxes, etc.		3.99
	Money spent to finance subsidiaries + investments		45.81
	Unamortized debt discount		8.24
	Money deposited with government departments, etc., to protect the employee in case of accident, and other deposits		–
	Construction fund		4.29
3. Investments	Money invested in subsidiary and allied companies whose assets are not consolidated with Crane Company's		1.22
	Other assets		6.05
4. Fixed assets	Money invested in lands, buildings, transportation facilities, plants, and equipment. Original cost to the company was		1,099.43
	From this amount we subtract an estimated loss of value due to wear and tear during their lifetime (accumulated depreciation)		580.69
			518.73
	Total assets (total of what we owned)		$1,042.25

(simplified and interpreted by J. J. Brown)

CRANE COMPANY
which shows how we stood at the year end

	Liabilities (*what we owed*)	(Millions)
1. Current liabilities	Money owed to employees (accrued salaries)	$ 91.13
	Money which we owed to others for goods and services rendered	86.67
	Money which we owed to banks for loan	9.71
	Money which we owed for federal, provincial, and local tax obligations	14.01
	Money which we owed for principal repayments and interest charges on money borrowed, payable within one year	8.04
	Total current liabilities (amounts owing which must be paid out of our current assets). The difference between our current assets and current liabilities is known as working capital and represents amount of funds readily available to operate the business.	$ 209.57
2. Mortgage and debenture debt	Money borrowed by mortgaging our assets and future earnings to expand our business, and other indebtedness not payable within one year	349.71
3. Other liabilities	Deferred income taxes (depreciation)	22.16
	Operating reserves and deferred credits	27.78
	Preferred shares	2.33
	Minority interest and capital leases	59.35
	The total of all the above liabilities (total of what we owed)	$ 670.94
	The difference between the above figure and the total of what we owned is what we were worth.	
	Common Shareholders' Equity	
4. Capital and surplus	Money invested by our shareholders in the 9,949,472 shares of $6.25 par-value capital stock outstanding	62.18
	Difference between par value and the actual price paid by original shareholders (capital surplus)	41.64
	Money that shareholders have left in the business, accumulated from earnings over the years. This is not cash, since the money is invested in property, accounts receivable, materials, etc.	267.48
	Total net worth	371.31
	Total of liabilities and net worth	$1,042.25

All figures are rounded, hence totals may not be exact.

the company has paid out in advance for services to be received some time in the future. A third kind of asset is investments made by the company in other companies. The fourth type is fixed assets, normally the largest single figure. This includes all the lands, real estate, plant, and machinery owned by the company. This figure is set down at how much these properties actually cost the company, and then an amount representing the extent to which the properties are worn out is deducted from the original sum. This second amount is called "depreciation". The net depreciated value of the properties can be very large or very small, depending on how long the company has been in business.

The Liabilities Side

The liabilities, too, are of several kinds. First come the current liabilities, such as the money the company has borrowed from banks, and other short-term debts that must be paid back in less than one year. The second type is long-term debt – money borrowed by the company by issue of bonds and debentures. This is debt repayable in periods longer than one year.

Next are the miscellaneous liabilities, which can assume many forms depending on the industry and the type of company. By adding up all these kinds of liabilities, you get a figure which shows how much the company owes.

Capital and Surplus Statement

By subtracting the total amount owed from the total amount owned, we get a figure called the company's net worth. The total of the liabilities plus the net worth of the company must equal the assets of the company. In other words, the balance sheet balances.

Equity

To find the equity of each share of the stock, we add up all the assets of the company on the left-hand side of the sheet and get a figure of, say, $1,042 million. We subtract from this the total of all the liabilities of the company ($669 million) and also the value of any preferred stock that comes ahead of the common, in this case $2 million. This subtraction gives us an amount of $371 million. Since there are still 9.9 million shares outstanding, we divide this into the figure for assets minus liabilities and get an apparent equity for each common share of $37.

The market price may not bear much relation to the apparent equity, but as a sort of minimum precaution you should know before buying any stock what dollar value of actual resources you are buying per share. This is particularly important when you are buying a share of a public utility, because its earnings rate is regulated by law, and the amount it is permitted to charge is often determined by the value of the assets it owns.

When the assets of a company are selling at twice their replacement value and three times the adjusted equity, the smart money stays away. With enough capital, the company would buy producing facilities at market, incorporate a company, and then sell the assets at the current mark-up to suckers. This is why you should pay attention to adjusted equity.

Adjustment of Apparent Equity

Say an oil company in its balance sheet has written down (depreciated) its refinery from $30 million to $5 million over a ten-year period. Yet for tax reasons and for operating efficiency the refinery has been upgraded every year in order that it will do exactly the same job as a new refinery built today at a cost of $70 million. Thus you must *add* back $65 million to the asset figure. The refinery is a hidden asset. Another hidden asset, harder to judge and value, is oil in the ground, proven, probable, or prospective.

Another type of adjustment is required when a company owns shares of another company. It is normally carried on the books at acquisition cost (high or low), but it must be valued at current prices and the difference adjusted for.

Other types of companies in which you should look very closely at the adjusted equity are financial companies and banks. Since their assets are mostly in very liquid form, you should know how many dollars' worth of assets you are buying for each dollar paid for the shares.

THE INCOME STATEMENT

The idea of the income statement is to tell you where the money came from and where it went. Like the balance sheet, this is set down on a yearly basis. The basic question answered in the income statement is: Does the company make money? But there are other subsidiary questions of almost equal importance to which it provides clues.

If you look for the sources and application of funds in the income statement of the average annual report, you will find, as you did in the case of the balance sheet, that much of it is unintelligible because of the special language used. In the sample statement in Figure 22 we have translated as many of the terms as possible into

FIGURE 22: **Crane Company Income Statement***

CRANE COMPANY
Income Statement (the money we received and what we did with it)
Year Ended December 31, 1979

WE TOOK IN	(Millions)
From the sale of our products and services	$1,573.1
From miscellaneous sources	5.8
	1,578.9
IT COST US	
For raw materials and supplies consumed, and expenses incurred in making and distributing our products	1,397.3
For taxes of all kinds – federal, provincial, and municipal, in Canada and overseas	12.4
For borrowed money – interest on bonds, debentures, bank loans, etc.	38.3
Money set aside to provide for replacement of plant, machinery, and equipment when they are worn out or of no further use	73.8
We deducted for minority interest in profits of subsidiary companies and miscellaneous	2.0
WE DISTRIBUTED	
To owners of preferred shares	0.8
To Crane Company shareholders in cash dividends	14.4
To shareholders as 2% stock dividend	5.5
	1,543.78
THERE REMAINED	
A balance to be kept in the business for expansion of the company's operations	$ 35.1

*Once again, all figures are rounded, hence totals may not be exact.

simple English. This statement is divided into four sections. The first deals with where the money came from. The second shows how much the company had to put out in order to do business. The third shows how the difference between income and expenditure was distributed to various interested parties, and the fourth shows the balance retained in the business in order to finance expansion.

One income statement taken alone doesn't tell very much, but a series of such statements, going back five years, can be very valuable in showing whether the trend of earnings is up or down.

ORGANIZING YOUR INFORMATION

In order to make your information taken from the annual report more easily usable from year to year, you should assemble two balance-sheet items and six items from the income statement. This could take the form shown in Figure 23.

This table is full of information you can use to help you make up your mind whether you should buy the shares at a given price. Crane Company is easy, because there are almost exactly 10 million

FIGURE 23: **Digested Five-Year Summary, Crane Company** ($ millions)

	1979	1978	1977	1976	1975
Apparent equity	371	335	326	287	242
Working capital	248	221	240	218	223
Net sales	1,573	1,227	1,133	1,087	1,119
Depreciation	74	51	44	36	36
Operating profit	102	68	67	81	126
Interest	43	30	24	23	16
Income before taxes	67	50	79	77	114
Adjusted earnings	55	35	66	48	64

Note: These figures come from the company's own statements, not from the simplified forms above.

shares outstanding. To get the "per share" figures, all you have to do is move the decimal point one place to the left. Thus you can see immediately that, at the recent price of $35 a share, you can buy the company for less than its adjusted equity ($37.47) and for only about 50 per cent more than its working capital ($25.05). If you have been looking at its figures for the previous five years, you will notice that Crane habitually writes down its assets so drastically, and is so conservative in its treatment of its liabilities, you can be sure that both of these balance-sheet items (equity and working capital) are in fact *more* than stated.

An alert reader will have noticed that there is a difference in our methods of arriving at equity figures for Crane and for Gulf Canada. On page 186 we added back depreciation to get a more realistic figure, because the Gulf refineries are in operation, competing successfully with the most recent types. Also, we felt we should make some allowance for oil and gas still in the ground. In the case of Crane, with its record of very conservative valuation, we

FIGURE 24: **Digested Five-Year Summary, Gulf Canada** ($ millions)

	1979	1978	1977	1976	1975
Apparent equity	1,639	1,419	1,288	1,152	
Working capital	661	478	535	472	439
Net sales (revenues)	3,058	2,584	2,357	1,954	1,730
Depreciation, etc.	123	89	82	73	71
Operating profit	517	375	406	341	
Interest	25	26	21	8	9
Income before taxes					
Adjusted earnings	288	187	184	167	176
Number of shares	227.48 (million)				
Earnings per share	1.27	.82	.81	.73	.77

Note: Figures from actual company statements.

are content to use their published figure of $371 million, and not to add back any depreciation at all. We have even ignored the effect of the doubling in value of the Atlantic Richfield shares they hold.

The items from the income statement are equally reassuring. Cash flow of $12.90 (earnings plus depreciation) per share is high, and the trend over the five-year period is good. The growth of net sales is good, being both rapid and reasonably steady.

Now let's read the annual report and make the five-year summary table for an entirely different company, Gulf Canada (Figure 24).

Using the materials in these two tables, we can make a comparison of the two companies. Both shares happen to be selling at the same price of $35 in mid 1980.

In addition, you could look at growth in cash flows for the two companies over the five-year period and get about the same results.

The reason for making up these five-year histories is not to make you into an amateur historian but to make it possible for you to see what is likely to happen in the future.

Looking at Figure 25, we can see that a dollar invested in Crane bought five times as much equity and nine times as much working capital as a dollar invested in Gulf Canada. In addition, the three income-statement items in the case of Crane are more solid and reassuring. (Market-price changes in the subsequent year and a half appeared to bear us out. Gulf Canada fell in price to $12, while Crane went to $47, then down to $30, and held at $32.)

This is what investment analysis is all about. You need to be able to anticipate future earnings. By looking carefully at what earnings have been under various circumstances in the past, you develop a

FIGURE 25: **Comparison of Crane and Gulf Canada as Investments**

	Crane	Gulf Canada
Equity per dollar invested	$1.02	$ .21
Working capital per dollar invested	.71	.08
Cash flow per dollar invested	.37	.05
Growth in working capital (5 years)	11%	50%
Growth in apparent equity (5 years)	53%	

skill in figuring out what they are likely to be next year and the year after. This, when corrected for market price, gives you ideas about what to buy.

SOME OVERSIMPLIFIED APPROACHES TO BE USED WITH CAUTION

Even the above material on balance sheets and statements of source and application of funds is complicated enough to make the average investor wonder whether the game is worth the candle. Like the algebra student struggling with the binomial theorem, you may be saying in a plaintive voice: "There must be some *simpler* way."

There are simpler ways, but like most simple things they must be used with great caution. These five piecemeal approaches are: 1. the price-earnings ratio; 2. the cash-flow ratio; 3. the current-yield method; 4. trading on the equity; 5. buying stocks that are below liquidating asset value.

1. *The Price-Earnings Ratio*

The most widely used of the crude and often misleading yardsticks is the price-earnings ratio. If a company has a net income of $2 per share, it can be alleged that a fair price for the stock would be $20, since ten times earnings is about right for this particular industry. (This is the sort of thing you will learn as you familiarize yourself with an industry.)

As a minimum requirement, the price-earnings method should be used with five-year-average earnings, not the earnings of one year. The $2 rate mentioned above may be exceptional. An average over at least a five-year period should be taken.

In addition, however, the whole theory of price-earnings ratios may well be questioned on several grounds. First of all, net earnings are not usually a sufficient base to use for appraising a stock. The net profit shown on the company's statement is not by any means a complete measure of the earning ability of the company. Moreover, the price-earnings ratio ignores the whole question of quality. Its strict application would lead us to the conclusion that a stock priced at five times earnings is cheaper than a stock priced at ten times earnings. Actually, of course, the difference in risk between the two stocks may justify all the difference in price.

2. *The Cash-Flow Ratio*

Some of the difficulties inherent in price-earnings ratios may be overcome by using income plus non-cash expenses as the demonstrated earning ability, rather than income alone. This cash-flow ratio is more accurate because it takes into consideration the provisions made by the company for depreciation, depletion, amortization, deferred income taxes, and other non-cash expenditures. From an accounting point of view, these expenses have been written off, yet are available for use by the management. Companies whose shares can be bought at a low multiple of cash flow deserve further study.

3. *The Current-Yield Method of Valuing Stock*

Many people feel that if a company pays a good dividend, its stock can be valued by capitalizing the dividend at a certain rate. Thus, if a stock pays $10 a year in dividends, and you feel that it can be capitalized at 10 per cent, a fair price for the stock on the market would be $100. The theory behind this reasoning is that in a stable company, the income will continue for ten years at the $10 rate and you will have your money back. Better still, the dividend should increase enough each year to cover inflation at least. If you feel that the risks are such that you should get your money back faster, you capitalize at a higher rate, say 15 per cent or 20 per cent.

The difficulty with this approach is the impact of taxation. You must figure out exactly what the net annual dividend will amount to in your particular case. If you are a Canadian taxpayer buying the shares of a Canadian corporation, you get the dividend tax credit. In the case of a low-income investor, this might make the dividend tax-free.

The choice of a U.S. company by a Canadian taxpayer means that the gross dividend has to be adjusted for currency differential between U.S. and Canadian dollars. You must also allow for the 15 per cent withholding tax, although there is an agreement pending to lower it to 10 per cent. It is these *net* dividends that must be capitalized in order to compare stocks on a "yield only" basis.

Most people like dividends, but they may be a bad sign. Compare the two companies A and B. Both are selling their equity at $10 a share, and both earn $2. But A pays out $2 in dividends and B pays nothing. Which is the best company for the shareholder? Take the situation at the end of one year. After taxes, the shareholder of company A has $1.50 left after taxes and owns a share worth $10. The shareholder of company B has a share worth $12. And this difference cumulates every year, speeding the growth of company B and its shareholders.

Today, when most income is taxed at a higher rate than capital gain, the dividend-paying potential of a company is much more important than the actual current dividend. In fact, this idea can be set down as a firm rule. The lower the dividends currently paid, the stronger is the company's dividend-paying potential. Thus, by paying too much attention to the company's current rate, we are using a method that is not merely incomplete, but gives a misleading impression of what will happen in the future.

4. *Trading on the Equity*

One approach to investment in common stocks that has been used successfully by people who can afford the higher risks involved is called trading on the equity. To explain how this works, let us consider two companies whose capitalizations look like this:

Conservative Capitalization		Leveraged Capitalization	
Debt	$100,000,000	Debt	$400,000,000
Preferred	0	Preferred	$100,000,000
Equity	$500,000,000	Equity	$100,000,000

(If you are unfamiliar with the word "leveraged", don't panic. Be patient and read the explanation that follows.)

In the leveraged capitalization, the equity shareholders are using other people's money to the extent of $5 of debt and preferred shares to each $1 of their own. If the company is able to earn 20 per cent on its invested capital, and pay only 10 per cent for the $400,000,000 it has borrowed, and 15 per cent for the 100 million preferred shares (these dividends must be paid out of the company's after-tax earnings, and thus are a less desirable means of financing), then it is clear that the shareholders will do much better under the leveraged capitalization than will the bondholders and preferred shareholders. Under the leveraged capitalization, the shareholder has the chief call on any profit growth that may be made. On the other hand, if things go badly with the company and it is taken over by the bondholders, the equity may well be wiped out. In the conservative capitalization the equity owner has a relatively minor opportunity of benefiting from good times, but on the other hand the risk of being wiped out is negligible, because there is little debt.

5. *Common Stocks Selling for Less Than Their Working Capital*
Every company has a liquidating value. This is a sum of money that remains after the physical assets of the company, such as plant, have been sold and all debts have been paid. It sometimes happens that nobody wants to buy common stocks. With the scarcity of buyers, the price of stocks falls to a point where the market price per share is less than the net liquidating value per share. In fact, during the market slump after the Second World War, many American stocks could be bought at a price lower than the actual cash per share in the company's till. An outstanding example of this was Curtiss-Wright, which in 1948 could be bought for $5 a share. At this time the company not only had $15 a share in cold cash, but owned all the immense plant and equipment that had been successful in earning up to $10 a share in the previous eight years.

This was not by any means a once-in-a-lifetime opportunity. In 1958 American Motors was selling for $8. It had cash working capital of $10 a share in the till, and an adjusted equity of $20 a share. A college professor we know bought at $8, sold at $40, and then watched in chagrin as it went on to $80 a share. Today it is nearly bankrupt. We all missed the opportunity for a short sale at $80.

Ten years later, in 1968, Crane Company was selling between $44 and $61. The working capital was $48 a share and all the other quality and growth parameters looked good. The shares were split 2 for 1 in 1972 and 1976, and 2 per cent stock dividends have been paid most years. As a result, a continuing shareholder has 5 times as many shares, selling now at $35 each.

In 1978 Wheeling-Pittsburgh Steel was selling for $15. The working capital was $35 a share. Second-best earnings ever in 1979 resulted in a cash flow of over $20 a share.

In 1988. . .? There's sure to be another.

Stocks that are selling for less than their working capital seem on the surface to be magnificent bargains, and sometimes they are. But before buying such a stock you would have to look behind the figures see what is actually going on. Such low prices often indicate that stock buyers have lost confidence in the company management. If the management is not changed (and it is very difficult to take over a company and change its management), it may gradually dissipate all the working capital and the stock will be worthless. As we have said, pinpointing good management is the key to successful investing in common stocks. A good management does not ordinarily leave large amounts of cash standing idle in the company. It finds ways of using the money, either for expansion of its own company or for acquisition of other profitable lines.

Great fortunes have been made by seeking out situations where a company has undervalued its physical assets on the balance sheet or has large amounts of cash in the till. By quietly buying up the shares of the company at low prices, the new group obtains control. With a controlling interest in the company, the group is able to fire the incompetent management and pay itself a resounding dividend, which more often than not pays all acquisition costs. But in order to work a successful takeover you have to have millions of dollars at your disposal.

6. *Common Stocks Selling for Many Times Their Apparent Value*

Can you live with success in the extreme? Well, if it's *too* extreme, you can have your broker borrow shares you don't own, and sell them short. Some technical details are explained in Chapter 17, but immediate current examples might be mentioned. Take Kellogg as an illustration.

The company has "motherhood" characteristics galore:

1. Nearly forty years of increasing sales and earnings
2. Impressive market share for its products around the world
3. Fully recognized by investing institutions as successful by every measure

Here are some calculations:

	$million	*Per Share*
Apparent Equity	683	
Adjustment for Accumulated Depreciation	494	
Adjusted Equity	1,177	$9.55
Net Income, Year 1985	281	
Depreciation for 1985	75	
Adjusted Earnings	356	$2.90
Market price of shares, October 1986	50	
Calculations per $ Invested		
Adjusted Equity	.19	
Adjusted Earnings	.058	

Something to consider while you munch your morning cornflakes!

A list of other stocks meeting a stringent *overvalued* criterion would include: Dun and Bradstreet, Marsh and McLennan, Syntex, Telecommunications, Cray Research, Pall, Tambrands, Commerce Clearing House, U.S. Health Care Systems, Shared Medical Systems, Pic'n Save, IMS International, Maxicare Health Plans, and New England Business Service. For each company

1. its market capitalization (price per share times shares outstanding) exceeds latest year sales;
2. earnings are less than 5 per cent of the price, i.e., price-earnings ratio exceeds 20;
3. the share price is at least five times the apparent equity "book value";
4. institutions (usually mutual funds) own half or more of the issued shares (so it can't be argued that the merits of the company have gone unrecognized).

Perhaps you'll fancy yourself as a David, setting out to select a Goliath. Remember, it will take lots of backbone, nerves of steel, and a good-sized mental slingshot to establish and maintain a short position in such well-known, successful, and respected companies.

CHAPTER FIFTEEN

Industry Studies

Every good that is worth possessing is paid for in strokes of daily effort. WILLIAM JAMES (1842–1910)

The conservative investor, before he buys for the long term, should make a fairly detailed study of the industry in which he proposes to invest. Ideally, this study should include technical, marketing, and financial aspects of the business, but as a minimum it must undertake intrinsic-value analysis of the industry leaders.

A workable system of security analysis must fulfil two basic requirements. First, it must be based on an adequate, but not overwhelming, body of carefully digested statistics. Second, it must be possible to subject these statistics to a comprehensive series of meaningful tests. These tests will have as their end result a clear picture of a company's policy and prospects, the degree of risk attached to it, and where it stands as an investment in relation to other companies in its industry.

There is a great need for a popular system of financial analysis that can satisfy these two requirements. We need a technique that is basically simple, yet provides enough information that judgments about the company are adequately based on facts. The statistical raw materials used must be readily available from company reports. The company analysis must be of a type that can be applied widely. Most important, the system of analysis used must leave the investor with a specific directive telling what to buy, hold, or sell.

The method that follows is the best system of security analysis we know. Conventional methods leave much to be desired. Either they engulf the user in a mass of undigested figures and charts which he has no way of using, or they place too heavy a reliance on time-honoured but often misleading indicators such as the price-earnings ratio, capitalization, or yield.

The basis of the system we follow is the balance sheet used as the source of "book value", and a simplified statement of "source and application of funds", from which we figure cash flow. A study of consecutive annual reports of the company permits the user to fill out a table. These columns of figures, one horizontal line for each year, contain the essential statistical information about the company. Two special columns giving the ratio of net earnings to book value, and of net earnings plus depreciation, i.e., "cash flow", to book value, are also worked out, using the figures in the other columns.

With a little instruction, anyone can learn to condense the information given in the company's annual report into one line in a table. Armed with these sets of figures going back five years, you can obtain a good picture of the company's financial condition and policy, as well as its relationship to other companies in the industry.

As in all financial statistics, a certain degree of caution is required in filling out the columns. For example, a degree of finesse is sometimes required to sift out certain hidden earnings and reserves.

One important attraction of this method is that the financial statistics for each company require only *one* line a year. This means that the pertinent statistics covering many companies can be set down in little space. The financial statistics for ten companies in one industry can be reduced to a common denominator and set down side by side for ready comparison. Analysis of a number of companies in a single industry leads to a clear understanding of the problems and policies of different managements working in that industry.

Our "object all sublime" is to come up with three basic numbers:

1. equity per dollar invested
2. cash flow per dollar invested
3. working capital per dollar invested

You know how many dollars you are investing, but the equity and cash-flow figures cannot usually be taken directly from the annual report. The "apparent equity" given in the report has to be changed to "adjusted equity" using the methods described on pages 186, 194-5, and 198-9. (Sorry the topic has appeared in three places, but different industries have different valuation problems.)

In the same way, "cash flow" (income plus depreciation) must be subjected to analysis and changes to get "adjusted cash flow".

The "working capital" figure is usually easy to find, and can be taken directly from the annual report.

What is book value? It is simply another term for net worth, net assets, shareholder interest, or equity. It is the number for the apparent value of the company's common shares, if all the assets were sold at their stated value and all the liabilities paid off at their declared price. As mentioned in the last chapter, this is called liquidation. The book value, upon liquidation, is the amount that the shareholders will get, except for any taxes that might be levied.

Is book value a good measure of the value of a company's shares? We think so, provided only that certain adjustments are made. Both hidden assets and hidden liabilities have to be ferreted out and added in. For example, the oil industry traditionally leaves out of its balance sheets the value of its gas and oil reserves that are still in the ground because of the difficulty of accurately measuring something unseen. In addition, all industries tend to undervalue their assets, such as mills, private railroads, and airplanes, keeping them in their books at prices substantially below replacement cost. These assets must be properly valued, at current market prices, and the difference added to the balance-sheet figure, to get "adjusted equity".

When we go to analyse an industry, we first try to arrive at a figure for "adjusted equity per share". We can divide this number by the current market price of the shares to get our first criterion: the "adjusted equity per dollar invested". This figure allows us to compare any company with all other companies in its industry.

The only part of this technique that is not simple arithmetic is adjusting the figures for assets and liabilities given in the annual report. It is sometimes difficult to find out exactly what an asset is worth. Similarly, it is often impossible to get an exact figure showing how much a company's liability is understated or overstated. But if you use the same valuation rules for all companies in an industry, you cannot go too far wrong. The object of the exercise is not to come up with absolute figures, but to reduce the companies to a form in which they can be compared.

Before going on to tell you what industries we are going to subject to a careful look, perhaps we should tell you the industries we are going to ignore, and why.

In the first edition of this book we had a section on banking in which we ended up recommending three banks: Commerce, Montreal, and Mercantile. Mercantile has since been forced to merge, but it had honest figures, so you could see a year before that it was going under and had time to get out. Even if you weren't watching, the price that was allowed the shareholders at the merger got them out with a small profit. Commerce and Montreal have both done well. If you bought them, you have a profit.

Nevertheless, now, only five years later, we are suggesting that you keep away from banks entirely, except perhaps if you want to sell them short. Some horrible things have happened in the past five years – things that reflect not only on the intelligence, but on the basic honesty of Canadian bank management. First of all, dumb decisions about Dome Petroleum and loans to Mexico have cost the banks some six billion dollars. When you subtract this huge amount from the combined assets of the six major Canadian banks, you notice quite a hole. This alone precludes any recovery, ever, for Canadian banks. Even at the consumer level, Canadian banking has become a disaster area. Most banks now charge you for taking out your own money. In other words, they are making *us* pay for their six billion dollars of bad loan decisions. Maybe they will succeed in hiding this fiasco from the general public, but even if they do, there is no reason to think that the management of banks has improved, or that they will not hand out billions of dollars to the next Dome Petroleum that happens along.

The second reason for not investing in bank securities is that three banks have gone bankrupt – the first Canadian bank failures in over sixty years. Finally, and worst of all, the government and court investigations of the management of the bankrupt banks produced revelations that make us think you should keep well away from such people. There were a dozen scandals, but all you need to know is that the annual reports of the Canadian Commercial Bank and the Northland Bank, audited by "respectable" Canadian accounting firms, failed completely to disclose the financial condition of the companies. For these reasons we think you should stay out of this tarnished industry, no matter what the prospects, and no matter what rosy figures are put before you in the annual reports.

Another industry we do not recommend is Canadian energy. Why not? This is easy. The government is in it, so serious businessmen should keep away.

Why not Canadian mining? We are usually looking for disaster industries, and this certainly qualifies. But many countries have handled their natural resources better than we have. Just because we are physically close to the big U.S. market doesn't mean we are in the best position to grab it. Also, there are environmental problems that we don't seem to be able to get our minds around. Asbestos would be a perfect subject for farce if it hadn't killed so many people and made so many lawyers rich. Besides, we use arsenic to treat gold ores. This may one day return to haunt us. There has been a basic decline in commodity prices – therefore a certainty of price recovery. But you can still buy nickel at less than the cost of production, which is not confidence-building.

Why not forest products? Because it is really an international business. Besides, the facts are hard to get at. Noranda, owned by the Bronfmans, is in both mining and forest products.

SOMETHING CONCRETE

Let's have you begin with a solid, essential industry – cement. There are four basic steps to follow, once an industry is chosen.

1. *Define the industry.*
For a start, see *Value Line* and any encyclopedia at the city library. You will learn:

Cement is made from crushed limestone or oyster shells (lime, alumina, silica compounds) heated to 1600 degrees F. to produce a fused clinker, later ground with gypsum into a fine power. It serves as a binding agent in concrete, which is a mixture of cement with aggregates (gravel, slag, sand), and water.

Cement is very heavy. Transportation costs are high relative to the value of the product. As a result it is usually marketed within two hundred miles of the manufacturing plant, unless barges or special carriers are used.

Total sales of the U.S. and Canadian cement industry are probably less than $6 billion (that's small), but essential (most construction requires it).

2. *Find out who is involved.*
Ten companies are listed in *Value Line*, alphabetically, with their annual capacity in millions of barrels. The U.S. barrel is 360 pounds, the equivalent of 4 bags of 90 pounds each; the Canadian barrel is

350 pounds, 4 bags of 87½ pounds each. That's for Portland cement. For some reason masonry cement is different. It is sold in 70-pound bags, 4 to the barrel, making 280 pounds.

Company	*Capacity* (million tons/yr)	
Calmat	3.2	
Florida Rock	nil	(readymix & aggregates only – see definition)
Giant Group	1.4	
Gifford Hill	3.8	
Ideal Basic	5.4	
Kaiser Cement	4.0	
Lone Star Industries	10.3	+ 4.2 in South America
Moore McCormack	2.7	
Southdown	3.7	
Texas Industries	2.3	
	41.0	

Let's drop Florida Rock *and* let's add other cement companies: Canada Cement Lafarge, 5.8-million-ton capacity (largest Canadian producer); its parent in the United States, Lafarge, 13.0 million tons; St. Lawrence Cement, 4.6 million tons; and Lake Ontario Cement, 1.1 million tons. I found the three Canadian companies in the *Financial Post* cards at the library, and Lafarge in *Moody's Industrial Manual* and *Standard and Poor's*. The *Globe and Mail* of October 21, 1986, focuses on the purchase of Lake Ontario Cement by a French firm and identifies the world's largest firms.

1. Holderbank Financière Glaris firms (Switzerland)
   – controls St. Lawrence Cement
2. Blue Circle Industries (U.K.)
3. Lafarge Coppée (France)
   – controls Lafarge (U.S.), which owns Canada Cement Lafarge
4. Ciments Français (France)
   – now will control Lake Ontario Cement

To simplify our task, let us concentrate on the North American companies and limit our study to those with over $150 million sales in 1985.

3. *Rank the top companies by sales and determine equity and earnings (in $M)*. Adjust each of the latter and calculate sales, adjusted equity, and adjusted earnings on a per-share basis.

FIGURE 26: **Table of Basic Statistics, North American Cement Companies**

Company	1985 Sales	Equity	Accumulated Depreciation	Adjusted Equity	Common Shares Outstanding
	($M)	($M)	($M)	($M)	(M)
Lafarge	944	312.5	435.3	747.8	38.7
Lone Star Industries	872	516.9	396.7	913.6	14.5
Canada	750	287.3	466.7	754.0	—
Moore McCormack	584	209.6	347.0	556.6	8.8
St. Lawrence	493	189.5	276.9	446.4	5.6
Gifford Hill	434	152.0	203.0	355.0	8.6
Calmat	405	336.1	204.5	540.6	15.0
Texas Industries	344	181.8	186.1	367.9	8.1
Southdown	326	246.2	211.1	457.4	8.6
Ideal Basic	293	d.206.6	583.0	376.4	14.0
Kaiser	248	135.7	134.5	270.2	7.3
Lake Ontario	183	57.4	66.3	123.7	4.3
	$5,876			$5,959.6	

Some useful notes:

–Equity pertains to common shares, so preferred-share values must be deducted from total shareholder equity.

– Adding back accumulated depreciation does imply that the facilities are now worth the original cost plus retained earnings. However, it gives a clearer and more comparable figure than equity alone.

Notice that sales do not *usually* exceed adjusted equity.

– "Common Shares Outstanding" refers to the most recent reported number (not an average).

Already something has been learned: the relationship between sales and adjusted equity is approximately dollar for dollar. This means that *a dollar of capital expenditure is necessary in order to generate a dollar of revenue.*

Next, for the latest year (1985) find the stated earnings (net income after taxes) and adjust these by adding back non-cash expenses (write-offs like depreciation, amortization, deferred taxes) in order to find cash flow or adjusted earnings.

FIGURE 27: **Adjusted Equity, Adjusted Earnings, North American Cement Companies**

Company	1985 Sales	Adjusted Equity	Adjusted Earnings	Sales divided by Adjusted Equity	Adjusted Earnings divided by Sales	Adjusted Earnings divided by Adjusted Equity
	($M)	($M)	($M)		(%)	(%)
Lafarge	944	747.8	46.7	1.26	4.9	6.2
Lone Star	872	913.6	85.7	.95	9.8	9.4
Canada	750	754.0	81.4	.99	10.9	10.8
Moore McCormack	584	556.6	78.2	1.05	13.4	14.0
St. Lawrence	493	466.4	59.9	1.06	12.1	12.8
Gifford Hill	434	355.0	44.0	1.22	10.1	12.4
Calmat	405	540.6	55.1	.75	13.6	10.2
Texas Industries	344	367.9	50.3	.94	14.6	13.7
Southdown	326	457.4	63.4	.71	19.4	13.9
Ideal Basic	293	376.4	d.3.0	.78	—	—
Kaiser	248	270.2	22.0	.92	8.9	8.1
Lake Ontario	183	123.7	18.7	1.48	10.2	15.1
	5,876	5,959.6	602.4	Average .99	Average 10.2	Average 10.1

By calculating, we can determine two further analysis ratios: adjusted earnings as a percentage both of sales and of adjusted equity.

The latter can be considered a measure of management's effectiveness in getting results for shareholders – the so-called "bottom line".

Despite its name, Ideal Basic has failed in this respect, since the year's adjusted earnings are negative, and bankruptcy or major refinancing is expected because of their two new but badly designed cement plants.

Those cement companies having oil revenues (Southdown, Moore McCormack) achieved better results. Overall, 1985 offered opportunity for a 10 per cent return (adjusted earnings divided by adjusted equity).

By using the takeover prices (parentheses, Fig. 28, Column 2) for Gifford Hill and Lake Ontario (September 1986 and October 1986 respectively), we can get an indication of what price other companies are prepared to pay for assets and earnings. Without a takeover offer, shares of cement companies are now selling at less than their adjusted equities and at five to six times their adjusted earnings.

4. *Apply your criteria.*
What about you?
If you are to achieve a 50 per cent to 100 per cent increase in your investment within a 2-to-5-year period (Ackerman's Objective), you must find an investment selling at two-thirds of its adjusted-equity value.

Putting it another way, you are seeking to buy assets worth $1.50 for each dollar you invest.

Seven out of twelve cement companies meet this test.

Your earnings criterion requires at least 20 cents of adjusted earnings for each dollar you invest. *Four* of the dozen companies meet this test.

***Moore McCormack* appeals because both its adjusted equity and its adjusted earnings are highest relative to present share prices. The company's management appears to be effective in generating earnings.**

FIGURE 28: Adjusted Equity and Adjusted Earnings Per Share

Company	Shares O/S	Oct. '86 Price/Share in $	Adjusted Equity Per Share	Adjusted Equity Per $ Inv.	Adjusted Earnings Per Share	Adjusted Earnings Per $ Inv.	Adjusted Earnings + Adjusted Equity (%)
Lafarge	38.7	9.5	19.	2.03	1.20	.13	6.2
Lone Star	14.5	29.	63.	2.17	5.90	.20	9.4
Canada	—	—	—	—	—	—	10.8
Moore McCormack	8.8	21.	63.	3.01	8.90	.42	14.0
St. Lawrence	17.6	20.	28.	1.30	3.40	.17	12.8
Gifford Hill	8.6	(32.)	41.	(1.29)	5.10	(.16)	12.4
Calmat	15.0	40.	36.	.90	3.70	.09	10.2
Texas Industries	8.1	26.	45.	1.75	6.20	.24	13.7
Southdown	8.6	36.	53.	1.48	7.40	.20	13.9
Ideal Basic	14.0	2.	27.	13.50	d. .20	—	—
Kaiser	7.3	21.	37.	1.76	3.00	.14	8.1
Lake Ontario	4.3	(36.25)	29.	(.79)	4.30	(.12)	15.1

FIGURE 29: **The Six Most Attractive Cement Companies on a Per-Dollar-Invested Basis, October 1986**

Company	Price Per Share in $	Adjusted Equity Per Share	Adjusted Equity Per $ Inv.	Adjusted Earnings Per Share	Adjusted Earnings Per $ Inv.	Adjusted Earnings divided by Adjusted Equity
Lafarge	9.5	19.	2.03	1.20	.13	6.2%
Lone Star	29.	63.	2.17	5.90	.20	9.4%
Moore McCormack	21.	63.	3.01	8.90	.42	14.0%
Texas Industries	26.	45.	1.75	6.20	.24	13.7%
Southdown	36.	53.	1.48	7.35	.20	13.9%
Kaiser	21.	37.	1.76	3.00	.14	8.1%

Lafarge has the advantages of size, and its assets are selling at a low price because it has not yet generated the results that can be expected in this industry.

Lone Star and *Kaiser* are also attractive on an asset basis if the investor is prepared to wait for better earnings to develop.

IS STEEL A STEAL, STILL?

In the first edition of this book, we hoped to establish a principle encouraging investor interest in industries in trouble. We said:

> Whenever there is increasing "viewing with alarm", it is time for a good look at an industry. When the industry leaders themselves say that they are in danger of going under, the situation becomes even more interesting. Pots of money were made by people who refused to believe what all the news media were saying: that the Dutch would allow KLM to go bankrupt, that the Americans would let Pan Am Airways go under, that the British would really say goodbye to Rolls-Royce. These days there is universal agreement that the U.S. steel industry is on its last legs; subsidized foreign competition, government regulation and punitive taxation, bad management, union greed, inflated transportation costs, and environmental-pollution laws have combined to do it in. This is the atmosphere of gloom and doom that produces bargains for the careful investor.

Here's what has evolved since that time.

1. The largest steel company (now called USX) has merged Marathon Oil, Texas Oil & Gas, and U.S. Diversified Group, becoming considerably less steel-dependent. Some of its obsolete steel capacity may not reopen after settlement of the current strike. Takeover ("raider") interest has put the stock on the most active list.
2. The second-largest company (LTV) has merged with Republic Steel and is in Chapter XI of Bankruptcy Proceedings (ensuring protection from creditors while a plan of financial reorganization is worked out).
3. Bethlehem Steel has continued to cut back its out-of-date facilities and to sell off its non-steel operations. Dividends on prefer-

FIGURE 30: **Basic Parameters of the North American Steel Industry (in millions)**

Company	1985 Sales	Year-End Shares	Adjusted Earnings	LT Debt	Equity	Accumulated Depreciation	Adjusted Equity
USX	19,823	123.4	1,607.	6,370	5,405	10,262	15,667
LTV	8,199	88.6	d. 144.	(2,137)*	364	777	1,141
Bethlehem	5,177	52.0	187.	1,195	786	4,484	5,270
Armco	3,733	68.0	144.	629	887	1,696	2,583
Inland	2,999	25.5	55.	847	870	2,178	3,048
Stelco	2,434	34.0	189.	572	980	1,452	2,432
National Intergroup	2,370	23.0	57.	521	912	149	1,061
Dofasco	1,993	53.9	265.	395	1,234	1,007	2,141
Algoma	1,176	14.6	44.	660	590	771	1,361
Wheeling	681	5.1	d. 258.	(527)*	d. 51	617	566
	$47,985		2,146.				35,370

*Prior to bankruptcy filing

FIGURE 31: **Per-Share Data**

Company	Sales/ Share	Adjusted Earnings per Share	LT Debt per Share	Adjusted Equity per Share	Adjusted Earnings divided by Adjusted Equity (%)
USX	156	13.02	52.	127.	10.3
LTV	93	—	(24.)	13.	—
Bethlehem	98	3.60	23.	101.	3.5
Armco	55	2.12	9.	38.	5.6
Inland	118	2.16	33.	120.	1.8
Stelco	72	5.56	17.	72.	7.8
National Intergroup	103	2.48	23.	46.	5.4
Dofasco	37	4.92	7.	42.	11.8
Algoma	81	3.01	45.	93.	3.2
Wheeling	133	—	(103.)	111.	—

FIGURE 32: **Per-Dollar-Invested Data, North American Steel Industry**

Company	Oct. '86 Price per Share in $	Sales	Debt	Adjusted Equity	Adjusted Earnings
		(per Dollar Invested)			
USX	26	6.00	2.00	4.88	.50
LTV	2	46.50	(12.00)	6.50	—
Bethlehem	7	14.00	3.29	14.43	.51
Armco	6	9.17	1.50	6.33	.35
Inland	19	6.21	1.74	6.32	.11
Stelco	23	3.13	.74	3.13	.24
National Intergroup	15	6.87	1.53	3.07	.17
Dofasco	24	1.54	.29	1.75	.21
Algoma	14	5.79	3.21	6.64	.21
Wheeling	9	14.78	(11.44)	12.33	—

red shares are not being paid. The common shares sell at one-third of the price a year ago.

4. Armco Steel has also cut back its steel capacity, closed its iron-mining operation, and sold off its non-steel business.
5. National (now National Intergroup) has sold half its steel subsidiary to a Japanese steel-maker. Its other operations are not related to steel.
6. Wheeling-Pittsburgh Steel has been in Chapter XI, Bankruptcy, since early 1985. The union is no longer running the company. The principal owner has taken charge and after negotiating a lower wage rate is planning how to capitalize on the specialized modern technology now in place.
7. The Canadian steel-makers, while more modernized than their U.S. counterparts (Algoma is an exception), may be facing restricted entry into the U.S. market.

See *Value Line*'s excellent description of this industry's extended difficulties.

Does any of this encourage your investment interest? Possibly not, unless you are contrary-minded, and are prepared to seek out the prospect of a "pony in the horse manure".

In case you are, here is a partial display of updated parameters, presented as an offer of encouragement of further practice in industry analysis.

Perhaps the Japanese steel-makers will extend their entry to North American steel production and show us how to upgrade and manage these businesses effectively. We thought so in 1982, and we still think so.

NORTH AMERICAN AIRLINES

For a third stint at exercising our analytical skills on an industry, let's look at airlines. Here are five basic reasons for the industry to deserve investment attention at this time.

1. It constitutes a prime business, offering efficient and economical travel over much of the planet.
2. The U.S. segment has been growing remarkably, generating nearly 50 per cent more revenues than it did five years ago.
3. The three major cost items – labour, fuel, and interest – have shown significant decreases over the last year or two.

   Labour costs are lower thanks in large part to the pioneering efforts of People Express. From an idea in 1981 to most New York departures five years later, employee ownership (non-union), high productivity, and low-low no-frills fares, the company has achieved one of the lowest possible cost structures and has shown the way for its established veteran competitors. After a mistaken romance with Frontier Air, the company has faltered and is being absorbed into Texas Air, a low-cost carrier which owns Continental Air and NY Air, and is acquiring Eastern Air, to become the largest of all airlines in the U.S.

   Fuel prices are down fifty per cent over the last twelve months, with further declines likely. The OPEC cartel has loosened at the seams and basic economics appears destined to prevail as a guiding force in world energy supplies.

   Interest costs are less owing to several factors discussed elsewhere.

4. The technology has become somewhat stabilized, with a variety of quieter, fuel-efficient planes available.

FIGURE 33: Basic Parameters of the North American Airline Industry

Company	1985 Sales	End 1985 LT Debt	End 1985 Equity	Accumulated Depreciation	Adjusted Equity	Net Income	Depreciation	Adjusted Earnings
TEXAS	1,944	1,641	115	400		31.6	88.1	119.7
Eastern	4,815	2,244	204	1,985		6.3	306.5	312.8
People	978	675	90	85		d.27.5	49.0	21.5
	7,737	4,560	409	2,470	2,878	10.4		454.0
UAL	6,383	2,686	1,555	3,439	4,994	d.122.5	540.7	418.2
AMR	6,131	1,992	2,180	1,810	3,990	345.8	336.9	682.7
DELTA	4,684	716	1,287	2,039		259.5	349.1	608.6
Western	1,306	360	177	408		35.5	57.4	92.9
	5,990	1,076	1,464	2,446	3,910	295.0		701.5
NWA	2,655	538	947	1,356		73.1	182.6	255.7
Republic	1,734	540	196	420		69.2	76.5	145.7
	4,389	1,078	1,143	1,776	2,919	142.3		401.4
TWA	3,725	2,001	435	1,637		d.208.4	220.9	12.5
Ozark	480	116	121	112		.6	23.1	23.7
	4,205	2,117	556	1,749	2,306	207.8		36.2

PAN AM	3,484	781	449	902	1,351	d.292.2	208.3	d.83.9
AIR CAN	2,723	1,259	513	1,194	1,707	d.14.8	192.5	177.7
US AIR	1,765	448	954	399	1,354	117.1	77.2	194.3
PIEDMONT	1,527	626	501	280	781	66.7	105.2	171.7
CP AIR	1,128							
PSA	780	608	178	184	362	26.8	51.3	78.1
SW AIR	680	410	466	173	639	47.3	53.6	100.9
ALASKA	433	244	161	74	235	25.9	16.3	42.2
Jet America	102	58	6	8	14	d.8.5	4.3	d.4.2
	535	302	167	82	249	17.4		38.0
WARDAIR	473	190	31	153	186	11.0	23.3	34.3
PWA	352	6	287	100	387	13.4	19.9	32.3

5. The financially strong, better-managed companies have been and are aggressively pursuing the opportunities afforded them by deregulation.

Following the basic steps:

1&2. *Define the industry* and *Find out who is involved.* Determine U.S. and Canadian carriers for which information is readily available. This will mean those covered in *Value Line* plus Wardair and PWA, which are covered in *Financial Post* cards. Air Canada, a Crown corporation, publishes a report, but its shares are not traded and the information on CP Airlines, Eastern Provincial, and Nordair is well buried in the annual report of Canadian Pacific Limited. Some of the five basic reasons for investment attention at this time apply to the Canadian companies. However, the companies are dominated by our national airline with its excessive costs, high fare structures, and resistance to change characteristic of government enterprises. European and Pacific Rim airlines compete in some of the same markets, but with minor exceptions (KLM is one) comparable data are not easily accessible.

3. *Rank the top companies by sales and determine equity and earnings.* Adjust each of the latter and calculate sales, adjusted equity, and adjusted earnings on a per-share basis.

Here comes a basic decision – namely, to include the merging company's 1985 data with the data for the larger of any merging airline. Thus, the largest airline company (Texas) will include the data from Eastern and People Express, although these are not yet a part of Texas Air. Nor is Western yet a part of Delta, nor Jet America yet a part of Alaska. Such treatment will give a more meaningful current picture of the competing companies.

A couple of observations at this stage:

1. Although borrowed funds are almost as important as planes and passengers, some airlines are much more financially secure than others. Contrast Texas or Pan Am with NWA or Delta.
2. Depreciation is such a major item that stated net income has little to do with the "bottom line" results.

FIGURE 34: **Adjusted Equity and Adjusted Earnings, North American Airlines**

Company	Present Shares O/S (In Millions)	Sept. '86 Price/Share	Adjusted Equity Per Share	Adjusted Equity Per $ Inv.	LT Debt Per $ Inv.	Adjusted Earnings Per Share	Adjusted Earnings Per $ Inv.	Adjusted Earnings divided by Adjusted Equity (%)
TEXAS	26.8	30	107	3.56	5.67	16.94	.56	21
UAL	43.6	57	114	2.00	1.09	9.59	.17	8
AMR	58.7	55	68	1.24	.62	11.63	.21	17
DELTA	51.8	42	75	1.75	.50	13.54	.32	18
NWA	26.8	48	109	2.27	.83	14.98	.31	14
TWA	40.8	22	56	2.54	2.36	.89	.04	2
PAN AM	133.6	5	10	2.00	1.20	d.62		
US AIR	31.8	35	42	1.20	.40	6.11	.18	15
PIEDMONT	18.5	43	42	.98	.79	9.28	.22	22
PSA	7.8	30	46	1.53	2.60	10.01	.33	22
SW AIR	33.2	22	19	.86	.55	3.04	.14	16
ALASKA	12.3	20	19	.95	1.00	3.43	.17	18
WARDAIR	3.6	20	51	2.55	2.25	8.72	.44	17
PWA	12.2	19	31	1.63	.47	2.64	.14	9
AIR CAN								10

Finding a dollar and a half of value (adjusted equity) per dollar invested is easy at the time of writing. *Nine of the fourteen companies provide this,* with six companies providing over two dollars of "value" per dollar invested.

The companies with over twenty cents of adjusted earnings per dollar invested are: Texas, AMR, Delta, NWA, Piedmont, PSA, and Wardair. Those with *both* $1.50 of value and $.20 of adjusted earnings are: Texas, Delta, NWA, PSA, Wardair.

Thus, by using explicit criteria, we are able to narrow considerably the investments "eligible" for our portfolio.

For most airlines, the annual financial statements disclose the expenditures for fuel and for labour (Wardair is an exception). Here is a comparison (1985 data) of the four U.S. companies that meet the two tests above.

	As a percentage of revenue		
	Fuel	Labour	Fuel and Labour
Texas	23%	30%	53%
Delta	20%	38%	58%
NWA	25%	29%	54%
PSA	15%	27%	42%

This additional consideration helps to narrow the choice even further.

It is to be hoped that this outline of essential steps will "get you off the ground" in your own study of an industry.

CHAPTER SIXTEEN

Attention to Growth

To perceive things in the germ is intelligence.
LAO-TSE (604?–531? B.C.)

The kinds of shares that protect to some extent against inflation are the so-called "growth" stocks, and what we need to look for is a "growth situation". Two of the things we have to keep in mind in looking for shares of this type are:

1. An expanding industry
It goes without saying that the moustache-cup industry is not going to grow. What we need to find is an industry that is relatively young, yet firmly established, and whose prospects for the future are good. Such industries as oil, chemicals, light metals, air transportation, electrical equipment, drugs, insurance and finance, or household equipment probably fall in this class.

2. A solid company
When you have chosen an industry, the next problem is to choose one or more of the companies in that industry whose prospects of growth are good. You should avoid new companies like the plague. Most new companies fail – and soon. You should choose a company that has been in existence long enough to have a solid foundation in the form of a good financial history. You can get the annual reports of the company going back ten or fifteen years, and see whether the amount of property the company owns has increased with the years, or whether the company has expanded at better than the average rate for its industry.

In choosing a company it is best to avoid small companies, because they have fewer resources of management skill – or money

– and thus are less able to stand competition. This is offset to some extent by the fact that smaller companies are usually faster on their feet. But by and large the bigger company is the safer bet. Not only does it have large resources of manpower and money, but it has diversified products, and plants in many parts of the world. These give it stability to ride out economic storms.

In size of company, a compromise is in order. The largest company in the industry is likely to be torpid, the smallest paralysed by its problems. Try picking about the third-largest.

However, be careful. The natural human thing to do when you find yourself established in a business is to build over-capacity. This discourages rivals from entering the business, so you can lead a comfortable life with minimum competition. But over-capacity often leads to slackness, and you find yourself saddled with obsolete plant and equipment. The Japanese and the Koreans are making your product by modern methods, and are underselling you by 50 per cent right in Montreal. In this event you have to rush to Ottawa or Washington to get the government to raise import duties. This tells you why you should not rush to buy Dominion Textiles, Cannon Mills, or J. P. Stevens, in spite of their strong asset positions.

The price of every stock in the market tends to get pushed up and down unrealistically by the emotional excesses of people who buy and sell. Our problem is to pick a time for buying when the price represents a fair value of the share you are buying.

WHY GROWTH STOCKS GROW

The market price of a true growth stock will rise from $1 to $10, and then from $10 to $100 a share, and perhaps more. This rise takes place for two reasons: growth of earnings, and growth of investor regard.

The rise caused by the growth of earnings is easy to understand. If a stock earns $1 a share, it should be worth more than $1, and when it earns $10 a share it should be worth more than $10 and some allowance for its rate of growth. But by the time earnings have reached this point, the stock is more likely to be selling at $50 to $100.

The reason for this is the growth of investor regard. There are hundreds, even thousands, of stocks selling for \$1, and your baby is lost in the crowd. There are not many stocks, however, that have moved from \$1 to \$10 a share and held their gains. Thus the stock becomes known to a wider public, and when the public gets to know about anything, it always goes to extremes. So the stock begins to sell at three times earnings, then at ten times, and finally at thirty times earnings. The great danger of growth stocks is that you will be swept along with the crowd and betrayed into paying too much. At thirty times earnings you are discounting many years of prosperity. And remember that the business world, unlike many other aspects of our society, is still highly competitive. The basic idea in choosing a common stock is to pick a well-managed company in an expanding industry, and then wait, cash in hand, for the moment when you can buy its shares at a fair price.

INVESTMENTS THAT GROW FASTER THAN CHILDREN

One reason for investing is so that you will be able to give your children all the education they will take. This costs money, especially if your children happen to be bright. What you need is an investment you can forget about for ten years and then find that it is worth many times what you paid for it. One investment that does this is well-chosen growth stock.

In 1962 Dr. Ackerman, looking for a place to put his children's baby allowance, did a study of Getty Oil and concluded that the stock would eventually be worth \$200. So in late '62 and early '63 he bought the shares at an average price of \$20. They were sold in 1977 for \$160 a share, when the children began to need money for college.

One of the hardest things to do in finance is to recognize growth stocks in the early stages. Nevertheless, it can be done if you know how, and if you are patient enough to keep trying. In looking for a growth company, always satisfy yourself on the following general points:

WHO IS BEHIND THE COMPANY?

It is your task to find people who are as careful with your money as you would be yourself. Wealthy people who enjoy building young companies as a challenge are ideal managers of your money. Here again, J. Paul Getty would have been a great man to follow. He bought his shares of Tidewater Oil during the Depression at 10¢ a share. Wealthy men do not need, nor do they want, to take anything for themselves, and they can afford to follow policies that maximize growth. They can attract the best people as managers, they have sufficient money to see things through, and they take exactly the long-range approach you want in investing for your children.

They may not pay much in dividends, as they do not need dividends themselves, but to the extent that the company can reinvest dividends more profitably than you can after paying taxes, this policy should suit you fine. It assures your company faster growth than that of the competitor with a large dividend-payout policy.

Management salaries that are too high are a bad sign. Large stock options for management, over the long run, lead only to dilution of the common equity. Adequate salaries and adequate options at or above the market price of the shares (and not given when the price is depressed) should be looked for. Large option agreements sometimes make for high stock prices shortly after, but it is doubtful whether such companies make very good long-term investments.

Management of an Ontario trust company used to annually pay itself 2½ times as much as was given to all the shareholders combined. This is the kind of management to avoid.

Successful investments are often found in the stocks of companies controlled by a family or a small group of individuals who work well together. Shareholders who have bought stocks of this type have rarely paid too much for them. This is easy to explain. The group that controls the company has as its objective the company's long-term development. They want to reinvest their savings in their own company, and they do not need dividends. When the largest shareholders believe their company is a good investment, they want to buy more stock at a fair price. Moreover, a low-dividend policy very often leads to a low valuation in terms of intrinsic worth. You must watch that this policy of keeping the stock at a low price is not overdone, and you must have some assurance that the management will think of the small shareholders when the time is right. Ethical management will not promote the stock of the company, but they will also not withhold information, or try to keep the shares artificially depressed.

Another likely place for successful investment is the Canadian subsidiary of a well-established U.S. company. The big company provides capital as needed, marketing skills, high technology, and hand-holding to get the beginner started. Canadian companies of this type that we mentioned in the first edition of this book have done very well over the past five years: Fruehauf has moved from $12 to $26, Kelsey Hayes from $5 to $25. Other examples are Goodyear, Campbell Soup, Budd Canada, Canadian Occidental, Celanese Canada, Du Pont Canada, Scott Paper, Greyhound Lines Canada, Gulf Canada, Hayes Dana, Imperial Oil, Nabisco, Shell Canada, Texaco Canada, Sears, TIE/Telecom, Teledyne Canada, and Xerox Canada.

With these general observations on growth stocks, and some stress on the importance of the management group in growth companies, let us look now at the specific problem of finding a growth stock at a fair price.

STAGNATING COMPANIES

These are often very good investments if your timing is right. If you can buy just before a good new management comes in to make better use of capital, assets, and people, you will be right for the right reasons. Crane Company was a stagnant plumbing-fixture company until it was found by Thomas Evans, who became a major shareholder and made the company into the world's largest manufacturer of valves, an integrated steel company, a building-products manufacturer and distributor, and a major producer of cement.

Crane is our classic illustration of how management with principles can help the growth of shareholder equity, and make an excellent investment out of an otherwise quiet company business. Here is the story with the basic principles emphasized.

CRANE COMPANY: PEOPLE WHO DID IT OUR WAY

Figure 35 plots the growth of equity per share (broken line), working capital per share (solid line), and high and low of market price per share (dotted lines) each year from 1957 to 1979. The left

side of the chart shows a striking anomaly, with both equity and working capital well above the price of the shares. Twenty years later, at the right-hand side of the chart, the lines have come into a more normal relationship.

We say Crane is a fine growth stock, yet over the years the lines have dropped if anything, or at best have remained about the same dollar level. Why is this? The explanation lies in the three blank vertical sections, representing two-for-one share splits in 1964, 1971, and 1975. On each of these occasions shareholders doubled the number of shares they owned, but the price of each one was cut in half. Based on the original 1957 low near 20, today's low (1980), had there been no splits, would be near 160.

Thomas Evans came to the Crane Company in 1958 as president and significant shareholder. Twenty-one years later he was still chairman and in charge, although the long-time president was retiring, to be succeeded by a new generation, Evans by name. Let's look at Crane to see how a really excellent management functions while directing the growth of a company over many years.

Some outward and visible signs of growth are evident. The company has a billion dollars of assets now, well ahead of the $224

FIGURE 35: **Crane Company**

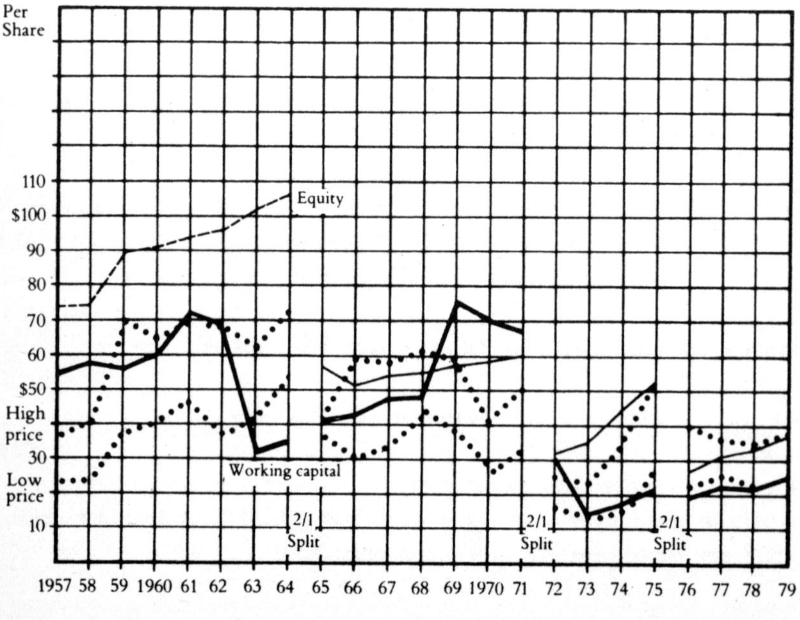

million at year-end 1958. Sales, then $336 million, totalled one and a half billion in 1979. (This is an annual rate of growth of 7.38 per cent compounded.) Both years had the same ratio of sales to assets. Here are some other growth statistics:

Shareholders' equity	$174 million to $371 million, up 113%
Net income	$ 5 million to $ 55 million, up 1000%
Cash flow	$ 11 million to $132 million, up 1100%

The company has done well, but how have the investors fared? In 1958 the shares traded between $23 and $40. With 2,372,624 shares outstanding, that is a market valuation of $55 to $95 million. At year-end 1979, the ten million shares were trading at $33, that is, $330 million.

Could you have shared in this growth? Yes, if you had purchased 100 shares at $35 then, you would have received $12,600 in cash dividends and could sell your present holdings, including stock dividends and splits, for $45,100. For an investor, that is the best growth statistic of all.

Ignoring dividends, which over the years amounted to over three times the original investment, the profit of $41,600 ($45,100 less $3,500) over twenty-one years amounts to nearly 13 per cent cumulative per year.

Remember first of all the model at the beginning of Chapter 14. We shareholders expect management to fulfil these four roles:

- assemble enough assets
- obtain enough production from the assets
- sell the production profitably, keeping costs in line
- deal responsibly with human relationships – employees, shareholders, customers, the general public

These roles have been played in a masterly fashion at Crane. In addition, the following specific business principles have been used by the management in making the company an investment vehicle par excellence:

1. Always acquire assets at a discount.
2. Close down or sell any unprofitable activities.
3. Strengthen profitable activities.
4. Develop back-up sources of supplies of raw materials.
5. At the right price, sell what isn't strategic.
6. Emphasize cash flow rather than net income.

Principle No. 1: Acquire assets at a discount.

The graph (Figure 35) sums up the major events in the financial life of the Crane Company between 1958 and 1979. For a financial man, these lines tell all, but for the ordinary person some interpretation and extrapolation is needed. First of all, why did Thomas Evans and Gurdon Wattles look at Crane instead of some other company? The answer is simple, and leaps without equivocation from the left-hand side of the chart.

In both 1957 and 1958 the shares sold at less than half their apparent equity value, and well below working capital. This was the case despite the stock-option incentives held by eighty-six officers and key employees on 101,710 shares, which usually is a good strategy for holding share prices up.

Having bought lots of shares and achieved effective control of the company, the management noticed that there was lots of cash in the till. So they started looking around for places to invest the company money. They looked and looked, but couldn't find anything as attractive as their own company shares. No one else was offering shares of a solid money-making company at prices well below the working capital. So they set up a long-term program for investing the company's surplus working capital, whenever possible, in Crane shares.

This provided immediate benefits for the remaining shareholders, because each year the profits would be split among fewer shareholders. Figure 36 gives the year-by-year figures showing the extent to which this Principle No. 1 was observed:

Other assets purchased over the twenty-one-year period amounted to a billion dollars. Some of the companies purchased were closely associated with Crane's line of products – Chapman Valve, National U.S. Radiator, Midwest Piping, Glenfield and Kennedy, Flowmatics, Chempump, Reff Plastics, Classic Brass – allowing the business to implement Principle No. 3 by expanding its valve-manufacturing capacity by 50 per cent. The company is now well ahead of world-wide competition in this field.

Some of the billion dollars went toward putting the company into new activities – as significant producers of essential materials in steel (CF & I Steel), in building products (Huttig Sash and Door), and in cement (Medusa Corporation). The latter three acquisitions now (1980) have assets of $700 million, sales of nearly a billion dollars, and an operating profit of over $60 million.

FIGURE 36: **Crane Company Purchases of Its Own Shares**

Year	Number of shares purchased by Crane	Portion of initial shares at beginning of period following stock splits in 1965, 1972, and 1976
1959	856,784	
60	28,410	
61	104,860	
62	97,300	
63	92,850	
64	42,700	
		1,222,904 equals 51.5% of 2,372,624
1965	101,620	
66	12,700	
67	20,600	
68	16,500	
69	48,300	
70	16,000	
71	47,700	
		263,420 equals 12% of 2,081,200
1972	110,800	
73	170,000	
74	433,888	
75	470,611	
		1,185,299 equals 23.3% of 5,076,405
1976	755,900	
77	381,100	
78	462,400	
79	200,000	
		1,799,400 equals 17.9% of 10,030,897

Additional investments were made as timely bargains became available – Briggs Manufacturing, Alliance Ware, Westinghouse Air Brake, North Jersey National Bank, Anaconda, and Zapata. Conversely, when eager buyers appeared, Crane was willing to sell. For example, Atlantic Richfield acquired Anaconda in 1977, providing Crane with $25 million cash and 1,800,000 shares of Atlantic Richfield. Over half of these shares were still held in 1980, and were worth twice their purchase cost.

Principle No. 2: Close down and sell any unprofitable activities.

Principle No. 3: Strengthen profitable activities.
These two principles were implemented by retirements (the closing of losing activities) and sales amounting to over $400 million. To quote *Moody's Industrials Manual*: "Since 1969 the basic Crane business has made several changes. The investment in building products has been reduced with the discontinuance of heating and air conditioning products and cast iron bathtubs. Crane Supply has emphasized the marketing of industrial products and distributing products to commercial building rather than to residential building markets." In 1979, two of Medusa's cement plants were closed, while an 80 per cent expansion and modernization was undertaken at the largest, most modern, and best-located plant.

Principle No. 4: Develop back-up sources of supplies of raw materials.
CF & I Steel is fully integrated. It has its own coking coal, iron ore, limestone, and dolomite, its own railroad, extensive water rights, and over 350,000 acres of land. Medusa Corporation has accumulated a plentiful supply of aggregate materials to market along with its cement.

Principle No. 5: At the right price, sell what isn't strategic.
Briggs Manufacturing was sold a year after purchase, as was North Jersey National Bank. Alliance Ware went after two years, Westinghouse Air Brake to a competitor, American Standard, and Anaconda to Atlantic Richfield at an excellent profit.

Principle No. 6: Emphasize cash flow rather than net income.
This helps minimize tax exposure and tightens up the balance sheet so that assets do not become overstated. Over the twenty-one years Crane has claimed depreciation and amortization of $486 million. During the last ten years such write-offs have exceeded net income. Current examples of this practice are the 2 per cent allowances for receivables and over $80 million reserve for inventories. Plant and equipment have been written down to less than half their original

values. Coupled with funds realized from the sale of less profitable activities, substantial money for fresh investments was generated internally. The basic figures are listed in the following table.

(In millions of dollars)

Year	Depreciation & Amortization	Retirements & Sales	Capital Expenditures
1959	8,494	19,326	7,603
60	7,457	13,533	17,002
61	8,000	10,172	29,743
62	8,383	5,620	8,069
63	7,606	3,882	11,318
64	8,316	6,197	12,109
65	7,846	9,547	5,747
66	8,124	12,272	23,229
67	8,632	4,874	16,605
68	9,145	11,444	15,513
69	14,354	9,590	317,068
70	22,458	30,023	56,911
71	26,837	17,218	57,827
72	28,277	23,156	38,372
73	30,163	60,130	48,315
74	34,879	75,634	45,828
75	35,784	18,551	52,458
76	36,380	30,910	82,530
77	44,192	44,628	93,190
78	53,271	5,883	57,403
79	77,514	10,412	85,315
	486,112	423,002	1,082,155

Principle No. 7: Keep cash dividends low.
Over the past ten years, only 25 per cent of Crane's net income has been paid out as dividends. But shareholders were not forgotten. Two-for-one share splits occurred in 1965, 1972, and 1976, plus a 20 per cent stock dividend in 1966 and 2 per cent in shares for twelve recent years. This policy respects the fact that taxes on capital gains are less than on income, and that a well-managed company can

make better use of income than can investors who are growth-oriented.

Use the seven management practices as test questions for each company in *your* investment portfolio. If "your" company management is not acting in accordance with these principles, fire them (if you have the voting power), or sell your shares to some investor whose interests don't include growth in value of his investment. Worse yet are companies whose management violates any or all of these seven principles. They pay premium prices for assets, using external financing, expand what is unprofitable, and sell off the company's heritage. In order to provide the illusion of growth they manipulate depreciation and inventory-valuation policy so as to display continuously rising earnings numbers. Increased cash dividends are paid out while new investment capital comes from the banks, insurance companies, or unsuspecting shareholders. For example, in 1945 the then management at Crane sold 160,000 shares at a price of $102 a share, then treated those particular shareholders to a 50 per cent decline over the next fifteen years. If your investments have such management in evidence, avoid them for what they are – the investment equivalent of a social disease.

We have left the Crane story from 1958 to 1979 substantially as we wrote it in the first edition, because Crane is still the locus classicus of successful long-term solid growth. But this does not mean that you should go out and buy Crane as a growth stock today. The new president has ideas diametrically opposed to those of his father, and the company has moved away from steel and has de-emphasized cement and plumbing-ware, pushing into electronics and frontier technology. Crane is still buying back its own stock, so the policies are clearly successful so far, but it remains to be seen how they will work out in the long term.

CHAPTER SEVENTEEN

Risk and Risk-Taking

Be bold, be bold, be not too bold. EDMUND SPENSER (c. 1552–99)

While speculation is by definition more risky than investing for intrinsic value, there are degrees of risk in any speculation. In other words, you can be intelligent about speculation and take steps to minimize the risk.

This is a large subject, but its elements can be covered under ten headings. By considering these important points about any speculation you are looking at, you can at least focus your mind on the key areas. If the answers are unsatisfactory, the speculation should normally be left to someone else.

1. Is there *any* intrinsic value?

Time after time, mining promotions are sold to the public on the basis of a company with total assets of $50,000 in cash selling five million shares at $1 each. One very simple calculation can demolish a company like this. The intrinsic value of the stock is $50,000 divided by 5,000,000, or 1¢ per share. The other 99¢ you are paying is for the hope that maybe this company can scrape together large capital sums for equipment which will enable them to see whether or not there is any gold on their property. This is a long shot by any definition of the term.

2. Is there any apparent floor price at which buyers are always available?

Sometimes the existence of large physical assets or proven oil reserves in the ground sets a floor price below which the stock of a company will not sink. For example, take a company that has proven reserves of a million barrels of oil in the ground, and oil is worth $15 a barrel. If the company has issued a million shares and they are selling at $10, they are not likely to go lower. Normally, there are buyers around looking for bargains like this, and these buyers will snap up the shares when the price sinks below the value of proven assets.

3. How large is the floating supply of the stock?
The larger the floating supply, the less violent will be the swings in its market price. Say, for example, that a million shares are issued by a particular company. Of these, 300,000 are in the hands of the original promoters, and 600,000 have been bought by the public at a high price and then locked away in safety-deposit boxes and forgotten when the price collapsed. This leaves 100,000 shares as the floating supply. A stock of this kind will be extremely volatile, because a very small amount of bidding for the small floating supply of 100,000 shares will quickly drive the price up. Such situations are an investor's paradise.

Canadian subsidiaries of U.S. companies are often interesting for this reason. The U.S. parent owns most of the shares, and so these shares are off the market. Hence, when anything interesting happens to companies like Fruehauf Canada or Kelsey Hayes, the very thin market emphasizes stock rises. There is very little stock available, people begin bidding for it, and the jump is not commensurate with the news that caused the upward move to start.

4. How has the market price moved in the past?
The price-volume pattern of the shares over a period of time can give you important indications about the bona fide nature of the security. If the volume is very steady week by week, and the price of the stock is rising gradually, this normally indicates a sound situation. If, on the other hand, there are drastic fluctuations in the weekly volume, and equally drastic price fluctuations, it is a bad sign. It can mean that some price manipulation of the shares is taking place.

5. Who is behind the company?
If the shares of a company are held by wealthy and respectable people who are investing for the long pull, this is an excellent sign. There is a difference between building up a company and promot-

ing a stock. Building up a company is not like selling soap, and publicity is the last thing needed. If the management is really concerned in building up a long-term asset, it wants to keep the price of the shares as low as possible so that members of management can buy more for themselves. Thus, the fewer people who know about the company, the better.

This is why a good place to look for undervalued securities is on the unlisted market. The fact that shares are not listed on any exchange is a clear indication that no one is interested in promoting their sale to the public. The basic question is: Does the company act for the benefit of shareholders or is it being run as a device to permit inside members of management to make profits by speculating in the stock? The way to answer this question is to see who the large shareholders and management members are. Promoters are well known by name to most members of the financial community. If the company you are looking at is loaded down with promoters, you should leave its shares alone. If, on the other hand, the shareholders and the people managing the company are men who are experts in that particular industry, and who have a history behind them of building up solid companies, then you know that you are on the right track. In a genuinely low-price issue there is never any pressure to sell or to buy. You will find no peddling of stock to the public. Rather, you will find the opposite: a very close-mouthed attitude on the part of management, simple annual reports, and no publicity stunts in the newspapers.

For example, Kelsey Hayes, a wheel manufacturer at Windsor, had an astonishing rise in price between 1973 and 1978 that was fully justified by progress in the company. Yet it is a company almost unknown to investors to this day. Their plain annual report deserves serious study.

Fruehauf of Canada is another small company whose shares at $25 should be looked into with care. Why?

a. Its assets are still selling at a discount. The time to buy a summer resort is not at the height of the season in July, when the grass is green and the sun is rippling on blue waters, but rather in February, when it is boarded up and buried in snow, and unmet mortgage payments are disturbing the owner's sleep.

Fruehauf had an equity per share of $18.50 at the end of 1979 and of $27.50 in 1985. The working capital per share was $15.60 then, and is an estimated $25 now.

b. These assets are not just numbers, they are useful. The company is the leader in its field, and has been consistently the leader over a long period of time. Truck-trailer manufacturing is a business with an ongoing demand.
c. Fruehauf earnings are sufficient to provide a good return at present prices, perhaps 15 to 20 per cent of the share price.
d. The company is well managed. Their profit margin on sales has averaged 5.7 per cent over the past ten years, while sales have more than doubled.
e. Expansion has already occurred. Production capacity has been doubled.
f. The company was able to finance its expansion on a short-term basis, thus remaining free of long-term debt.
g. Management comes "on the cheap". Total costs for the top officers and directors are less than the usual salary for a single corporate officer.
h. Attention has been paid to growth of equity, which has increased 50 per cent in the past seven years.
i. There are very few trading shares. The parent company in the United States owns 2,446,000 of the 2,705,775 shares outstanding, and the management own about 30,000. That leaves only about 200,000 shares for investors – a very thin market. This is unlikely to attract mutual funds or wild-eyed share promoters.
j. We like a company that has shown it knows how to make money during a strike. We also like a company whose parent is sympathetic, and occasionally waives its right to a dividend.

6. Is there any prior capital?
A rule for intelligent speculation is never to buy a stock that is not preceded by some bonds or other evidence of debt. In other words, what you want to do, whenever possible, is to buy into leveraged situations. If the equity of the company is small in relation to its debt, buying the equity in the form of common shares gives you a cheap call on very large assets.

What you need to look at is not the market price of the stock, but the dollar price of the assets controlled by each share of stock. If 500,000 shares selling at $1 follow a debt of $8 million, then each share controls at least $16 worth of assets.

When the public buys common stocks of a speculative nature, it usually does just the opposite. The average investor buys stock with no debt, and therefore no leverage. Under these circumstances, the only call he has is on the money put in by the public, and this sum is usually relatively small. What happens in most stock promotions is that the promoter gets the leverage, using the public's money.

There is another reason why you should always demand that some sort of debt be ahead of any common stock you buy. This is because the amount and the nature of the debt is a good indication of the strength of the company. If a bond house will lend money to the company, or if a bank will lend it money, you can be sure that there are some assets to back up the company's claims. If there is neither debt nor bond issue, watch out.

7. Can you buy the shares for less than the working capital per share?
If you can, this is a good sign. True, the working capital can disappear very quickly into the middle distance, even with an honest management, but that is one of the risks you have to take.

8. What is the trading like in the stock?
Market action is another important indicator. Has the stock quieted down after a flurry? Has everyone sold who wanted to sell? If so, it is now free to go up.

9. Crooks.
Once they get into the management of a company, it is very hard to get them out with empty pockets. Even after thievery is exposed and the crooks are out, a serious question remains: Can the new management get the company going again?

10. Governments.
The same as crooks, but not as smart. When civil servants get into a business, the intelligent investor gets out. Provincial governments vie with each other to see which can make the most idiotic move, and perhaps even outdo the feds, the greatest boondogglers of all time.

When you pause a moment to think about it, it is inevitable that a business run by civil servants should go bankrupt. The reason these men are in government, rather than in business, is precisely that they don't like business and don't think the way businessmen think. All they have is money – *your* money – and what a mess they make with it, at best disrupting legitimate companies, and at worst putting them out of business.

The Canada Development Corporation bought Connaught Laboratories from the University of Toronto and Venturetech from private owners for prices well above market at the time. Texas Gulf Sulphur was then acquired, also at prices well above the market. But the greatest triumph of all was the National Energy Plan. The official position of the government was that oil prices were going to $65 a barrel by 1985. They wanted to share in this bonanza. Canada had to have its own oil company, no matter what. So Petrofina became Petrocan, courtesy of the ever torpid Canadian tax-payer, and the Belgians were very happy to go home with all that money.

The Ontario government, not to be outdone, insisted on buying Suncor at a very generous price. But when the smoke cleared, they found they had inadvertently agreed to a dividend payment to others that left the company in less than robust financial condition.

The government investment company in British Columbia, BCRIC, distinguished itself by buying MacMillan Bloedel from Canadian Pacific Investments (CPI) for well above the market price, and their purchase price for Canadian Cellulose is at least twice what it is worth. An option to buy Kaiser Resources at a high price was allowed to expire. A few weeks later they brilliantly closed the deal at 150 per cent of the option price. Manitoba has distinguished itself by putting an initial $18 million of the taxpayers' money into Saunders Aircraft (known in that province as Squanders Aircraft). This government can't even learn by experience. They sank another $19 million into Saunders, when any high-school student could have told them the case was hopeless.

La Belle Province is famous for Sidbec, and many others. Nova Scotia is famous for Clairtone and heavy-water plants. New Brunswick rests its case on Bricklin. Just what Canada needed: a new $40,000 sports car, designed and built by amateurs. No wonder it attracted government support!

There is a great book to be written about Canadian governments (provincial, federal, and local) in business. But we are not going to write it. We both have weak stomachs.

WHAT IS A FAIR REWARD FOR TAKING RISKS?

It goes without saying that you want to be paid for all your trouble, work, and rue. People who take considered risks are very rare, and people with rare skills should expect to be well paid by society. But the question is: how much? What is a fair return for betting your own post-tax money on a well-considered risk that the ordinary man wouldn't touch? I would say as a rule of thumb that your upside gain should range between five and ten times your investment. If you can't envision getting five to ten times your money back over twenty years, forget it. Dr. Ackerman takes the view that a satisfactory return would be 50 per cent to 100 per cent over a period of two to five years. At first glance there would seem to be a conflict between these views, but there really isn't. The fair rate of return on an investment depends largely on how much of it is borrowed money. The great thing about finance is that you can add risk the way a cook adds chili peppers. Season to taste. The more borrowed money you use, the higher your margin at the brokers, the higher the risk, and the higher the potential profit should be. This is called "the magic of finance".

PROTECTING PAPER PROFITS AND PROFITING BY RISK-TAKING

Since we are discussing risks and risk-taking, this is probably the place to elaborate on something we mentioned in our early chapter on brokers – methods by which the investor can, through his broker, attempt to protect his paper profits and make profits on risk-taking.

Sometimes you are lucky enough to buy just at the beginning of a long bull market. When this happens, you begin to wonder whether it wouldn't be wise to sell all your shares and take your profits. On the other hand, the market has been going up for six months, and shows no sign of losing its steam. One way to have your cake and eat it too in this situation is to give your broker a special type of order known as the "stop loss" order.

Say you have a stock which has gone from $50 to $70 a share. You give your broker a sell order for the stock at $66½ (5 per cent below the market price). Thus, if the market drops, your stock will be sold automatically and your paper profit will become realized.

True, you could have sold at 70, but then you didn't know whether the market was going up or down. If, on the other hand, the market continues to rise and your stock goes to 80, you then adjust your stop to 5 per cent of 80, at 76.

Depending on what you think the prospects of a continued rise are, you use 5, 10, or 15 per cent stop. Less than 5 per cent is not recommended because you are liable to be sold out in one of the minor daily dips of the stock and lose your position. The 15 per cent level, of course, is the safest, but the insurance costs you more.

Another danger of stops is that your broker may be asleep. When the market price comes to your stopped price, the stop-loss order becomes a market order. That is, it is an order to the broker to sell the stock at whatever he can get on the market. In a rapidly declining market, with the ticker-tape falling sometimes an hour behind actual transactions, a sell order placed at market might take place at a price much below your stop. This, however, is a very rare occurrence. The risk of its happening is almost negligible if you are dealing in well-known listed stocks. Putting stops on shares on which you have a paper profit is an excellent method of protecting your profits. The same method can be used to limit losses.

Selling Short

When you can't find any shares that meet your quality standards (and 1986-7 seems to be such a time), you should consider the possibility that the market is just plain too high. But don't let this keep you out of the market. There are still plenty of opportunities. Using exactly the same methods, but inverse criteria, you select those issues that are most *over*priced, i.e., that offer

- the *least* adjusted equity per dollar
- the *least* prospective earnings

Consider Polaroid late in 1969, selling at $120 a share. This meant that a company that had never earned $2 a share was judged by the market as being worth $4 billion. You felt that this was at least twice what the shares should be selling for, and you took action to back your judgment. You borrowed the shares from the broker and sold them short. Less than a year later the market proved you right, and you covered your short position by buying the shares at $60. Two years later you notice that the shares have again climbed to $120, so you short twice as much this time, having gained some confidence. You spend the next two years gleefully watching the stock fall to $20. (Your broker, meanwhile, collects two commissions and the interest on the loan of stock.)

Short selling is a great way to make money and retire early if your emotional make-up permits it. Short selling is relatively rare because it is emotionally difficult. It is easy to buy cheap and hope to sell dear. Everybody does it. But selling out everybody's favourite company at the height of a bull market when everybody is stuffed with great expectations takes character. Another difficulty: there is a built-in problem with the broker. *His* emotions are against it; besides, it is extra work. He has to find and borrow the stock for you to go short with.

After going short, the way to protect yourself against a runaway stock and instant bankruptcy is *not* to use stops. They are too slow. Rather, get your broker to phone you when the stock reaches 10 per cent above your purchase price. When this happens you have to evaluate the stock again. Has something new happened? Even if it hasn't, maybe you should cover your loss and wait for another opportunity to short the stock again.

The history of Kentucky Fried Chicken is a classic illustration of how to go short, when to do it, and how to follow up.

This is written in standard brokerage-house language. Try your hand at understanding this language now, because most of the new material about companies you look at from now on will be written in this language.

In August 1969 Dr. Ackerman sent out the following memo to his clients:

The Thresher case for selling short

Kentucky Fried Chicken $40 to $45

(listed NYSE-KTY 1969 price range 35 to 49¾)

(a) Plenty of shares – 9.8 million Market valuation $400 m(illion)

(b) Nominal asset values – book value 33.6 m (3.40 / share)
as of March 31 / 69 includes $6.8 m intangibles
–property and equipment 24.5 m
–working capital 1.9 m (=$.20 a share)
Shares are selling for over 10 times net assets.

(c) Sales for the year ending September 30, 1968, were $80 million. This is a healthy increase from $46 m the year before; and for the 6 months ending March 31, 1969, sales were $58 m, up from $35 m. Thus shares sell for 4 or 5 times present sales. *At an annual increase of 50 per cent, it will be fiscal 1972* before sales equal the present market valuation of the shares.

9 months ending June 30

Sales	$ 93 m	vs	$58 m
Net	$ 8.4 m		$ 4.8 m
(per share)	.85		.50

(d) The company's 9 per cent profit margin is unlikely to be improved as it encounters stronger competition in the fast-food franchising business. Entry into roast beef operations, motels or nursing homes indicates a levelling off of chicken operations despite managment's estimate of 4,000 chicken units by the end of 1973 (from 2,400 now). Foreign expansion and small town expansion promise higher cost structures. While the fish and chip units (100 now, 270 scheduled) appear promising, their volume is lower and this company does not have the distinctive lead in the field. Earnings per share were $.78 in 1968. Expect $1.25 in 1969 and perhaps $2.00 in fiscal 1970. *Shares sell for over 30 times expected 1969 earnings.*

(e) *Trading on the exchange indicates distribution of shares.* The Chairman's sale of 400,000 shares at $48.50 on June 5th was preceded by net sales of over 25,000 from other officers and directors during the last year and has been followed by 4 block trades totalling 147,000 at prices from 45 to 38½.

(f) Anticipated decline – perhaps 30 to 40 per cent in a dull or declining market.

Jerry Ackerman

NOTE: Canadian brokerage firms appear to find it difficult to borrow this stock.
FURTHER NOTE: On August 25th, *Barron's* began a series on fast-food franchising entitled "Speculative Bellyache?" listing 133 firms, mostly newcomers to the field.

What happened? Dr. Ackerman and several of his clients sold short and the stock promptly went up from $45 to $55. Clients who had shorted in the low forties called to ask plaintively, "How long, O Lord? How much money can we lose?" One out-of-town client lost his nerve and liquidated at the peak, losing $15 a share. The few who had the emotional strength to hold on watched the price decline steadily over nine months to $10 a share. Then the company was bought by Heublein for about $20 a share. Never has Dr. Ackerman been so right for the right reasons.

On February 26, 1980, the *Globe and Mail* "Report on Business" had the headline: "Oil and Gas issues lose ground in a move believed long overdue." An analyst was quoted: "I have been trying to tell people the issues have gone too far. Gulf Canada fell to $173.50, but if it were not for the East Coast holding, the shares would probably be trading about $100 less than the current price. This price puts a value of $4.5 billion on Gulf's interest, based on 45.5 million shares. I think the company will make a good profit on its East Coast interest, but to put a value of $4.5 billion on it is too much."

On the same page was the story of the injured Newfoundlander coming out of his coma in the hospital and asking immediately: "How is my Mobil stock doing?" Mobil is the drilling operator on the wells where Gulf Canada owns 25 per cent and 18 per cent. On February 28, Dr. Ackerman, awakening from *his* coma, verified the calculations in the article and then sold 100 shares of Gulf short at $173.50. This transaction required the deposit of 60 per cent of the price, or $10,800 (including commission), with his broker.

It was only a matter of days before the stock had risen another $20 to $193.50, providing a hair-raising replay of the Kentucky Fried Chicken affair ten years before. However, Irish stubbornness prevailed, and he hung on until the share price retreated to $153.50 on March 23. The position was covered, and Dr. Ackerman got a cheque from the broker for $1,658.47, the net difference between the sale and the purchase price, less commission, plus his original investment of $10,800. This was a percentage gain of 15.35 per cent in twenty-four days. Had he held on one week more, the profit would have been twice as much.

Another way to achieve similar results with less risk was to buy a "put" option giving him the right to sell 100 shares of Gulf Canada at $180 a share until November. The cost, including commission, was $2,550 on February 29. On March 25 the option itself was sold to another buyer for $3,800 less commission, or $3,732, while the stock price was $145. The gain: $1,182 on an investment of $2,550, or 46 per cent in twenty-six days.

Understanding Puts and Calls

One method traders use to limit losses and protect gains (called hedging) is through the buying of "puts" and "calls".

A "call" is an option which permits you to buy a given number of shares at a fixed price within a fixed period, usually ninety days. Say you think a stock is going to go up, but it sells for $50 a share and you don't have that kind of money. You can back your judgment by buying an option to buy 100 shares of the stock at today's price within ninety days. This call will cost you perhaps $200. If you are right and the stock goes up 25 points, you make $2,500 profit on an investment of $200. If you are wrong, and the stock either goes down or stays the same, you lose your $200. Thus, call options are a pleasant and harmless way of speculating in the market. They fulfil the basic requirements of putting a definite floor on your losses, yet do not limit your potential gains, except for the time limit.

A "put" is an option to sell. Puts are used chiefly to protect a paper profit. Say you have 100 shares of a stock which you bought at $50 and it has now jumped to $80. You think it is going to $100, but you want to protect your paper profits already made. For, say, $500 you could buy a put on the stock, entitling you to sell your shares at today's price any time within the next 90 days. If you are right and the price continues upward, you will have lost your $500 paid for the put, but the increased price of your stock will offset this. On the other hand, if you are wrong and the market price goes down, your paper profit is guaranteed in cash. From this you must subtract the cost of the put, but even so you will have a substantial profit.

People with large portfolios of stocks can make money painlessly by selling calls to hopeful speculators. If the calls are not exercised, they make a clear profit; if they are, the portfolio is better balanced, and the proceeds of the sale are larger than they would have been if the stock had been sold in the conventional way.

The market is less liquid than you want when you can buy only calls. You want to be able to go both ways, depending on your view of what is really happening.

Writing Calls and Puts

Remember, both puts and calls can be bought and sold. When you sell, you are said to "write" a put or call. If you think the market is going down and you want to get shares at a discount from the market price, you may write a put option on 100 shares. You will be paid immediately for the option, and if the stock does decline sufficiently before the termination date of the option, you will be forced to buy the shares at the price mentioned on the put.

If you really want to gamble, you can "go naked" and write a call option on shares you don't own. You are betting that the stock will not rise, that you will get paid for the call, yet not have to deliver. In theory, puts are better than calls because stocks go down abruptly, while they tend to rise more gradually.

In June 1980 Dr. Ackerman was spending a lot of time on the telephone to his broker instead of pulling his weight in writing this book. Taxed with this behaviour, he said: "Look, this is the chance of a lifetime. Writing calls on Gulf Canada today is like setting up wooden milk bottles at the midway while the barker eggs on the next country bumpkin to try to win a stuffed panda bear for his girl."

I asked: "Why?"

He replied: "Because:

a. The shares are not worth what they are selling for.
b. Short-term call options (August 1980) are selling at magnificent premiums even for a striking price (minimum exercise price) well above the present market.
c. Stock-split news (5 for 1) has already been announced.
d. The parent company has decided to sell off ten million of the newly split shares.
e. The Canadian dollar is suffering because U.S. interest rates are considerably higher.
f. Consensus opinion is that a recession, if not a depression, is imminent."

So, with the shares at $140 and $130 and $150 he wrote naked calls expiring in August with a striking price of $170, pocketing $4,300 cold cash. What easy money. The stock could not possibly rise against such prevailing negative factors. However...you guessed it. It did. The split stock hovered between 28 and 30 until the ten-million-share sale appeared at $26.75 a share. It sold out within a day, and within a few days the shares moved up above 34. And Dr. Ackerman still had an obligation to supply shares at this price. By this time he had lessened his exposure by buying an option for 100 shares at a cost of $170 and another for $190. He also sold two more options at $262. Finally, before any financial disaster, he bought the rest back, escaping with his shirt. He still claims Gulf Canada was not worth $34 a share and the world now agrees with him, the quotation being $12.

While most investors and many brokers are unfamiliar with puts and calls, once your portfolio has become substantial, the writing of options on it can be used to improve the annual performance figures.

WHY WE ARE BEARISH NOW ABOUT THE STOCK MARKET

- Five years ago inflation was bad but everyone was aware of it. Now people think it has gone away.
- Consumers are still willing to borrow at extremely high rates.
- Unemployment has stayed high.
- Government deficits have increased rather than decreased.
- In Canada the largest majority mandate ever given to a party has been dissipated, with nothing to show for it.
- While crisis literature has disappeared from the bookstores, the financial crisis leading to an economic crisis is only on hold.
- Commodity prices are very low, and some are below the cost of production.
- National and international banks are still willing to lend on the basis of rising commodity prices. Not only has this jeopardized the legitimate borrowing power of good enterprises, but it has brought into question the solvency of major financial institutions. Were the Bank of America to collapse, there would be a high likelihood of financial panic.
- We have a majority government that participates with enthusiasm in the great Canadian passion for being diddled.

CHAPTER EIGHTEEN

Portfolio Construction

Unless the Lord build the house, their labour is but lost who build it. PSALM 127, i

HOW MANY ISSUES? THE PROBLEM OF DIVERSIFICATION

Whether you should have all your eggs in one basket, and then watch that basket very closely, or whether you should spread your eggs among several baskets, is the question. Strong feelings are held on this problem, and strong feelings expressed. Benjamin Graham of Columbia took the conventional view that diversification, properly carried out, will make up for many of the mistakes inevitable in security analysis. Cabot, then head of the State Street Investment Fund in Boston, tended more to the view that the investor should make few commitments and watch them carefully. Loeb, author of *The Battle for Investment Survival*, took an uncompromising one-basket approach. He felt you should buy only one stock, and this only after careful study of the entire industry and its member companies. If this one commitment failed to turn out well, you should sell the stock and choose another.

There is something to be said for all these approaches. Excessive diversification is the coward's way out of investment problems. Some mutual funds, for example, buy nearly everything on the list, so they can never be accused of having missed a good bet. On the other hand, choosing one stock out of a list of thousands is pyramiding risk on risk. There is first of all the risk that the entire market may be in a bear phase in which prices are falling. Second, there is the risk that the industry you have chosen is in a temporary decline. Third, there is the risk that the company you have chosen within that industry is not the best performer.

The new investor especially might find it best to have three or four stocks in the portfolio. Then, if two are torpid, and one is going up and one is going down, he feels more comfortable. When you are more experienced and gain confidence, concentrate further and take big positions in single stocks.

Your attitude on diversification may well change as you grow older. In other words, there is no one-word answer to the question: Should I diversify? The young man whose basic need is to build capital fast must take the risk inherent in having all his eggs in one basket. On the other hand, the middle-aged investor who is comfortably off does not need to take this risk, and certainly the older investor who requires income from his securities for support in his old age would be very foolish not to diversify to some extent.

The basic rule about diversification is "concentrate". Don't let the fact that you own more than one security lull you into thinking you don't have to concentrate. You are not running a mutual fund.

There are several *kinds* of diversification, and we recommend and practise two of them. The first is a diversification among types of investments. We say you should have an RRSP which you will administer, buying mostly Canadian common stocks, and a second group of investments for capital gain that may include U.S. common shares, or real estate, or a small business.

A second type of diversification lies within each of these classes. Your RRSP Canadian common-stock portfolio can consist of one to five companies. One point in favour of five is the see-saw relationship of different industries. During a recession, building starts are down, but collection agencies, tobacco, and liquor stocks thrive. During a boom, retail merchants thrive, but gold mining languishes. Given the broker-commission economies of buying in 100-share lots, you will probably buy only one or two companies, at least at first. When you have more money to spend, if your analysis of the company remains favourable, you will buy more shares of the same two companies.

As for the investments for capital gain, *over*-diversifying is the real risk. It takes time to develop real expertise on any investment. You have only so much time. If you split your available time among ten investments, each one is going to be *under*-investigated, and therefore more risky.

THE PROBLEM OF LOW-PRICED VS. HIGH-PRICED STOCKS

In theory, the price of a stock you buy shouldn't matter. A thousand shares of a dollar stock, ten shares of a hundred-dollar stock, and one share of a thousand-dollar stock should behave exactly the same on the market, if the intrinsic value of the three companies is the same. In actual practice, however, this does not seem to be the case. When a stock gets up over fifty dollars, it tends to be bought by a different class of investor; similarly, stocks priced under ten dollars are the favourite of a class of investor that is easily scared out of the market.

Thus, the fluctuations in high-priced stocks normally reflect true changes in the industry or the company. At the opposite end of the scale, in stocks selling for less than $10, the price fluctuations mean much less. In many cases a severe drop means that the investors who are holding the stock have become terrified and want to get out at any price.

The argument in favour of stock splits, where a stock selling for $100 is split five for one so that each new share sells for $20, is that the $20 price attracts more small investors. More people have $20 with which to buy a share than have $100. This change, of course, does not affect the real value of the shares in any way. When you look at the history of stock splits, you find that most splits have been anticipated by an increase in the market price because of pre-split rumours. It is difficult to say whether this rise should be attributed to the new, seemingly low price of the stock, or to the mere fact that during the stock split the company achieved considerable publicity. Publicity alone will cause activity in a company's stock.

One thing to be said in favour of buying low-priced instead of high-priced stocks is that their volatility creates opportunities for the investor. Any stock of a solid company that reacts excessively to bad news can be picked up at bargain prices near the bottom of the drop. Similarly, the same stock can be sold at a considerable profit when it has again reacted excessively to good news. If you have firmly fixed in your mind the price you think the stock is worth, you can have a fixed policy of selling at a reasonable level above that price and buying it whenever it reaches a reasonable level below that price. This is how one-stock specialists operate, and many make a living in just this way.

Other things being equal, we tend to favour lower-priced rather than higher-priced issues in the average portfolio. This is partly for the reason of their volatility mentioned above, and partly because the low-priced stocks have further to go. A $100 stock seems to go easily to $150, at which point a 50 per cent profit can be taken. A $1,000 stock going to $1,500 is a rare event, yet the percentage rise of the two is exactly the same.

A good rule is to master your emotions, especially fear and greed. The way to do this is to be generous at the extremes. The stock is going down and down. Nobody wants it. Buy it. Take in the stray cat. When the stock has gone away up, be generous again. Let your fellow citizens enjoy the pleasure of owning it.

PSYCHOLOGICAL PROBLEMS OF BUYING AND SELLING

In forming your investment policy, you must take into consideration not only the characteristics of individual stocks and the stock market, but your own characteristics as a human being. People are so constituted that they find it very difficult to sell stocks if the market is rising and very difficult to buy if the market is falling. This is just the opposite to the human reaction to bargain sales in every other field. When your local department store has a sale, you rush down and try to buy products at marked-down prices. When the bottom falls out of the stock market and stocks are a gift, nobody wants to buy.

For this deep-seated psychological reason, portfolio management is very difficult unless you have certain regular techniques which you force yourself to use once a month, or at least quarterly. You must have, first of all, a regular program of portfolio review. At this time you go over every security you hold and justify your decision about it, whether to hold, sell, or buy more. One of the most difficult attitudes to cope with in investing is epitomized by the phrase "wait and see". People who wait and see eventually find out what they should have done, but by that time it is too late to do it. In investing, you have to look into the future as best you can, then act.

The difficulties of selling are at least as great as those of buying. You develop a loyalty to a particular stock, especially if you have held it for some time. For good portfolio management you must be ruthless and not allow your feelings to interfere with your analysis of the stock's prospects. Selling at a loss is particularly difficult, because not only are you parting with the stock, but you are admitting that you have made a mistake. Most human beings hate to do this. Yet the ruthless selling of a stock on which you have had a loss, and the placement of the money into something that has a prospect of profit, are the first rules of portfolio management.

Ideally, most conservative investors are looking for a single stock or a set of stocks in which they can put their money and forget it. They want something that they can buy and hold and ten years later come back to and find that the market price has doubled. But, in an imperfect world, this ideal investment is very difficult to find. True, there have been periods in the past when almost any stocks, bought at exactly the right time and held for ten years, would have doubled. But these were the accidental result of a conjunction of sharply rising markets, high levels of economic prosperity, and widespread interest in the stock market. These three factors are seldom in conjunction for extended periods.

PORTFOLIO CONSTRUCTION

We have now covered the three basic raw materials required before we can attempt to put together a portfolio of securities. These are: analysis of individual stocks to get an idea of their intrinsic value; analysis of market action to find out what other investors think about the stock; and the forming of an investment policy.

With these basic requirements in hand, you are in a position to put together an investment portfolio that is precisely suited to your individual needs. The course you choose in investing depends on two major factors:

1. Individual investment aims
2. The amount of time you have available for study

To arrive at a set of investment aims that is reasonable for you, it is important to consider all aspects of your financial situation rather than just your investments. A person's financial affairs must be seen as a whole. The first question is: Where does your money come from now and what will be your sources of income in the future? Obviously, if you work for a large corporation, where promotion up to middle management levels is almost automatic, your source of income is more secure than if you are self-employed. Next, you should look at your current and future expenses. These must bear a reasonable relationship to your current and future income. Any major capital expense (such as building a house) contemplated for the near future must be taken into account. In addition, if you are in debt, or if there is anyone dependent on your income, you should carry adequate term life insurance, and, to be on the safe side, you should have a reasonable reserve in cash or bonds set aside for emergencies.

The second factor is the amount of time you have available for study of securities, and your interest in the field. This, of course, will depend to some extent on the amount of money you have to invest. If you have several hundred thousand dollars, and are fascinated by the subject, you can make a career of simply managing your own money.

If you have neither the time nor the interest, you have three main alternatives. You can go to an investment counsellor and pay him for managing your portfolio, you can buy a mutual fund, or you can do it yourself.

Investment Counsel

The value of advice is always in direct proportion to the expertise of the giver, and in indirect proportion to his personal involvement. That is, the advice you get from a broker or an underwriter may be expert, but since he is paid for his trouble by means of a commission on everything you buy or sell, it is unrealistic to expect him to give you totally unbiased advice. The investment counsellor, since he is paid for pure service, and has no financial interest in whether you buy or sell, is in a position to give relatively unbiased advice.

The basic problem in using the services of investment counsel is picking out one that is good. When you choose a medical doctor, even if you pick a name at random out of the telephone book, you at least know that he has passed a prescribed course of study at a recognized medical school and that he is a member in good standing of the Medical Society. With investment counsel, in most countries, you have no such assurance. Anybody can set up a business in this field without having to prove any educational qualifications or any experience. In many provinces, investment counsellors are licensed, but this is more or less a formality, designed only to eliminate the most obvious frauds. The licensing is also used as a threat to pushers of penny stocks. In big cities the word soon gets around about who is good in investment counselling and who is not, but in less sophisticated communities anything goes.

Everything depends on how good the investment counsellor is, and this can be judged only by results. Over a reasonable period of time, a good investment counsellor should be able to do substantially better than you have been able to do yourself, and also should beat the records of the mutual funds. If he can't do this, you should fire him and get another.

Like other human beings, even a good investment counsellor will make mistakes. But these should be relatively infrequent and less serious in dollar value than the mistakes you make yourself. No matter what your investment aims turn out to be, whether you want capital growth, safety of principal, or income, a good investment counsellor should be able to achieve the objective. He has the advantage of having your account under constant supervision and he knows your investment aims. If he is careful to keep open all his channels of communication with the investment community, he can take advantage of opportunities that the ordinary investor would not hear about. In addition, being a generally well-informed financial man, the investment counsellor will be watchful of tax angles.

The major disadvantage of the investment counsellor, apart from the fact that he may be no good, is high cost. This is particularly true if the portfolio is small. A counsellor cannot charge much less than $1,000 a year for managing a portfolio. If the amount of money at stake is only $10,000, this means that a reasonable return of 5 per cent in dividends, plus 10 per cent capital gain, returns only 5 per cent net to the client.

On the other hand, if the portfolio is $100,000, the usual counsellor's fee of 1 per cent to 2 per cent of the net asset value at the end of the year is quite small in relation to the benefits obtained. And in times of severe market turmoil a cool-headed investment counsellor should be able to save you from a wipe-out. (See the Investment Club example, pp. 265-6.)

MUTUAL FUNDS

Mutual funds are usually bought by amateurs for the same reason that they own "permanent" life insurance – some hot-shot salesman has stuffed it down their throats.

The way a mutual fund works is that it sells its own shares to the small investor, and with the proceeds buys shares in a well-diversified list of companies. Dividends from these companies are paid to the mutual fund, which in turn distributes them to its own shareholders after deducting its profit and the cost of doing the business.

An open-end mutual fund can have an unlimited number of shareholders, and guarantees to buy back its shares from the individual investor at any time. Thus, if the market value of all the shares it was holding on a given day were $200,000,000, and the mutual fund had issued 20,000,000 shares, each share would be bought back at a price of $10. On the same day the fund might ask $11 for each of its shares. The difference between these two prices is called the "load" and is the amount that the mutual fund receives for providing its services to the individual investor.

The closed-end mutual fund has a fixed number of shares like a manufacturing company. These shares rise and fall on the market, depending on what investors think of the prospects of the mutual fund itself. The price of closed-end mutual funds on the market can be either higher or lower than the actual asset value of the industrial shares it holds at any time.

Another distinction between kinds of mutual funds is whether or not they use any leverage. Some mutual funds are empowered by law to borrow from banks and invest this borrowed money in stocks when they think stock prices are going to rise. Therefore, if the rise does take place, leverage companies make more money than if they had used only their own funds. But conversely, if the market falls, leverage companies lose more money than non-leverage.

The advantages of the mutual fund to the small investor are personal reassurance ("hand-holding"), convenience, simplicity, automatic reinvestment of income, some market guidance, and dollar averaging.

The convenience and simplicity of investing by means of mutual funds arises chiefly from the fact that you can pay $25, $50, or $100 a month and the mutual-fund company does all the rest. Some mutual funds even have a life-insurance feature that guarantees to finish your payments if you die before completing the two- or three-year savings plan.

Such features make mutual funds very popular during all market booms.

Disadvantages of Mutual Funds

Like everything else, mutual funds have their serious disadvantages. The most obvious is the loading charge that must be paid in addition to the annual fee of ½ per cent to ¾ per cent for the management of the fund, and all the brokers' commissions and taxes. This charge may be equivalent to between 1½ and 2 years' dividends. That is, you have to stay in the fund nearly two years before your money begins earning any interest at all. A charge of 9 per cent is undoubtedly high, and, moreover, in the case of open-end funds, both buying and selling charges have to be paid in advance. Anything over 5 per cent for the round trip is too much, even if the fund's performance is outstanding. Some funds with good growth records charge less than this. And the strong trend is to "no load" funds.

These funds are sold at a price that contains no front-end load, and no salesman's commission. You have to seek them out and buy them of your own free will. Your reward for going to this extra trouble is that you buy them at a price that gives you an even start.

Open-end funds have the unique disadvantage that, because of their very nature, their timing must always be wrong. The incoming money must be invested immediately. People usually buy mutual funds when they have money and when confidence is high. This is usually the best time to sell common stocks, not to buy them. On the down side of the market, the situation is even worse. When the underlying stocks start to decline, mutual-fund holders start to worry and many of them get out. This means that the fund must sell its stock holdings in a soft market at low prices. Precisely at the time they should be buying, they are forced to sell.

In addition, fund managers are prone to the lemming syndrome. At the New York bar where they meet to compare notes, word spreads that Unmitigated Brass is a sell. After lunch there is a wave of panic selling, spreading to other funds.

Perhaps the worst feature of mutual funds is that in a free-falling market they cannot possibly protect themselves for long. Nor can the individual owner of a fund protect himself, because they are impossible to sell short.

Hidden Costs in Mutual Funds

Before buying any mutual fund you should find out about the fee taken by management. Look not only at salaries but at the total expenses of the fund in relation to the capital. Don't pay too much attention to a galaxy of big names on the board. Make sure that the managers are respectable people, and that their record with the fund has been good. Big names make for very conservative investments. Moreover, none of the big men have any time available to spend on the fund. They merely assure you that the manager is honest. This is very important, but it doesn't assure competence.

FIGURE 37: **A Mutual Fund Record**

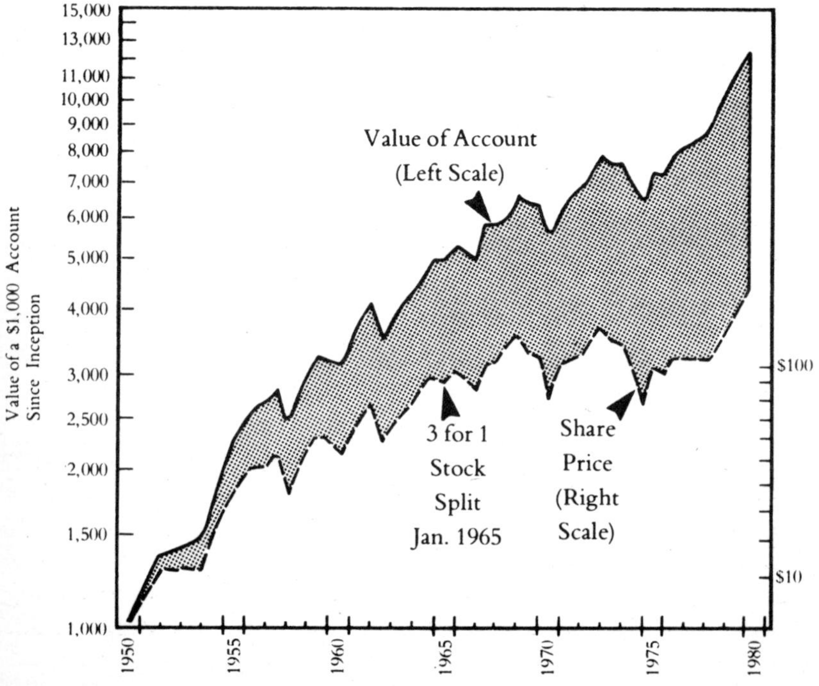

Performance of Mutual Funds

Most mutual funds have made up exhibits proving that their growth records are better than those of other mutual funds. This is done by choosing standards and starting dates and lengths of time that best suit the purposes of the particular mutual fund they are trying to sell. The graph in Figure 37 is a typical example of this type of promotional literature. To facilitate comparisons, the Toronto Stock Exchange 300 Composite Index is shown in Figure 38.

Graphs of this sort are perfectly accurate, but should be read with caution. For example, you should ask yourself how good the investment would have been if you had put in $1,000, not in 1950, when the market was down, but in 1969, when it was up.

Seen over a period of years, the performance of the average mutual fund leaves much to be desired. Its capital increase has not usually kept up with the 7 per cent cumulative inflation, so that in terms of real buying power the dollars you can take out of a mutual-fund investment today buy less than the dollars you put in. Nor has the average fund kept up in terms of income. Most funds still earn only 4 per cent to 5 per cent on their invested capital, and this is not enough, especially at a time like today when as high as 10 per cent can be obtained on sound industrial bonds.

Performance of mutual funds can be compared in several publications. Wiesenberger, in New York, publishes a monthly survey of all U.S. mutual funds, separated by type of fund, in which monthly results are compared. This survey can be seen at major libraries. *Barron's* and the *Financial Times of Canada* both publish studies of mutual funds showing how each one compares in results with all the others of its class. These come out quarterly.

Riding the Coattails of a Fund

While the industry does not abound with splendid examples, there are a few mutual funds that are outstanding performers. This is directly traceable to the men running them. The T. Rowe Price funds are worth the study of any investor, not necessarily to buy the shares, but to help you set up an accepted list for your own use. A study of the holdings of the mutual funds that have had outstanding growth records in the past will provide you with many ideas about what stocks are worth special study currently.

By comparing their portfolios from year to year you can see what expert investors have agreed to buy and sell. Most funds will send you a report giving a list of their holdings each year.

FIGURE 38: **Toronto Stock Exchange 300 Composite Index**

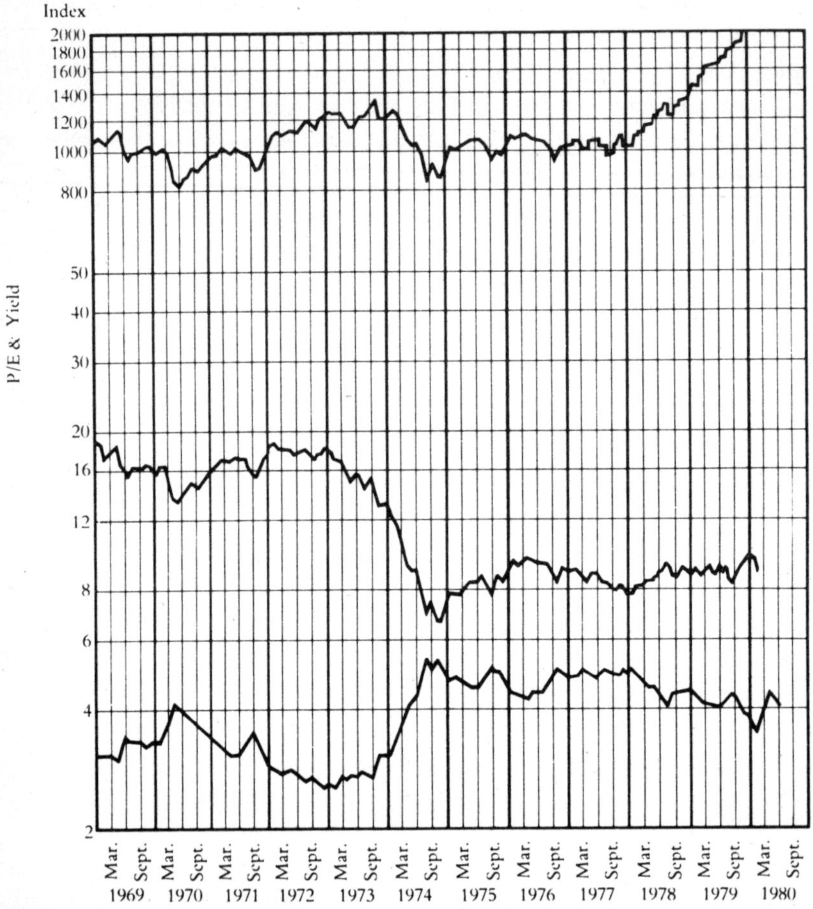

The figures on this chart are of three kinds, and happen to fall into three ranges, so they can be put on one chart. The TSE price index (ranging from 800 to 2,000) is at the top; the price-earnings ratio (ranging from 20 down to 7) is in the middle; and the yield (3% to 5%) is at the bottom. Time runs from left to right.

DO IT YOURSELF – BUT NOT ALONE: INVESTMENT CLUBS

Whenever the stock market experiences a pronounced rise, people make money from it. People who make money can't resist telling their friends. This causes their friends to get into the stock market willy-nilly, and, even if they lose, they tell their friends they won. This causes more friends to get into the stock market, and we have a market boom.

At times of booming market prices, people want to get together to brag and compare notes. For this reason there has been a vast increase in the number of investment clubs. There is now an American Association of Investment Clubs, and such clubs are said to number over twenty thousand in the United States and Canada. Such clubs are often aided and abetted by the local broker, who can see commissions flowing his way from the increased interest in common stocks. Others are formed spontaneously when people get together to catalogue their triumphs and disappointments in the stock market.

More often than not, the investment club is a classic instance of the blind leading the blind. Carlyle's observation "You can't get wisdom out of a ballot box" applies with even greater force to finance than to politics. If you assemble twenty people who know nothing about finance, they will still know nothing about finance when they leave, no matter how long they stay. Thus, the average investment club has only a social function, and this function could be fulfilled just as well by calling the club the Basin Street Chowder and Marching Society.

One type of investment club, however, that is not entirely without merit is the one in which certain types of professionals – chartered accountants, lawyers, architects, and engineers specializing in various industries – meet together to discuss specific investments. This focusing of several different professional disciplines on the problem of investing can often work out well. One prerequisite, however, is a financial man to provide the meeting with the factual material it needs, and to direct the discussion into the areas that bear directly on whether or not a given security is a "buy", "sell", or "hold".

Treat your participation in an investment club either as

1. a lark (not to be confused with the goose that will lay the golden

egg); or as 2. a group of serious-minded investment students committing hard-earned dollars to well-researched ideas (the group of airline pilots* who bought, for $100,000, the number 4 position on the Canadair Challenger later worth $7 million); or as 3. a system whereby the club hires investment counsel and adopts a monthly check-off system so substantial amounts of money will be added each month. Here is an example of the latter:

The Freezin Investment Club of Winnipeg (not its real name) hired investment counsel in mid 1969. This was just in time to share in the overall market decline, and when the dust cleared, the members had lost 10 per cent of their investment in five months. Again, during the panic of 1973-4, the results overall, after five years of hard work, were a disastrous 26 per cent and 18 per cent loss. Most investment clubs without counsel would have been eager to disband at the first opportunity to "get out even". Not this one. After ten years the results are much better than the average mutual fund, and well above the long-term goal of 1 per cent increase a month. Here are the actual figures:

Compare the percentage loss or gain column above with column five of Figure 40, remembering that the results are not strictly comparable because Freezin received new investment money in ten years out of eleven. Nevertheless, Freezin compares very favourably with most long-term growth funds over this eleven-year period.

EMPLOYEE SHARE-PURCHASE PLANS

There is strong feeling among members of management and labour alike that it is a desirable thing for the employee to own a part of the company in which he works. Share ownership seems to contribute to a high degree of solidarity among members of a company, and often leads to high morale. Share ownership gives the employee a chance to improve his personal fortunes as the fortunes of the company improve.

For these and other reasons companies that have inaugurated employee share-purchase plans have had a high degree of success.

*Canadair executives claim this story is apocryphal, but even if it is, the principle is sound.

FIGURE 39: **Results of Freezin Investment Club, Over Eleven Years**

End of	Invested	Total Invested	Value	Gain	%	Time (in months)
1969		10,617	9,573	−1,043	−9.8	5
	+4,500					
1970		15,117	15,925	+809	+5.3	17
	+6,750					
1971		21,867	25,764	+3,897	+17.8	29
	+4,800					
1972		26,667	32,768	+6,101	+22.8	41
	+5,200					
1973		31,867	23,487	−8,380	−26.2	53
	+2,400					
1974		34,267	28,239	−6,028	−17.6	65
	+3,300					
1975		37,567	37,892	+325	+.1	77
	−2,400					
1976		35,167	44,900	+9,733	+27.7	89
	+5,600					
1977		40,467	78,212	+37,745	+93.3	101
	+4,000					
1978		44,467	118,038	+73,571	+165.4	113
	+5,280					
1979		49,747	167,200	+117,453	+236.1	125
	+570					
July 1980		50,217	184,700	+134,483	+267.8	131

To encourage participation, employees are often allowed to buy shares in their company below market prices. This is good for the employee, but hardly fair to the other shareholders.

We encourage this, too, as a means of beginning a portfolio, as long as your company and its shares meet the tests we have outlined. And, once you are under way with an investment undertaking, we think it's a sound idea to learn something of other companies and other industries as potential portfolio candidates.

FIGURE 40: **Results of Some Long-Term Growth Funds**

	Total Net Assets 3/31/80 ($ Million)	3 Months 1980	Year 1979	5¼ Years 1975 to 3/31/80	10¼ Years 1970 to 3/31/80	Classification of Assets (Percent) 3/31/80: Cash + Govt.	Bonds + Prfd.	Common Stock	Percent Yield Last 12 Months
B. Long Term Growth Income Secondary									
AMCAP Fund	100.1	−8.3	51.9	293.5	147.8	21	0	79	2.3
AMER Birthright Trust	59.7	−1.1	32.9	65.1		3	0	97	Nd
AMER Growth Fund	20.6	−2.5	53.1	210.6	169.6	11	42	47	3.P
AMER Leaders Fund	47.6	−2.7	14.9	78.3	36.4	38	0	62	5.6
**Anchor Growth Fund (1978)	121.0	−9.0	22.1	73.1	−12.1	9	0	91	2.8
Armstrong Associates	4.9	−8.9	25.7	225.4	103.4	33	0	67	4.8
Axe-Houghton Stock Fund	66.1	−7.2	23.8	63.3	60.7	19	0	81	2.7
Babson Investment FD	211.1	−6.1	17.2	54.8	45.1	4	0	96	3.4
Beacon Growth Fund	8.2	−3.3	16.7	53.4	−9.6	13	6	81	4.3
BLC Growth Fund	9.4	−9.8	27.2	112.4	45.5	1	0	99	2.6
Capital Shares	29.4	−9.7	54.5	190.2	47.5	0	3*	97	1.P
Cardinal Fund	11.8	−8.0	23.2	135.4	40.4	7	1	92	3.4
CG Fund	104.6	−7.7	24.3	94.8	66.2	7	0	93	3.9
Charter Fund	22.7	−3.7	44.5	266.3	254.2	29	0	71	2.6
Chemical Fund	775.0	−7.2	24.9	56.7	48.0	6	0	94	2.2
Colonial Growth Shares	54.6	−6.3	38.6	71.6	18.0	9	1*	90	2.6
Common STK FD of ST BDSMTGE	29.4	−7.9	18.4	73.0	19.6	21	0	79	2.4
Companion Fund	77.8	−7.1	24.8	100.4	61.1	10	0	90	4.3
Country Capital Growth	37.0	−8.5	20.0	55.7	21.4	7	0	93	3.2
De Vegh Mutual Fund	53.3	−4.4	30.3	95.0	58.0	23	0	77	3.2

Drexel Burnham Fund	34.3	−4.5	23.5			28	12*	60	4.6
Dreyfus Fund	1,316.1	−6.3	25.6	122.0	68.3	9	2	89	4.0
Dreyfus Number Nine Fund	32.4	−4.5	47.9	246.8		5	1	94	0.8
Dreyfus Third Century Fund	46.7	−3.3	60.3	269.7		12	2	86	1.4
**Eaton & Howard Growth Fund (1979)	26.2	−6.3	34.6	119.4	10.6	1	0	99	1.0
**Energy Fund (1970)	271.7	−2.4	50.0	182.1	149.0	29	1*	70	3.5
Farm Bureau Growth Fund	29.3	−4.5	18.5	124.1		27	7	66	3.6
Fidelity Asset Invest. Trust	9.7	−6.4	18.6			5	12*	83	1.1
Fidelity Destiny Fund	132.9	−11.2	35.2	270.0		2	2*	96	2.9
Fidelity Trend Fund	501.6	−12.0	26.6	91.6	24.2	1	0	99	3.4
Fiduciary Growth Associates	61.6	−11.2	86.1	234.0	94.3	1	0	99	1.4
First Index Invest. Trust	73.3	−4.1	18.1			0	0	100	5.5
First Investor BD Appreciation	27.0	−7.0	11.4	**	**	(4)	101	3	8.7
**First Investors Option Fund (1979)	29.1	−7.6	16.3			(5)	0	105	5.5
Foursquare Fund	5.9	−4.0	20.6	79.3	39.5	11	4	85	2.9
Franklin Growth Series	7.2	−10.9	8.3	47.0	15.0	(1)	6	95	1.6
Gateway Option Income Fund	12.7	−6.2	15.4			(2)	0	102	3.8
Growth Fund of America	74.9	−10.1	45.8	219.1	78.0	11	0	89	1.2
Growth Industry Shares	28.6	−6.1	30.1	122.2	59.5	4	2*	94	1.7
Guardian Park Ave Fund	21.8	−4.2	29.2	221.2		36	9	55	5.4
John Hancock Growth Fund	27.4	−4.8	34.0	81.4	5.9	2	0	98	1.2
Investors Research Fund	10.8	−3.7	18.7	89.9	96.1	60	0	40	2.1
Investors Variable Payment	348.1	−6.8	22.3	78.9	17.9	13	0	87	3.9
Ivy Fund	35.2	−3.0	30.9	89.6	15.6	11	1*	88	4.6
Johnston Capital Appreciation	184.7	−2.8	20.1	85.1	49.0	27	1*	72	5.1
JP Growth Fund	16.5	−3.4	17.6	116.5		12	0	88	4.8
Kemper Growth Fund	124.7	−6.3	41.1	192.7	111.9	22	1*	77	2.3
Keystone K-2 (Growth Fund)	103.8	−4.2	17.7	75.0	31.9	15	1	84	4.5
Keystone S-3 (Growth)	89.4	−7.9	30.9	143.3	66.9	3	0	97	2.4
Lehman Capital Fund	24.6	−9.1	46.0			17	2	81	2.3

FIGURE 40: **Results of Some Long-Term Growth Funds (cont.)**

	Total Net Assets 3/31/80 ($ Million)	3 Months 1980	Year 1979	5¼ Years 1975 to 3/31/80	10¼ Years 1970 to 3/31/80	Classification of Assets (Percent) 3/31/80: Cash + Govt.	Bonds + Prfd.	Common Stock	Percent Yield Last 12 Months
Lexington Research Fund	77.7	−6.9	32.1	121.7	57.8	7	2*	91	4.3
Lindner Fund	8.2	−9.8	28.5	306.1		1	2*	97	2.7
Loomis-Sayles Cap. Dev. Fund	45.5	−6.2	27.3	116.3	66.9	3	0	97	2.4
Magnacap Fund	5.0	−11.5	27.5	92.0		9	0	91	3.8
Mairs & Power Growth Fund	11.2	−10.9	19.4	116.9	58.4	2	0	98	3.7
Manhattan Fund	47.0	−8.2	33.8	54.7	−53.6	30	2	68	1.6
Mass Capital Develop. Fund	34.7	−7.6	52.8	191.0		10	0	90	3.0
Mass Investors Growth Stock	644.5	−4.2	26.2	74.2	26.6	6	0	94	2.4
Merrill Lynch Basic Value FD	78.5	−8.0	31.4			4	0	96	5.4
Merrill Lynch Special Value	38.8	−15.2	25.7			1	1	98	3.4
Midamerica Mutual Fund	33.1	−4.9	22.7	113.6	22.6	26	0	74	5.3
Mony Fund	10.4	−5.7	19.1	54.8		7	0	93	3.8
Morgan (W.L.) Growth Fund	190.5	−7.5	19.3	141.4	96.0	1	0	99	3.7
Mutual Benefit Fund	18.5	−5.1	11.9	59.4		27	0	73	5.0
Mutual Investing Found-Growth	25.4	−10.4	21.7	108.0	11.5	7	0	93	2.7

Approximate percent change in net assets per share with capital gains and income dividends reinvested total return.

CHAPTER NINETEEN

Some Final Words About Investing Risks

And we are here as on a darkling plain
Swept with confused alarms of struggle and flight.
MATTHEW ARNOLD (1822–88)

Conventional "wisdom" about investing results in conventional failure. Most people in our society reach retirement age without sufficient investment capital to provide adequate levels of living for the fifteen years they are likely to survive. Usually their inexperience and fears keep them from gaining any protection from inflation, and from enjoying their retirement years.

The following case is a bit exceptional and contains two worthwhile ideas for a reader planning an investment program *during* retirement. What we are saying is: "It is never too late."

During the 2½ years just prior to retirement, a university professor talked to Dr. Ackerman. Her prospect was a pension income of $7,700 per year, including two university pensions totalling $6,400 and over $100 a month from Old Age Security and the Canada Pension Plan, to begin in 1969. Even without dependants, and even for a scholar supposed to get satisfaction from intellectual rather than material things, this is hardly an adequate income.

Fortunately, something could be done by taking new risks with the capital accumulated through thirty-five years of patient frugality. The big job was for the investment counsel to persuade the client to accept different and unfamiliar risks. Most of us like best the risks we *know*. If we are used to losing our capital on government bonds, that's what we want to do. From December 1965 to August 1968, the portfolio doubled in size, from $42,500 to $85,700, using about $15,000 of borrowed money and investing less in bonds and mutual funds, and more in shares and convertible debentures. With the 1969-70 market crash for both shares and bonds, the equity fell to just over $50,000. But the worst was over. During the subsequent ten years, with only modest supplements to the pensions, this woman has lived exactly as she wishes financially – summers at the lake, new boat and motor, new car when needed, and plenty of intercontinental travel when winter winds blow. Her investment portfolio exceeds $250,000, allowing quite nicely for increases from inflation, past and future, and providing the sense of security we all deserve to have after retirement but few achieve.

How did this come about? The client was persuaded to accept two risks that were unfamiliar to her: 1. To invest in securities that had potential for growth. 2. To borrow to do it.

A skilled counsellor can persuade you to try some unfamiliar risks, but only you can decide about a major factor we call "liveability".

The ultimate test of an investment, after availability, prospective earnings, and risk of losing capital and purchasing power, is this liveability. It is a highly personal, emotion-laden test. Though quite often different from one investor to another, it cannot be ignored. The buyer of a building brags about picking it up at only five times earnings; the seller is happy to sell at 50 per cent above market value. The volatile common shares of a well-known company like Chrysler Corporation may bring ulcers to one investor, joyous excitement to another, and peaceful sleep to a third. Karl Marx was wrong. The informed willing exchange of value for value does not represent one loss and one equal gain. Antiques and art furnish examples galore. The pleasure of owning something that brings you joy is not diminished but rather enhanced because someone has discarded it or sold it for a nominal sum. Hence the pleasure of garage sales and city dumps.

When your portfolio becomes a bit too stolid, even for a Canadian, and you are tempted to buy some shares in a ground-floor venture or the latest tax dodge...don't. Instead, do a fresh analysis of your present holdings. Sell off the weakest and buy three times as much of the strongest, using borrowed money. If that doesn't keep you alert and on your toes, buy five times as much of the strongest. In this way you will review your analysis procedures and keep your interest from straying from the true investment path.

Lastly, about investment risks. We've tried to lessen yours by telling you what to avoid, showing you our investment principles, what information to seek out and where to seek it, how to analyse the data, how to develop and apply personal investment criteria, and how to live with your decisions. In short, all you need in order to do it yourself.

We hope these words have value for both novice and experienced investors over many years. The authors *are* interested in how you get along with the book and with your investment program. We are both in the education business in our own separate ways. If you found any part of the book hard to understand, we would be glad to hear about it. Conversely, if any part turned out to be particularly helpful, we are open for compliments, too.

If you are interested in subscribing to Dr. Ackerman's ongoing investment thinking (he may soon start an investment-comment style of newsletter), encourage him by writing to:

J. Ackerman, Suite 102, 1200 Pembina Highway, Winnipeg, Manitoba, R3T 2A7, or
Box 457, Annapolis Royal, Nova Scotia, B0S 1A0
J. J. Brown, Brookdale Farms, R.R.1, Namur, Que., J0V 1N0

APPENDIXES

APPENDIX 1: **Don't Pay More Than These Rates for Life Insurance.**

Annual Renewable Term Insurance

Renewable to Age 80

MINIMUM ISSUE – $25,000 ISSUE AGES 16-60

Annual Premiums Per $1,000 (Add $15 policy fee)						
				Banded Rates		
Issue and Attained Age*		Waiver of Premium		$25,000 thru $99,999	$100,000 thru $249,999	$250,000 or More
Male	Female	Male	Female			
	16		$ .16	$ 1.59	$ 1.49	$ 1.43
	17		.17	1.60	1.50	1.44
	18		.17	1.61	1.51	1.45
16	19	$ .09	.17	1.62	1.52	1.46
17	20	.10	.17	1.63	1.53	1.47
18	21	.10	.18	1.64	1.54	1.48
19	22	.10	.18	1.65	1.55	1.49
20	23	.11	.19	1.66	1.56	1.50
21	24	.11	.21	1.67	1.57	1.51
22	25	.11	.23	1.68	1.58	1.52
23	26	.11	.25	1.69	1.59	1.53
24	27	.11	.27	1.70	1.60	1.54
25	28	.12	.31	1.71	1.61	1.55
26	29	.13	.34	1.72	1.62	1.56
27	30	.14	.38	1.74	1.64	1.57
28	31	.15	.41	1.77	1.66	1.59
29	32	.16	.45	1.81	1.69	1.62
30	33	.17	.49	1.87	1.74	1.67
31	34	.18	.53	1.95	1.81	1.74
32	35	.19	.57	2.05	1.90	1.83
33	36	.21	.62	2.17	2.01	1.94
34	37	.23	.67	2.31	2.15	2.08
35	38	.25	.72	2.46	2.30	2.23
36	39	.27	.77	2.61	2.45	2.38
37	40	.29	.82	2.76	2.60	2.52
38	41	.31	.87	2.92	2.76	2.68
39	42	.33	.92	3.10	2.94	2.86
40	43	.35	.97	3.30	3.14	3.06
41	44	.38	1.03	3.56	3.39	3.31

Annual Premiums Per $1,000 (Add $15 policy fee)

Issue and Attained Age*		Waiver of Premium		Banded Rates		
Male	Female	Male	Female	$25,000 thru $99,999	$100,000 thru $249,999	$250,000 or More
42	45	.43	1.11	3.89	3.72	3.61
43	46	.50	1.21	4.26	4.04	3.89
44	47	.58	1.32	4.67	4.40	4.22
45	48	.67	1.44	5.12	4.80	4.60
46	49	.78	1.57	5.60	5.28	5.04
47	50	.91	1.71	6.11	5.78	5.53
48	51	1.07	1.86	6.64	6.30	6.05
49	52	1.23	2.03	7.21	6.86	6.61
50	53	1.42	2.21	7.84	7.49	7.24
51	54	1.63	2.40	8.56	8.20	7.95
52	55	1.88	2.61	9.35	8.97	8.72
53	56	2.15	2.82	10.23	9.81	9.56
54	57	2.44	3.04	11.21	10.73	10.48
55	58	2.77	3.26	12.33	11.73	11.46
56	59	3.09	3.49	13.59	12.87	12.55
57	60	3.41		15.02	14.10	13.84
58	61	3.74		16.61	15.71	15.32
59	62	4.06		18.38	17.42	16.98
60	63			20.30	19.27	18.78
61	64			22.38	21.25	20.71
62	65			24.60	23.36	22.76
63	66			26.95	25.59	24.93
64	67			29.43	27.95	27.23
65	68			32.04	30.44	29.64
66	69			34.78	33.04	32.19
67	70			37.69	35.81	34.91
68	71			40.88	38.84	37.87
69	72			44.45	42.22	41.16
70	73			48.28	45.87	44.75
71	74			52.39	49.77	48.58
72	75			56.74	53.90	52.63
73	76			61.31	58.25	56.90
74	77			66.11	62.81	61.36
75	78			73.47	69.80	68.05
76	79			81.69	77.60	75.66
77				90.76	80.24	84.09
78				100.90	95.85	93.46
79				111.88	106.29	103.63

*Rate at issue age applies whenever policy is in force as Decreasing Term.
Attained Age applies to policy and rates when policy is on Level Term.
Renewal only.

APPENDIX 2: **Why You Should Manage Your Own RRSP**

Investors Retirement #9452211 begin June 22, 1977
Annual payments in: $280 i.e., 5 units
Principle: MONEY EARNS MONEY
Application: The cost of paying in $280 / yr. is what that money would otherwise earn. Since other RRSPs earned 7 per cent to 9 per cent, let's use 8 per cent; i.e., the cost annually is 280 × 8 per cent = $22.40

	Capital Cost	Total Cost incl. forgone earnings	Accum. Value	Your Loss
After 3 years	$ 840	$ 909	$ 725	–184
5 years	1,400	1,642	1,400	–242
10 years	2,800	4,056	3,425	–631
15 years	4,200	7,602	5,875	–1,727
20 years	5,600	12,813	8,530	–4,283

That is, if you take a "normal" rate of return, you lose more and more every year. *or* You may otherwise only earn 6%.

	Capital Cost	Total Cost	Accum. Value	Your Loss
After 3 years	$ 840	$ 891	$ 725	–166
5 years	1,400	1,578	1,400	–178
10 years	2,800	3,690	3,425	–265
15 years	4,200	6,517	5,875	–642
20 years	5,600	10,300	8,530	–770

That is, if you take a tiny rate of return, you still lose from the beginning. *or* 4%? (that's the Investors "basic guaranteed" rate)

	Capital Cost	Total Cost	Accum. Value	Your Loss
After 3 years	$ 840	$ 874	$ 725	–149
5 years	1,400	1,516	1,400	–116
10 years	2,800	3,360	3,425	+ 65*
15 years	4,200	5,605	5,875	+270*
20 years	5,600	8,338	8,530	+192*

*Gain

Even if you think money is still worth 4%, you lose for the first 8 years. More likely 10%.

	Capital Cost	Total Cost	Accum. Value	Your Loss
After 3 years	$ 840	$ 927	$ 725	–202
5 years	1,400	1,709	1,400	–309
10 years	2,800	4,462	3,425	–1,037
15 years	4,200	8,896	5,875	–3,021
20 years	5,600	16,037	8,530	–7,507

From the minus signs along the right-hand column, you can see that this trust company consistently gets you annual losses. You can do better than this for yourself.

APPENDIX 3: **How Stocks Behave in a Crash**

A Dozen Good Common Stocks, 1929–1932

Company	1929	1932
Anaconda Copper	174⅞	3
A.T.&T.	310¼	70¼
Chrysler Corporation	87	5
DuPont	503	22
General Motors	224	7⅝
Montgomery Ward	156⅞	3½
New York Central	256½	8¾
Sears, Roebuck	197½	9⅞
Standard Oil of California	81⅞	15⅛
Standard Oil of New Jersey	83	19⅞
U.S. Steel	261¾	21¼
Western Union	272¼	12⅜

Source: Jerome B. Cohen and Arthur W. Hanson, *Personal Finance*, 4th ed. (Homewood, Ill.: Richard D. Irwin, Inc., 1972), p. 677.

The Biggest Losers of 1967–70

Company	1967–70 High	Mid-May 1970 Price	Percent Drop
Liquidonics	155	8	95
Levin-Townsend	68	5	93
Valley Metallurgical	68	5	93
Bio-Dynamics	111	10	91
Ling Temco Vought	169	15	91
Unexcelled, Inc.	68	6	91
Susquehanna Corp.	80	8	90
Elcor Chemical	80	9	89
Rucker Co.	66	7	89

The Biggest Losers of 1967–70

Company	1967–70 High	Mid-May 1970 Price	Percent Drop
Waltham Industries	55	6	89
Perfect Film	82	10	88
Tuco Labs	68	8	88
Conductron	75	10	87
Interphoto	62	8	87
Parvin / Dohrmann	141	19	87
American Export	70	10	86
Graphic Sciences	83	12	86
Home Oil	84	12	86
Gulton Industries	67	10	85
Intersystems	67	11	84
Litton Industries	115	18	84
Tracor, Inc.	75	12	84
TWA	91	15	84
Victor Comptometer	92	15	84
Zapata Norness	87	14	84
Collins Radio	115	20	83
Dennison Mfg.	80	14	83
EG&G	72	12	83
Jefferson Lake Petro	60	10	83
Optical Scanning	145	24	83
Sanders Assoc.	77	13	83
Trans-Lux	84	14	83
Vernitron	52	9	83
Boeing	112	20	82
General Instrument	83	15	82
Iroquois Industries	51	9	82
Lockheed	74	13	82
SCM	77	14	82
Talley Industries	66	12	82
Career Academy	54	10	81
Sunstrand	91	17	81
Keller Ind.	70	14	80
Monogram Ind.	82	16	80
Natomas	130	26	80
St. Paul Railway	69	14	80
Technical Operations	64	13	80
Western Air Lines	59	12	80

Source: Lehman Brothers, 1970.

APPENDIX 4: **Don't Pin Too Much Faith on Charts.** Note how this one differs sharply from the Dow Jones Index, and you will see how different samples give different graphs.

Standard & Poor's Stock Price Index
1941-1943 = 10

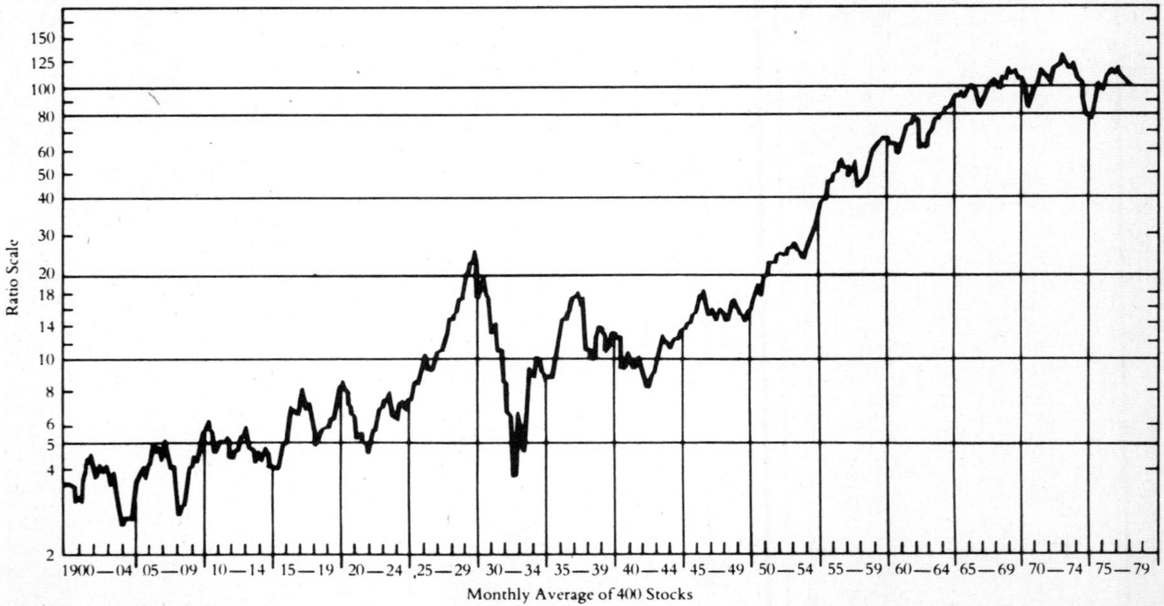

Source: Standard and Poor's Corporation, New York

Glossary of Financial Terms

Amortization Spreading a large expenditure proportionately over a fixed period of time.

Asset Anything of value owned by a company or an individual.

Balance sheet Statement of the financial worth of a business or organization which is divided into three parts – assets, liabilities, and ownership (equity).

Capital 1. What is owned by a company or individual minus what is owed at a specific time. 2. Total investments of owners (shareholders) of a business at a given time, which may be calculated by subtracting from the total assets all the liabilities of those other than the owners.

Capital assets Assets owned or held by a business of either a tangible or an intangible nature which are expected to be used or held over several fiscal periods (not including stock for sale).

†**Capital expenditure** An expenditure to acquire or add to a capital asset; an expenditure yielding enduring benefits.

†**Cash flow** The figure resulting from adding back to income items that do not affect working capital, such as depreciation and amortization. Used chiefly by financial analysts and not to be confused with "cash flow" as used in the cash flow statement.

Consolidation A parent plus one or more subsidiary companies which present financial reports for the group as a whole, not as separate entities.

Corporation A legal entity or corporate person with authority to operate under provincial or federal statutes, usually formed to make a profit. Owners are liable for the debts only up to the amount of their investment.

†**Current liability** A liability whose regular and ordinary liquidation is expected to occur within one year or within the normal operating cycle where that is longer than a year. A liability otherwise classified as current but for which provision has been made for payment from other than current resources should be excluded.

†**Deferred income taxes** The accumulated amounts by which income taxes charged in the accounts have been increased (accumulated tax allocation credit) or decreased (accumulated tax allocation debit) as a result of timing differences.

Depletion Gradual using up or consumption of a natural resource, recorded in the accounts.

Depreciation Gradual reduction of the cost of a fixed asset and gradual application of this cost to the expense of a business over the useful life of the asset.

Dividend Distribution to shareholders of a portion of the profits of the company.

†**Dividend coverage ratio** The ratio of the net income to dividends.

†**Earnings per share** The portion of income for a period attributable to a share of issued capital of a corporation. The calculation of earnings per share is relevant only with respect to shares whose rights to participate in the earnings have no upper limit.

Equity 1. A right or claim to the assets of a company. Both the owners and the creditors have equity in a business. 2. Amount that a business is worth beyond what it owes.

Expenditure 1. Spending. 2. Incurring a liability.

Fixed assets Property or equipment of a tangible nature owned by a business for use in its operations (not for sale), which is expected to have a useful life of several fiscal periods.

Income Difference between total revenue and total expense of a business for a given period.

Inventory A detailed list of items and their values owned at a specific point in time.

Investment Funds committed to something tangible or intangible in order to receive a return either in income or in use.

Liability 1. An amount owed to another, not necessarily due to be paid immediately. 2. An obligation to remit money or services at a future date.

†**Long-term liability** A liability which, in the ordinary course of business, will not be liquidated within one year or within the normal operating cycle where that is longer than a year.

†**Minority interest** 1. The equity of the shareholders who do not hold the controlling interest in a controlled company. 2. In consolidated financial statements, the equity in subsidiaries that is applicable to shares that are not owned by the parent company or by a consolidated subsidiary company.

Profit Total revenue less total expenditures for a period of time calculated in accordance with generally accepted accounting principles.

Ratio Relative size, expressed as the number of times one quantity is contained in another.

Retained earnings The portion of a company's aggregate income since incorporation which remains invested in the operation after distribution of dividends to shareholders.

Revenue Inflow of cash or receivables from customers or clients in return for goods, services, or interest on investments.

Subsidiary A company which is controlled by another company usually through its ownership of the majority of shares.

†**Working capital** The excess of current assets over current liabilities.

Write-off (verb) To transfer an item which was considered an asset to an expense account; for example, to transfer an uncollectible account receivable to bad debts expense. (noun) The item or amount reduced or cancelled.

Terms reprinted with permission from the booklet *ABC's of Accounting* published by The Certified General Accountants Association of Ontario, except for those marked†, which are reprinted with permission from *Terminology for Accountants* published by The Canadian Institute of Chartered Accountants.

Bibliography

ALLEN, LEON B. *Profits Without Forecasting*. New York, Gillen, 1952.

BROWN, J. J. *The Intelligent Investor's Guide to Real Estate*. New York, Putnam, 1964.

———. *Life Insurance, Benefit or Fraud?* Toronto, Longmans Canada, 1964. (Rev. ed. Academic Press, 1972.)

———. *Start with $100.* Toronto, Longmans Green, 1960.

———. *Winning the Life Insurance Game.* Toronto, Macmillan of Canada, 1985.

BROWNE, HARRY. *How You Can Profit from the Coming Devaluation*. New York, Arlington House, 1970.

———. *You Can Profit from a Monetary Crisis.* New York, Macmillan, 1974.

———, and TERRY COXON. *Inflation-proofing Your Investments*. New York, Morrow, 1981.

CASEY, DOUGLAS R. *Crisis Investing*. Beverly Hills, Ca., Stratford Press, 1980.

CLASING, HENRY K., JR. *The Dow Jones–Irwin Guide to Put and Call Options*. New York, Dow Jones–Irwin, 1975.

DREMAN, DAVID N. *Contrarian Investment Strategy: The Psychology of Stock Market Success*. New York, Random House, 1980.

ERDMAN, PAUL E. *The Billion Dollar Sure Thing*. New York, Scribner, 1973.

———. *The Crash of '79*. New York, Simon and Schuster, 1976.

———. *The Last Days of America*. New York, Simon and Schuster, 1981.

———. *The Silver Bears*. New York, Scribner, 1974.

(Read for the fun and excitement, not to learn about finance.)

Executives Bond Value Tables. Boston, Financial Publishing, 1966.

FARRELL, MAURICE L. *The Dow-Jones Averages, 1885–1970*. New York, Dow Jones, 1972.

GRAHAM, BENJAMIN. *The Intelligent Investor*. 4th ed. New York, Harper and Row, 1973.
_______, et al. *Security Analysis*. 4th ed. New York, McGraw-Hill, 1962. (Still the basic text if you are a serious student.)
LOEB, GERALD M. *The Battle for Investment Survival*. Rev. ed. New York, Simon and Schuster, 1965. (First published in 1935, this book has been in print continuously ever since.)
_______. *The Battle for Stock Market Profits*. New York, Simon and Schuster, 1970.
MALKIEL, BURTON G. *A Random Walk Down Wall Street*. Rev. ed. New York, Norton, 1973.
MAYER, MARTIN. *The Builders: Houses, People, Neighborhoods, Government, Money*. New York, Norton, 1978.
_______. *The Fate of the Dollar*. New York, Times Books, 1980.
The New Encyclopedia of Stock Market Techniques. Larchmont, N.Y., 1977.
RIEGEL, E.C. *Dollar Doomsday*. New York, Inflation Counsellors, 1941.
RUFF, HOWARD J. *How to Prosper During the Coming Bad Years*. New York, Times Books, 1978.
SARNOFF, PAUL. *Puts and Calls: The Complete Guide*. New York, Hawthorn, 1970.
_______. *The Wall Street Thesaurus*. New York, Astor-Honor, 1963. (Good, cheerful definitions of brokers' terms.)
SMITH, ADAM (pseud.). *The Money Game*. New York, Random House, 1968.
_______. *Paper Money*. New York, Random House, 1980.
_______. *Supermoney*. New York, Random House, 1972.
(Almost unique in the financial-writing field – a man who knows how to read and write the English language.)
SNYDER, J. CHRISTOPHER, and BRIAN E. ANDERSON. *It's Your Money: The Complete Guide to Personal Financial Planning*. 2nd ed. Toronto, Methuen, 1979.
Toronto Stock Exchange. *"300" Stock Price Indexes*.
VAN CASPEL, VENITA. *The New Money Dynamics*. New York, Reston, 1978.
Wiesenberger Investment Companies Service, 1980 edition. New York.

Want more? Go to your public or university library and consult:
ZERDEN, SHELDON. *Best Books on the Stock Market: An Analytical Bibliography*. New York, Bowker, 1972.

Index

PROPER NAMES, PLACES, AND PUBLICATIONS

SUBJECTS